Anna's Legacy

First Published in September, 2019 by

Willow Publishing

ISBN: 978-1-5272-4362-0

Jacket design: Gabrielle Morley
Cover Photo: Robert Wilson

Book Design and Artwork by Peter Miles

Printed by Printwize
Witham, Essex

special days for seriously ill young adults

Gate House, Fretherne Road
Welwyn Garden City
Hertfordshire AL8 6NS
Telephone: 01707 259 777
Email: willowfoundation.org.uk

Registered charity number: 1106746

All profits which may accrue from the sale of this book will be donated
in support of the continuing work of the Willow Foundation.

Jan
Remembering the amazing support
you and Dennis gave to Anna
during her illness and subsequently
for Willow.
With love and thanks Megs x

ANNA'S LEGACY

Her life with cancer and the creation of Willow

Megs Wilson

'In the midst of winter, I found there was,
within me, an invincible summer.'

Albert Camus

*This book is dedicated to the memory of Anna and Mitchell
and in grateful thanks to all who have worked for or
supported the work of Willow over the past 20 years*

Contents

Introduction

Grief comes along in so many guises. I was 30 when my mother died, and at a time when Bob and I had a growing family of our own. In spite of the feeling of deep loss I had to be practical and help my father, brother and sister make all the arrangements with the necessary detail, immediately after and for the months following her death. I appeared to cope brilliantly, but a year on I had what I can only describe as a 'nervous breakdown', attributed to delayed grief.

In 1998 our beloved and only daughter Anna died aged 31, and I could not even start to describe the physical pain that would engulf my body and the feeling of injustice that she had gone before me. For the five years of her illness we were there at her beck and call, willing to play any role, do any task, just to try and alleviate her suffering. With her death we were left with a huge hole in our lives, and one that could seemingly never be filled.

I had kept a diary over the period of her illness and, after she died, I decided to turn it into a printed personal narrative so that the close family could never lose the memory of Anna's all too short life – her personality, her need for fun, her attitude to cancer and her philosophy, which helped her though all that terrible and painful time. What I didn't realise was that by doing this, by recording the day-by day events and my own reactions to them, I was keeping her close to me, recounting the times we had at hospital and at home. It was hard to let her go, but it was my way of grieving for my beautiful daughter and the suffering she had to bear over those five years which led to her ultimate death.

Her personality and the way she faced her illness was quite remarkable and I felt it only fair that others in the family should be able to have her story to pass on to future generations.

Our daughter taught us much about living with serious illness, particularly at such a prime time of life. She should have been forging ahead with her profession as a nurse, starting a family, enjoying the energy that a 26 year-old is normally blessed with. Instead of which she had to cope with the shattering news of a rare cancer diagnosis and the effects of subsequent treatments.

She was determined that cancer would not define her and would not take away her ability to have the quality of life nor the fun that she craved. She would live with cancer on her own terms and she would take charge of whatever was thrown at her, laughing in its face.

She knew I would do something after her death with what I had learned and all she had taught me; she who had craved fun, laughter, family, days out, parties; she, who would always have something in her diary to distract away from the menace lurking beneath the surface of it all. She begged not to let her inevitable death destroy us, but that we should keep communicating and enjoying life for her sake.

It was at Christmas following her death when I said to Bob that if our daughter's special days worked for her, why shouldn't they work for others? And twenty years on we are happy to say that we have achieved this wish through the work of 'Willow', the charity we set up in memory of Anna, and so far, nearly 16,500 seriously ill young adults have benefitted from its existence by being able to have a Special Day of their choosing alongside their friends and family.

This book follows the course of Anna's illness, her remarkable attitude and the subsequent creation of that charity. Her words have been echoed thousands of times in letters received at Willow, from other seriously ill young adults, the majority of whom appear to have a similar defiant mind-set to that of Anna. They often tell us that their own Special Day took them back to a normality that had been so cruelly lost, and for that period of time and beyond, helped them cope with their situation by seeing the bigger picture.

This book is not only a tribute to our daughter and her amazing husband Mitchell, but to all those who have helped build Willow and further it's work and intentions through whatever means. Thank you all for creating a lasting legacy for Anna.

Megs Wilson
September 2019

Part 1

... from Life to Death

In the Midst of Winter

1 December 1998

We left the hospital with great reluctance. In the last few months Anna had never been alone overnight without one of the family being with her. Her pain had become so intense that she had to be moved every fifteen minutes to relieve that part of the body in contact with the bed. She hated disturbing the nursing staff so either Mitchell or myself stayed by her side in a bed or a chair whenever she had to go into hospital.

Bob and I were numb on the drive home, a journey which took only eight minutes; unable to speak, unable to communicate save for the unified thoughts that ran through our heads. We followed Mitchell's car to Gun Lane and entered the cosy cottage that had been so lovingly created over the last five years by Anna and Mitchell. Stoli came to greet us, having slept in the laundry basket since we left, and ran past our legs to her cat food in the kitchen.

The house was warm and comforting. It was Anna's sanctuary where she and Mitchell could retreat from the outside world, where she longed to be when she was away for any length of time, and where select family and friends would gather in gossip, discussion, laughter or tears. It was as orderly as Anna's Filofax and as relaxed as Mitchell's clothes. It was Habitat and country, tasteful and tuned.

The chair that had been Anna's preserve had recently given way to the settee. She was more comfortable lying than sitting since it took the pressure off her distorted hips, though it created other problems. In fact the only place that she found true relief was in a hot bath. In the weightless and warmth the pain would gradually subside leaving her feeling as though 'an angel was wrapping me in its wings'. Water had always been her friend whether it be for swimming or for drinking. She had been a natural in the pool, more like a dolphin than a girl, champion swimmer in both butterfly and crawl. She had a strong chest, broad shoulders and powerful legs. In competition to see who could swim the furthest underwater there was never any contest; Anna would always be able to outlast all-comers. The competitive Wilson spirit was never more tested than in the pool or in the five years when cancer became the challenger. The further her illness progressed the more water she would consume, until she was seldom seen without a bottle in her hand, drinking profuse amounts to help soothe her body.

Despite the cold she was always hot and the back door would be open not only for Stoli to run in and out of the garden but to bring air into the room and ease Anna's breathing. Being a cold person I was forever sitting on the floor with my back to the radiator, searching for warmth. We had grown used to Anna's temperature being 38, her pulse 140, her peak flow 130 and her breath rasping as she gasped for more oxygen. It had become the norm and since Anna simply shrugged her shoulders uncomplaining and assured us she was 'OK' we didn't let her see that we were concerned. What was the point? She was in the hands of the most respected surgeons and oncologists in London.

Mitchell disappeared upstairs. He went to the drawer in the table at Anna's side of the bed and brought the contents downstairs. He handed Bob an envelope. On the front, in immaculate handwriting, it said, 'Mum and Dad x'. On the reverse was written 'Not to be opened until after my death.' She wasn't dead. We could still feel her here in the house, smell her, hear her voice. Only an hour ago I had lain on her warm body kissing her face, feeling her cheek next to mine, smelling her hair. Anna was invincible – or so I had always believed.

She was my own 'Kelly-won't-lie-down', bouncing back time and again after every set back. For five years she had looked cancer in the eye, challenging it to do its worst and proving that she was the stronger – until now.

The hardest thing for Mitchell had been leaving her there by herself. *'Till death us do part'* was always a lifetime away even though it had stared them in the face for so much of their married life. As we stood over her lifeless frame, convincing ourselves that she was at last out of her pain, Mitchell took off the wedding ring that he had placed there six and a half years previously, handing it in turn to me. The same wedding ring that my father had placed on my mother's hand in 1935 to seal a loving marriage that was to last nearly forty years, only to be terminated by my mother's death from the same disease.

Our physical beings had finally been parted but the umbilicus could never be severed. Anna would always be our daughter and would always fill us with pride at the role her life had played in not only our own lives, but in our souls. We would forever be moulded by her spirit and vitality.

I had asked the doctor to make sure they took special care of her. It was somehow ironic that she should die in the hospital where she had trained and where her illness was first discovered. She had completed the circle.

Bob put the letter away for a time when it seemed more appropriate. Mitchell placed two more letters on the mantelpiece next to Anna's favourite picture of their wedding day, one marked 'John' and the other 'Robert'. They were both on their way over, so very shocked at the news of their sister's death. John had phoned my mobile just before he went into dinner for the Turner Prize ceremony. He had an overpowering feeling that he should ring so made his way to the nearest phone booth. 'Where are you Mum?' 'In the Lister.' 'What on earth are you doing in the Lister?' 'John, get to Robert's.' 'What? I can't hear you, the phone's breaking up.' 'Go to Robert's house John – Anna's died.' It seemed such a cold, callous way to tell him but I had little choice. I wasn't sure the line was going to hold. I had to relay information fast.

Dr Kite had come to the hospital to certify Anna's death and had then made his way back to the house. As her GP he had become a familiar figure at Gun Lane, popping in for a lunchtime chat, knowing Anna would always have a smile and Mitchell a joke. Once he could see Anna was stable he would sit and chat about the world laughing at Mitchell's wit and wisdom.

His wife was with him and so made herself useful in the kitchen with the kettle. She noticed the array of tablets lined up for the next dosage. 'Would you like me to get rid of these?' Mitchell nodded and opened the cupboard above his head, revealing enough morphine, steroids, antibiotics, anti-emetics and laxatives to stock a pharmacy for the next year. She found a couple of Sainsbury's carriers, packed them to overflowing and took them out to the car. Gradually the house began to fill with disbelieving family.

We had all been gathered before, only a few weeks ago, waiting in hospital for the impending death of Anna. The doctors had warned us that she wouldn't last the night following a haemorrhage during an operation. But, as on many occasions, she had gone on to prove them all wrong. The very next day she was sitting up in bed making sure that the secret party being planned for her father was still going ahead in two weeks. As always her unselfish spirit was concerned for others, never for herself. How had we coped last night? Who came to the hospital? Where did we sleep? Did we have a giggle?

It wasn't that Anna didn't take her life-threatening illness seriously; she just wanted to deflect attention away from the all-encompassing pressure that crowded our lives. She understood so completely just how much cancer could eat away at family life.

We were numb. We had often wondered how it would be. There could have been so many different endings. We would never have guessed this one. We had clung to each other for support, weeping uncontrolled tears, shocked at the events of the past few hours. We had travelled so many routes in so many years never knowing the final course or destination. It was not of our choosing.

We were worried how the boys would react. John, the elder, loved his sister dearly and found it hard to come to terms with the severity of Anna's illness. He would always be there for her and often showed his frustration at the seemingly relentless march of the disease. His world, as an arts journalist, was one of questioning and interpreting other people's imagination and creation. The course of Anna's illness was irrational and unpredictable and John could only feel anger at the impotence of the medical profession.

Robert had spent as much time as he could in the last few months with Mitchell and Anna. Being a freelance photographer his days were never regimented so he and his girlfriend Sarah had spent hours of quality time at The Brompton or at Gun Lane talking, laughing, playing games or painting nails! His sense of humour was tactile and infectious whilst his sensitivity ran deep. Anna had been his buddy since his birth. She would mother him, play with him, dress him up and share secrets.

As soon as they arrived we clung to each other. This time it was real. Anna had taught and given us all so much in the last five years that we will always share her spirit, but in the last three hours her physical being had been taken away. I was apprehensive of the boys' feelings.

'I'm so glad it happened as it did,' said Robert, nudging me out of my anticipation. 'The fact that you were all three with her, holding her, talking to her and helping her is just how it should have been. After all you've been through it wouldn't have been right for her to die any other way.'

'She never lost her dignity and never gave in. It is what she would have wanted,' said John.

How wise they sounded, how philosophical. Robert and John

comforted us in our grief and helped us to see the kindness of her death. It was strange but warming to feel role reversal in action.

Mitchell's family joined us all and together we spoke of the joy and the gift of Anna. Her life had been relatively brief, but in those thirty-one years, and particularly in the last five when she was dying, she taught us all how to live.

Tired and exhausted, Bob and I made our way home to try to find sleep. We opened the letter and tried to take in the contents through the haze of tears.

> *Mum & Dad,*
>
> *I'm sorry I've not been able to say things to you face to face and that it now has to be via a letter – it just always seems too hard, too emotional – and you know what I'm like about 'not letting my barriers down'.*
>
> *I love you both so very, very much – you have both been amazing – not only through this illness but throughout my whole life – I am so very proud of what you've both achieved, of who you are – you really have given us all everything you could – thank you!*
>
> *I'm sorry you've been the ones taking a lot of my anger/black moods etc – nothing was meant personally towards you – I should have been loving/hugging you both – you deserved better.*
>
> *Obviously if you're reading this, then the inevitable has happened. I'm really not frightened about it – we've all got to go sometime – and one day we will all be together again – it's just I'll probably be younger and better looking than the rest of you! Please don't let your lives stop or be ruined by this – you must carry on together – talk together – don't ever push each other away – please be happy – and don't forget I'll be there watching just to make sure!*
>
> *I love you more than you'll ever know. See you later!*
>
> *Anna x*

I have always prided myself on my ability to cope with situations. A dear friend, a university professor, had once told me that if they handed out Degrees in common sense I would have a first-class honours. My reasoning powers have always been one of my better attributes and this I shared with Anna. We used to joke that we may not be the most intelligent of people but we could usually work things out, given a little time.

How did I feel that first morning of loss? Was I numb? Wretched? Distraught? I can remember little, save the question that forever runs through my head. Why, after five years of staring death in the face, had it taken me by surprise? All the warning signals had been there yet Anna's life had been ripped from our world in a whirlwind of events. Yes, she had been very poorly yesterday, but how many times had we been there before only to watch her recover, crisis after crisis.

I had come to terms with the question 'Why Anna?' She, who was a truly beautiful child with laughing face, loving nature and Raphaelesque blonde curly hair, had been the epitome of freedom. For her to have been captured by such an insidious enemy was unjust. To see so many of the activities that she loved curtailed was heartbreaking, but to observe the way she balanced her life by finding ways round her limitations was inspiring. Her reasoning helped her to accept that the life that she had was still a gift and no matter how much the quality had deteriorated, it was there to enjoy.

People would ask of me, 'How do you cope?' I would answer that if Anna could deal with what was thrown at her, I had no excuse for not doing so. It didn't matter to me how many years we faced hospitalisation, treatments, bad news, good news, as long as we had Anna. But there is only a certain amount of trauma that a body can take and Anna was beginning to feel the strain.

She had been very aware that her time was running out. She had prepared us all in the final five weeks, in a way that only Anna could. After one such crisis she talked to us all at different times. 'I can't do this any-more. It's too hard.' Mitchell had said 'You don't have to do it for us. We'll be OK.' Seeing her in pain, struggling to breathe, enduring new symptoms and treatments weekly had taken its toll on us all and the dilemma of holding on-to life, no matter what the quality, or letting go was demanding.

During those five years our relationship was always strong, but severely tested. There were times early on when Anna needed to talk but couldn't empty her heart for fear of opening the floodgate of her emotions.

'Talk to me Anna,' I would say.

'I can't Mum, because once I open up those gates I'm frightened that I just won't stop crying. And I mustn't do that.' Sometimes, in the latter period, she *would* open up her heart and express her concerns not for herself, but for Mitchell, for her dad, for me and for her brothers.

I learned so much from my daughter about love, communication, acceptance, and about what is truly important. I was a mother to her all her life, but during the last five years my maternal skills were tested more than ever before. I learned to be there when I was needed, to back off when my presence was inappropriate, to suggest and have my ideas accepted or rejected, to be practical in my help or be silent in my company. But above all I learned that a mother's love is unconditional and unrelenting and that I would have walked through fire to exchange my life for hers.

Love Story

I always referred to the bedroom at 'Threepwood' where she spent her childhood and teenage years as Anna's room. The pictures and furnishings were the ones she chose and the walls were painted by her with a lot of help from Mitchell. This had been her private space filled with her treasures, where she had friends to sleep over and talk until the early hours of the morning. Where she could play her own music and dress in her own fashion.

This was where I found myself, searching for a piece of her presence, a slice of her person, trying to catch her well-remembered smell or hear her uninhibited laugh. Her wedding dress still hung on the back of the door, protected by the zipped cover that had preserved it for six years. The pictures of Marilyn Monroe in the pink and white room reflected the femininity of Anna; the signed photograph of George Harrison, a reminder of our wonder that Anna's era could appreciate the music of the Beatles, a generation apart; the fruit machine in the corner bought by Mitchell for her twenty-first birthday in the hopes that it would cure her addiction; the cupboard full of nursing textbooks, letters, cards and notes from Mitchell. Why had I never changed the room? Perhaps because once she was diagnosed I was fearful of obliterating my strongest memories of Anna.

It was the room where, when she was eighteen and very unwell with flu, Mitchell arrived wearing a grass skirt, a T-shirt and a flower garland round his neck. He had no means of travelling the three miles from Hatfield to Brookmans Park, so he stood by the roadside thumbing a lift unaware of the amusement he was causing to passersby. As he walked into Anna's room, eager to see her, he lifted up his shirt to reveal a huge smiley face painted on to his body. It had the desired effect and Anna burst out laughing in disbelief at Mitchell's attempts to cheer her up. His concern was so great that he insisted on sleeping on the floor next to her bed all night so he could be there for her. We had not known him long but were impressed with his humour and his obvious love for Anna – and we trustingly let him stay next to our daughter!

He sat there all night watching her sleep and only left her side early in the morning to go to the toilet. He returned to find me by her side holding a bucket into which Anna was being sick. Sod's law I suppose, but Mitchell had proved his devotion by his night's vigil.

We could see the effect he had on her, how much she loved him and how he shared Anna's relish for fun. Her face brightened when he was around, her body language changed and he was good for her.

Little did we know then that this would be the first of many of Mitchell's attempts to make Anna laugh in times of illness, to show her how much he cared and to lighten situations that could have weighed heavy with despair. On the wall by the mirror in her childhood bedroom is a small black clip frame. Sitting diagonally across the frame under the glass is a torn sheet from a diary. The date is Tuesday 17th December 1985. In Mitchell's handwriting the words '1 year' are written followed by;

'I'd do anything for you,
I'd stand out in the rain
anything you want me to,
 … just don't let it slip away.

A small red heart seals the page which meant so much to Anna.

The first sighting Bob and I had of Mitchell was on Anna's eighteenth birthday in 1984. We threw a party for all her friends but it was gate crashed by two noisy individuals dressed in American baseball outfits who proceeded to take over the centre of the dance floor and do their own thing. We were expressing our pleasure at what terrific friends Anna had when Bob said, 'As long as she doesn't end up marrying one of those zany lads.'

She did, and for that we will be forever grateful. No one could have made her laugh more or loved her more. Their path together was rocky and treacherous but Mitchell made it an adventure. Without any given direction they forged their way through uncharted territory meeting challenges head-on, not always succeeding, not always coping. But always there was laughter, a crazy pair who squeezed a little more out of life than the norm.

Our first formal introduction to him was by way of a car crash. We were having a quiet weekend away when a phone call summoned us back home. Anna had been involved in an accident and we drove the hour and a half home not knowing the details other than the fact that Anna was unhurt. We were greeted at our home by friends who had taken charge of the situation and calmed down the nerves triggered by the anticipation of her parents' reaction. We were, of course, thankful that no serious physical damage had been done. The car was upside-down only a hundred yards away from home and was a write-off, Anna having swerved to avoid another car coming out of a turning. Sitting at my daughter's feet, looking suitably chastened, was a stranger who had apparently been a passenger in the car. We were introduced to Mitchell and were immediately taken by his concern for Anna. Without the baseball kit we were ignorant of the fact that we'd ever seen him before. Certainly I would have remembered those dark brown eyes.

Neither had I realised that Mitchell was perhaps the main reason why Anna was not keen to train in any of the London teaching hospitals that had accepted her. The Lister hospital at Stevenage was only thirty minutes from home, modern and had well-equipped nursing quarters. She had always been a home bird so I never questioned her choice. Mitchell occasionally attended lectures at Stevenage College and took his private study time very seriously − in the nurses' home.

She qualified and began her career on the wards at the Lister. She very quickly gained promotion to staff nurse and gradually became disillusioned when administration duties took her away from the practical nursing that she loved. She was approached by the head of Community Nursing, enquiring if she would be interested in working in the community. Anna jumped at the chance, spent a year at the University of Hertfordshire studying for her diploma and was finally totally happy in her career.

On 26 September 1992 Anna experienced the happiest day of her life. She and Mitchell were married in the tiny church in Knebworth Park surrounded by friends and family.

'How am I going to get through my speech without becoming too emotional?' In speaking about his daughter Bob was worried that he would be unable to control the tears and felt that he needed something to aid his composure. His answer came in the guise of a piece of material. At the beginning of his speech he asked the guests to wave their napkins at the first sign of a quiver in his voice. It worked like magic and caused much amusement, even though there seemed to be more audience participation than was usual with the father of the bride's speech. It would set a precedent for the rest of our lives and whenever emotion got the better of us in a public place, a hankie would always be whipped out of the pocket and waved in the air, much to others' amusement.

No bride ever looked so radiant or as happy as Anna did. She was fulfilling her dream of changing her name from Anna Wilson and becoming Mrs Anna Carey. She danced in the dress that she had taken so much care in designing, to the music that meant so much to her and Mitchell. We cheered at the fireworks that Anna had ordered as a surprise for Mitchell and we all cried and waved them farewell as Anna drove, in her wedding dress, the few hundred yards to the gates of Knebworth House where they were to spend their first night as husband and wife, in a four-poster bed.

We had held our breath prior to the wedding, wondering if Mitchell would appear in the topper and tails outfit that Anna wanted him to wear. His changing appearance from one week to the next left us all amused and curious to learn what fashion style he would be comfortable with. His hair had been pony-tailed, Mohican, flowing and dyed, streaked, shaved, spiked, shaggy, short, and shorn. His clothes had been just as varied and twice as wild. I was quietly relieved when I caught my first glimpse of him in the church. Yes, he had conformed, but had rebelled by the shortest haircut so far.

It was a year later that Anna developed a cough that wouldn't go away. She'd had a bout of flu in September, hadn't smoked during it, so had taken the opportunity to kick the habit once and for all. Since she was preaching to her patients in the community on the evils of smoking she felt she had better lead by example.

The cough seemed to be getting worse the longer she was deprived of cigarettes and we assumed it was one of the symptoms of the body's repair system. By November it had become very troublesome and was often worse after she'd been climbing stairs or exerting herself in the lifting of patients. She was also finding that she was choking on food quite frequently and had got into the habit of helping her meals down by drinking water immediately she had swallowed. She mentioned a strange feeling she had in her throat as if something was stuck in it and would often ask me if I could see anything. I told her it was perhaps her throat tightening up from tension, so we took little notice since she had always been the healthiest of us all.

She'd also complained of a pain in the top right region of her back, as though she had pulled a muscle. I took her off to see our good friend Gary Lewin, a physio, who gave her some treatment and massage around the area that was causing her trouble.

Christmas for Anna always started in November when we would go on our shopping expeditions; 1993 was no different. We caught a tube train to Marble Arch and as we came up the steps and on to Oxford Street it began to snow, huge white flakes that decorated our hair. It was magical and timed perfectly for the start of our day. We walked into Selfridges and were greeted by John Lennon singing, 'And so this is Christmas'. She loved the preparations, the build-up, the atmosphere, her Advent calendar, finding my hidden present lists and the fact that her birthday was on 7 December.

Christmas was going to be special. It would be the first time for several years that all the family would be together on Christmas Day. Bob and I began the day visiting Bronwen, a dear friend who was near the end of her fight against cancer and was forced to spend it in hospital. On our way home Bob began to feel decidedly queasy and by the time the family started arriving he was rocking himself backwards and forward clutching his stomach.

For the first time since I can remember Bob, missed out on Christmas lunch. It is quite difficult to balance the cooking and timing of such a meal, combining all the family's likes and dislikes and bringing it to the table piping hot. But to do this *and* rush up and down the stairs to comfort the sick is quite demanding. So Sister Anna took over the duty in the bedroom. As soon as we could hear him in trouble, she would dash upstairs to comfort him and encourage him to try and aim his vomit or diarrhoea into the correct receptacle, whilst we all sang 'Hark the Herald Angels Sing' to disguise the obvious distress he was experiencing.

After pudding had been demolished I crept upstairs to check on the patient's condition. Bob had managed to sleep and was feeling a little more settled. He began to realise that Christmas Day had reached 5.45pm and he'd seen little of it except the bathroom and bed. The word 'presents' sparked the semblance of a smile and I went downstairs to summon the rest of the family to his bedside.

John and Jane, Robert and Sarah, Anna and Mitchell and I, dressed him in a paper hat, helped him pull a cracker and oohed and aahed as he opened each of his presents. We finally made a part of Christmas Day together.

It was at this time, when my dear friend Bronwen was close to death, that I started to write a diary. Another friend had fought a battle with the disease and come through to live the rest of her life being forever grateful for the advance of medical science. The tenuous hold on life that makes its presence felt in the approach to the middle years had set my mind thinking thoughts that I wanted to see on paper. My diary had started on 24 December 1993, the day that I had helped Bronwen into hospital for a last-ditch effort to give her quality of life. Little did I realise then that the diary would become such a companion, such a reflection, a third eye that would help me see round situations.

It is interesting to note our awareness of Anna's condition that Christmas Day.

> *Saturday 25 December 1993*
>
> *By 7.00pm Bob felt comfortable enough to go downstairs and lie on the settee to watch television. We reflected on the day and decided – yes, Christmas Day had certainly been different.*
>
> *The concern over Anna's cough was felt by us all. If that was what giving up smoking did, then better to carry on. Having had a bad dose of flu and not having smoked during it, she'd taken the opportunity to try and kick the habit once and for all, particularly knowing that she would want to start a family in the near future. She really hadn't felt the need to begin smoking again and I was delighted to say the least.*
>
> *Bob managed to share his virus with the rest of the family so we all spent a certain amount of time between bed and toilet over the Christmas and New Year celebrations. It was only then that we felt a little guilty at making light of his predicament on Christmas Day.*
>
> *Bronwen became weaker but more settled. She had come to terms with her condition and had decided to go with the flow.*
>
> *Thursday 6 January 1994.*
>
> *Bronwen was lying on the bed when I went to see her. I commented that she'd be rivalling the supermodels leg wise, but she laughed and said she'd rather she have mine. She looked quite the most beautiful that I could remember. The struggle had left her face, her skin was smooth and pale, her eyes relaxed. And she still had the eye-shadow on! As I left her I gave her a wave and she reached out her hand to me. I went to hold it and give it a squeeze. We had shared a good sense of humour and friendship that encompassed many similar interests. There was a kinship that couldn't be broken. My gut instinct was not to dwell.*
>
> *Bronwen finally released her hold on life on 9 January.*

The weekend before her funeral Bob and I decided to go to Christchurch for a couple of days' relaxation. We had owned a property on the south coast for fourteen years where we had many friends and had shared so many lovely family holidays. Anna and Mitchell came to Christchurch for the weekend. Her cough was no better, neither was her breathing. We went for a walk over Hengistbury Head on

Sunday morning with friends, but Anna struggled to keep up with everyone. Her wheezing out-volumed the noise of the wind and she was embarrassed that, being the youngest, she appeared to be the most unfit. Mitchell had made her promise to visit the doctor and she had made an appointment for Tuesday.

I phoned Anna to find out how she'd got on at the doctor's. He thought that she may have become asthmatic, although he couldn't draw any conclusions about the cough so he wanted her to have a chest X-ray at the Lister.

After the first X-ray had been developed she was called back twice to have side views taken. They said it was routine and she would have to wait the usual time for results.

On Saturday, an early morning call brought a very distraught daughter on the phone. Anna had opened a letter from the Lister asking her to attend a CT scan appointment on the following Monday at 10.00am She knew something was wrong. She had two days to worry, to imagine, to panic and to sweat.

I called on all my reasoning powers to find answers as to why she should have to go for a CT scan so soon after an X-ray? Maybe it was smudged; maybe she'd had a bleed in her back where Gary had applied his massage to her muscles. Maybe there was a fault on the film. These were the thoughts of a layman, so different from those of a nursing sister who had recently been attending a patient with TB. The weekend must have seemed an eternity for Anna.

In my anxiety I phoned Bob's niece's husband Rino, who was head of Clinical Administration at the Hospital. I told him that Anna had been called for a CT scan and he soon put me at my ease by saying that if it would help, he could meet us there and see that everything was OK. It would be helpful to have a medical mind alongside us to translate anything that we didn't understand and we thought that it might speed up communication.

He invited me into the 'viewing room' during the scanning of Anna. To my amazement I saw a large round shadow across the right central part of Anna's chest. I immediately informed them that I knew exactly what it was. *My* diagnosis was that she'd ruptured a muscle which must have bled and for which she'd been having treatment from a physiotherapist. I received a polite tap on the head followed by a condescending look and told that their theory was a little more plausible.

It seemed that Anna had a cyst emanating from somewhere near the trachea region which had grown to the size of an orange. 'Cyst' to me was a word that covered a multitude of ailments. However, I was appeased and told that since its shape was spherical it was 99.9% certain that it was benign and full of fluid. Was I relieved to hear that! Well I guess my imagination, colourful though it is, certainly didn't wander any further than the immediate facts.

Rino began to explain to Anna what they had found and her face slowly changed from interest to bemusement. They took us into the viewing room and showed us the cross-sections of the CT scan which now declared the cyst to be as deep as it was wide. To me it seemed to fill the whole of the top half of her chest and I wondered how on earth she could have gone so long without feeling more effects.

We went back into the waiting area where Rino explained that the only way to remove the cyst would be by a major operation, either by opening up her chest or her ribs. This seemed to shake Anna more than the diagnosis and the worry that had built up over the weekend began to fill her eyes. The Lister couldn't perform such operations but a Mr Alun Rees was a visiting consultant from Harefield and it would certainly be in his field.

We left the Lister a little heavier than we had entered. We were leaving with a cyst − a mediastinum cyst − the likes of which *we* had never heard of before.

As we arrived home Anna immediately phoned Mitchell who, in his usual concerned way, told the rest of his colleagues to go and stuff their work − his wife was more important.

Tears were never far away from our eyes, but Anna summoned up enough spirit to phone her boss Caroline to ask to see her that afternoon. She would have to make arrangements for sick leave. As we had a coffee and mused on the morning's findings, the front door was flung wide and in walked a huge bouquet behind which was a very solicitous Mitchell. 'Show me how to iron T-shirts and jeans and I'll be all right!'

'Ah, *Love Story!*', I said wistfully. We looked at each other and laughed at the comparison, comforted by the knowledge that Anna's problem was just a cyst.

It was only with hindsight that my remark to Mitchell proved to be so poignant. How it has returned to haunt me since. Anna, during her romantic teenage years, had so enjoyed the film *Love Story* starring Ryan O'Neal and Ali MacGraw about a young girl and her fight against cancer. She had wept buckets over the portrayal of the couple's love and the crazy things they did during times of relief and stress.

Seeing the CT scan had allowed us a little relief; relief that Anna's symptoms were the result of a known medical condition and that it was nothing more sinister than a large cyst. She was informed that a consultation had been arranged at the Lister for the following Monday with Mr Alun Rees, who also worked at Harefield, the renowned cardiothoracic hospital.

We sat waiting to be called amid the other thirty-nine patients in the clinic that day, each accompanied by a relative or two. We discreetly found three chairs round a corner where we could laugh and joke to keep the unknown at bay. Anna had a vision of Mr Rees - big, round and cuddly. Bob's vision was that of a red dragon spouting Dylan Thomas. Anna won. And he had a wicked smile.

He spoke directly to Anna and expressed his interest at the enlargement in her chest. In twenty years of thoracic surgery he had only ever seen two other cysts in the same position and both had been in the last three months. We were relieved that Anna would not be a guinea pig.

He explained that the cyst would have to be removed quickly since it was fairly obvious from the X-rays and CT scans that her trachea was being trapped and squeezed, making the passage to her lungs very restricted, hence the wheezing. Her oesophagus was also affected since it too was being pushed to one side, this was the reason she was having difficulty swallowing food.

He told Anna she was 'priority' and that she should have his next available bed in Harefield. We waited three days without a word before we decided to phone Mr Rees' secretary at Harefield to see if there was a problem. There was – she had only just opened his bag and hadn't yet looked at his notes from the Lister clinic. She found Anna's file and read out loud, 'Anna Carey, very urgent'. She would be in touch directly.

There are two urgencies in life. The one that is applicable to you or your kin and the one that applies to others. The former causes nervous stomachs, heart palpitations, and a general heightening of the senses. The other can be filed away under 'to do'.

Anna was instructed to report to Harefield the following Tuesday for an operation on Wednesday and those six days were the longest we'd experienced. Our earlier state of ignorance meant that we'd previously carried on with our lives without fear. Anxieties now filled our days and nights.

Anna was twenty-seven when the cyst was discovered. We have no idea when it began to grow. We had little reason to worry even when symptoms began to show. But now that we had seen the mass that had taken over the space in her chest, we were concerned but relieved. Relieved that within a few days it would be removed and that she would be able to get on with her life.

She and Mitchell had been married for a year and they had a very settled life. Mitchell had continued to try and educate others into the ways of relaxed dressing at his place of work. He won his case and converted a few along the way. His individuality and sense of humour made him attractive in the workplace and he was soon forging his way in marketing, lending his own brand of original thinking to a growing company. At his best, he could entertain a room full of people for hours on end. At his worst his insecurities closed him down.

Over the next five years his special qualities would sustain Anna through an unfolding game of snakes and ladders.

Everybody Hurts

I met a lady in the car park this particular morning. I was removing my wellies after taking the dog for her early morning walk.

'How are you doing?' the stranger asked.

'Just fine thank you,' I replied politely.

She realised the question needed more padding for me to understand that she knew of our recent loss. 'You're coping all right?'

I replied that we were under orders. Anna wanted us to go out and face the world and not let her death ruin the rest of our lives. So that's what we'd been trying to do.

'I do know who you are. You're Megs aren't you? How's Bob taken it?' I told her that he was finding it hard, but was trying to bury himself in his work.

'I know a little of what you are going through,' she confided.

Since Anna died this sort of conversation had occurred many times. I thanked her and remarked that it was surprising just how many people suffer tragedies that are unknown to others.

'Yes, my husband had an operation and something affected him during the anaesthetic. He suffered terrible depression afterwards then hanged himself.'

I expressed my shock. 'How do you live with that?' I asked.

'Well, that was my second husband. My first husband was killed in a plane crash.'

It occurred to me that hers was a life of torment that was known only to those friends and family around her. Our own loss had been recounted in newspapers, not because Anna's story was any different to thousands of others, but because her father was a familiar face through the world of football and television.

Bob and Anna had a very special relationship. She was always his little girl, no matter how tall she grew or how mature she became. It was the only birth of our three children that he was to witness and assist in. It was a very special moment at our first home, only sixteen months after her brother John had been born. Bob and the midwife made Anna's entry into the world as smooth as could be — considering she had the cord round her neck a few times. He was there at her birth and at her death.

She was proud of his achievements as a professional footballer and her passion for the game was ingrained from infancy. I would take all three of our children to Highbury armed with teddies, books, drinks and sweets so they could watch their father perform his heroics in front of 40,000 people. And on the days that he went off to face a rival team they would line up at the door as he left, kiss him and say a ritual, 'Good luck, play well, keep them out, have a good game.' They had no idea that this wasn't what all fathers did, and only became aware of his fame once they were subjected to playground banter.

But they knew he was special. Not just because he played in goal for Arsenal, but because he had time to play with them. He would teach Anna to dance, to rock and roll and to jive. And when it came to ballroom, he would lift her on to his feet and waltz her round like a rag doll, her stride joined at his socks.

The grass of our back garden was specially laid for football and cricket matches, all serious games that would often end in tears. Depending on the season the garden arena could become the Olympic Stadium, Wimbledon, Lords, Twickenham or Wembley. The Wilson competitive streak would reveal itself and flashes of temper on one side would spark a celebratory rampage on the other.

But the main ingredient that bound us as a family was our need for fun and friendship. We gelled as a unit, supported each other, encouraged each other and liked each other – most of the time. Anna, being the middle one, looked up to John and mothered Robert. She had a ready-made lifesize doll to dress as she wanted. Robert would often be seen in the more glamorous gowns from the dressing up box with lipstick and eye makeup smeared somewhere near the correct area.

The rivalry between John and his younger brother during their late teenage years became less intense once John had gone to college, and visiting John and his friends in their student squat, where responsibility was inconspicuous, became very appealing to Robert. By the time the three of them were adults they were great friends, choosing to socialise with one another and their respective partners, and all supporting Arsenal.

Bob's career as a professional footballer came to an end in 1974 and he made the transition to television the hard way. 'There's the chair, there's the camera, now talk about football.' By the time Anna's condition had been diagnosed he was an established and respected television presenter for the BBC with twenty years' experience. His frustration at no longer being able to play in goal was mitigated by his ability to teach and most of his mornings were spent out on the training grounds coaching the new breed of goalkeepers – after he'd presented the morning sport on *Breakfast News*.

February 1994

Thus it was that Bob would drive from Television Centre at 8.30am, arrive at Harefield Hospital to have breakfast with Anna and stay with her as long as he could before he left for training with Arsenal. The plan was that he would do the early shift, I would then take over later in the day after taking my aerobic classes and Mitchell could still go to work and be there for Anna in the evening. The rest of the family would visit as and when they could. Her stay in hospital would only be for a week or so and then she'd be home.

It didn't begin well. Harefield Hospital was a shock. Where did its reputation come from? Certainly not from its architecture or grandeur. Ward C East was not an easy place to locate. The staircase sat apologetically behind a wall and a vending machine. At the top of the stairs we climbed over the laundry trolleys and walked down the curving corridor that ran alongside the wards.

We were greeted pleasantly by the staff and taken to Anna's bed. If our hearts could have sunk deeper into our shoes then we'd have had palpitations in our toes. 'I can't be nursed in *this* bed! I just *can't*' One side was pushed up against the wall. The head of the bed had a sink behind it, the foot a locker separating the bed from the nursing station. The open side was the main thoroughfare between the corridor and the ward. I watched Anna's face change from apprehension to fear. 'This place is freaking me out!' I had never seen Anna this out of control. The Lister, being modern, had spacious wards, space round every bed, a locker and chair within reach of the patient. Here space was at a premium. Patient was close to patient, male and female.

The nurse was concerned at Anna's state, comforted her and offered her a side-ward, just for the night. She would have to return to the same bed after the op tomorrow for intensive nursing. After a couple of days she'd be able to return to the side-ward. This compromise was acceptable and Anna calmed. By the time Bob and Mitchell arrived she was back to her normal self, telling them of the various tests she'd undergone that day.

When we left in the evening Anna was in a better state of mind but it was an awful wrench to leave her in hospital. She waved from the window like the Princess in the Tower, a scene that would be repeated over and over again at other times, at other hospitals. It never became any easier.

Anna hated being alone. She preferred the company of others to help time pass and we were willing to be there. Thus it was that Bob was there to accompany her to theatre the next morning, give her a kiss goodbye and promise her that I would be there on her return to the ward.

The road to Harefield seemed longer than the previous day and my heart was beating faster than the passing cat's-eyes. I raced up to the ward intending to be by Anna's bed when she returned from theatre only to find her already back. She was sitting upright with her eyes half-closed, looking very calm for someone who had just undergone major surgery. No drips, no drains, no bandages. I bent over and kissed her head.

As she opened her eyes she said, 'They've not taken it out.'

I presumed the anaesthetic was creating delusions.

'Yes, all right darling, go back to sleep.' But the nurse confirmed Anna's revelation and told me Mr Rees would be up soon to see me.

Still in his theatre blues, Mr Rees introduced us to the senior cardiologist who was also gowned-up. He explained to Anna that they hadn't removed the cyst because they wanted to do some more tests. It appeared not to be what they had originally thought and the tests would necessitate her having an aortogram that afternoon.

When I questioned Mr Rees further, he explained that he didn't touch the cyst because in looking at her trachea through the bronchoscope, he had a 'bad feeling' about it. He felt that it would perhaps be better treated medically.

How should I interpret this? Was it good news or bad? I was confused. I pressed for more. I was told the cardiologist would perform the aortogram because there was just a possibility that Anna could have an aneurysm of the aorta. It would necessitate a few more injections, a tube being inserted through the femoral artery via the groin and dye being passed through the veins and arteries to see what was affected by this growth. Mr Rees flashed a reassuring smile and left saying, 'See you this afternoon.'

It was all so matter-of-fact that I had no way of knowing how I should react. I phoned Mitchell and he left work immediately. He and Bob arrived together, just in time to see Anna wheeled off once more. It enabled us to make our first visit to the League of Friends' Coffee Shop, a place that would become a haven of ham and cheese toasties.

Anna came back to the ward with a smile on her face and a hole in her groin. The four of us sat and talked through to the evening. The pattern was set.

The next day Anna was to have a biopsy under local anaesthetic. A needle would be inserted through her chest and lung. There was a possibility that the lung would collapse so Mr Rees and the team would be there just in case.

Mitchell and I retreated to the L of F in search of refreshment, away from all things medical. Here you could see emotions being shared and exchanged: relief, worry, gratitude, anger and bewilderment. But the common denominators were tea, coffee and toasted sandwiches.

Anna's return from the biopsy found her more subdued. The insertion of the needle had not been pleasant, rather like a knitting needle being pressed through cardboard. She had seen the piece of tissue as it came out and described it as being white in appearance. This would be the one and only time that Anna would come face to face with the vicious enemy that had invaded her body.

The only clue we had to her condition was the word 'biopsy'. We presumed that the cyst was not of a common type and that tests would suggest how it should be treated. We had no need to panic since we had been assured from the beginning that it was benign. We waited all day for Mr Rees to come rushing through the door waving the results saying, 'Right, we know what it is, let's get on with the treatment.'

He had no results. He could only guess what it might be from its position. An aneurysm had been discounted and his main concern was the growth, its position and its treatment. He threw the words, 'lymphoma' and 'Hodgkin's' into the conversation, but we were too naive to pounce. It wasn't until my journey home round the M25 that evening that those two words crept into my brain. Even with my limited medical knowledge I knew the association. How *dare* he suggest such possibilities as the cause of Anna's problem? Cancer just didn't enter the equation and I resented the surgeon's lack of tact in even allowing the thought to enter our heads.

We had reached the weekend and it was explained that since the labs closed down until Monday the results wouldn't be through until the beginning of the week. Anna was offered a side-room again and we took pleasure in transporting what was now a florist's dream to a more open space. The single room acted as a haven away from the comings and goings of the ward. Here we could relax and be ourselves, laugh, talk and play silly games. Battleships, cards and jigsaws began to fill the room, Mitchell having decided that the name of the game was not to get bored.

Sunday saw a surge of visitors sitting round Anna's television watching the Coca-Cola Cup semi-final, creating a real party atmosphere. That was until Mr Rees had been in and ordered Anna back to the ward. At no time was she to be out of the view of the nursing station because of the possibility of her choking. What *we* hadn't realised was that since her trachea had been reduced to one quarter of its size, it would only take one small coagulation of mucus to block her air passage.

Anna and Mitchell were visibly depressed and angry, wearied by visitors, fed up with waiting, anxious with uncertainty. Surely a new week would bring answers.

We had reached Valentine's Day and Bob was due at the King Edward Hospital to have his arthritic hips injected under anaesthetic. Bob and I called in to see Anna then drove into London in the snow. Mitchell was in charge at Harefield for the day.

The contrast between the two hospitals was very marked. Harefield, being an old fever hospital was almost claustrophobic in the proximity of beds, tables, chairs and staff. Privacy was at a premium and space was identified by corridors and areas for walking. Elbow room there was none.

The King Edward was a haven of silence. We were shown the library and asked to wait a while. Copies of *The Field* and *Countryman* were neatly displayed on the coffee table whilst the books and plaques on the wall welcomed you into the history of Sister Agnes and her good work for Officers and Gentleman.

Hospital porters are a cheerful breed, used to chatty banter with the patients as they wheel them to and from their treatments. They wear their overall with pride and are always on hand with a joke and a witticism. The porter at the King Edward was more of the hotel breed, subservient rather than friendly and one almost felt guilty for not giving him a tip. We were taken along the hushed carpeted corridor to a single room with bath and were asked to wait until Sister had time to see us. For all we knew there was not another patient in the building. The television was elevated for ease of viewing from the bed. The windows overlooked the backs of mews houses in Marylebone and the skyline of London roofs, but the triple glazing allowed only the silence of the inner walls to penetrate.

I went to use the loo but decided against it since I didn't want to disturb the neatly folded V-shaped end of the toilet roll. However, my bladder finally won and my conscience forced me to refold the paper after use.

Bob insisted he was going to be all right and encouraged me to return to Anna and not come back until the morning, when he'd be ready for home.

I drove back through the snow full of expectation, it being Monday, the start of a new week and certain that results *had* to be forthcoming today. How wrong I was.

Mr Rees and Asif, his registrar, came to see Anna, Mitchell and me. They once more apologised for the absence of information and told us that this was unusual to wait quite so long for the cultures to produce results. I asked Mr Rees if he had decided that once the results had arrived and were what he hoped to see, he would then go ahead and operate. We knew that Wednesday was his day for thoracic surgery and time was short. He then said, 'Oh no, I'm quite sure I won't be operating. Anna's treatment will be by chemotherapy and radiotherapy. This was the first indication that we were to travel down a road which none of us wanted to follow. It was the first real sign that the doctors were serious in their suspicion that Anna's tumour might be cancerous.

The void that Mr Rees left behind was cavernous. It left so much more room for rampant thoughts to come running into our heads, but still there was a feeling of disbelief. They could be wrong, after all, nothing had been found in the tests therefore that *had* to be a good sign.

I rang the King Edward to see how Bob was after his op. He was dozy but fine. He insisted I stayed where I was, knowing that I was better engaged with Anna than risking driving through the snow into London. Anna, Mitchell and I were quiet, apprehensive and slightly unnerved.

My journey home round the M25 was accompanied by a rhythm in my heart that was to be with me for some time to come. Adrenaline was pumping and a panic began to creep under my bones and into my chest where it was to stay for weeks. Getting home didn't help. Usually I had a warm body and comforting arms to sink into, but all I had was a cold bed and lots of thinking space.

The next morning Mitchell and I were in early to see Anna. Every day brought new expectations about a result and we felt that this *had* to be the day.

Asif and Sister Pam arrived and invited us into the restroom for a while. Yes, they had the results but they'd proved inconclusive. However, cancerous cells were present but were not identifiable. Further tests would have to follow and another biopsy was required. Mr Rees would be operating on Anna the next day to make sure he could extract more tissue from the mass than before. We were left to take our time in returning to the ward, allowing the news to filter into our minds, news that was going against the grain of all that we'd been assured. It was hard to take in. We didn't know what it meant. Our comprehension of the facts was smudged so we tried to clarify our minds by positive thinking.

I left Anna and Mitchell to talk together and went over to the League of Friends. It was full and only one table had an empty chair. I sat down with a coffee and my thoughts. I was still fighting the words I'd just heard and began to realise how frightened I was. I began to shake and desperately wanted Bob to be there. Where was he? Why wasn't he there to be with me? What was keeping him? Please, *please* make him come through the door. My wish was granted at a stroke and relief rushed through my veins as I saw him walking into the room. I tried to control my emotions but tears were too easy and they flowed in torrents. We went outside and sat in the weak sunshine that was beginning to melt the snow. We sat there long enough to talk and for my face to return to near normal before going back to the ward and Anna.

Bob had managed to get a taxi from London, a difficult journey in the snow. He'd had to stay in the King Edward to have aqua therapy and see the doctor before they released him. Anna was pleased to see him and they exchanged hospital news.

Mitchell began to prowl round brooding, we thought, over the news we'd heard earlier. He grabbed his hat and keys and said, 'I'll be back soon.' We presumed he'd gone to the L of F for a toastie and cigarette. Anna and Bob continued to swap stories. Hospitals had suddenly become the focus of our lives. Two nurses came rushing through the ward shouting 'Anna, Anna, come here, quickly!' They were laughing and grabbed Anna and took her to the window.

The ward was on the first floor of a semi-circular building that wrapped round an area of grass that had been white with snow. On the ground beneath the window the snow had been broken by large letters ten feet tall. The I and the U sat either side of a huge heart in the middle of which lay Mitchell looking up to Anna's window.

Anna's face beamed half with disbelief, but with total joy at Mitchell's act of love. The trolley ladies came bustling through to look at the graffiti in the snow and laugh and cry at the outward show of emotion. 'Who said that the age of romance was dead?' Joan, a fellow patient said it was the best medicine her heart had had since she'd been in hospital. It certainly helped us all look at the day in a different way.

Mr Rees arrived later that evening to explain to Anna what he was intending to do the next day. He would have to take the biopsy from above the tumour going in via the throat — suddenly the cyst's name had changed. It would entail her having another pre-med and another general anaesthetic. His intention was to remove as big a piece of tissue as he possibly could so that there would be no doubt about its exact nature. At last we felt we were moving forward. Soon we would know and soon Anna would be able to start the treatment needed to shrink the tumour in her chest. As the evening came, so did the frost, sealing Mitchell's artistic flourish into the snow for the night.

The next day a very dozy Anna arrived back on the ward with a dressing across her throat and a tube leading from a hole beneath the dressing, draining into a bottle. Mr Rees came up to the ward and took Robert, Mitchell and me to one side. He explained that the operation had been difficult. The tumour was sitting amidst main arteries and extracting the tissue had been 'a dicey business.' He had, however, managed to get two large sections which he felt should be more than sufficient for a decent histology. I asked him why he had thought that it might be a lymphoma.

'The position of it. However, I don't know that it is. I *hope* it's a lymphoma.'

'Why do you hope?' I asked.

'Because lymphoma is treatable. If it's something else then we're in the hands of the gods. It could well be something else'

Realisation was finally beginning to dawn on me though Mitchell, fortunately, did not take in the implications. I then asked Mr Rees what made him realise that it wasn't a cyst.

'Because of the way it's gripping Anna's throat. If it had been a cyst then it would merely have the action of pressing. It is clear from inside the trachea that the tumour is gripping and squeezing.'

I could feel my own body beginning to react. He was saying words that I didn't want to hear, explaining things that had only so far been possibilities, not probabilities. It was difficult to think, whilst looking at Anna lying there, that this huge tumour was taking over the space in her chest and gradually squeezing the passage of her breathing. She was so calm, quiet and peaceful.

We left Mitchell with Anna. Robert and I took ourselves to the hospital's main entrance where chairs were arranged around coffee tables. Rob and I sat and talked about Mr Rees' words. This was the start of the 'crying corner'.

It was another two days before we were given any more news. Anna was quite calm and spent her time completing a jigsaw that Mitchell had bought. Visitors came and went and the atmosphere was tense but controlled. Anna had been in Harefield for ten days, and she had been in as many beds, being moved from one part of the ward to another, depending on her condition.

Bob and I met Asif as we were returning from saying goodbye to the last group of visitors. He had just seen Mitchell and told him the latest histology findings. Mitchell had gone to tell Anna. The tests identified the biopsies as either lymphoma, cancer of the lung or cancer of the pleura. However, the cells were 'poorly differentiated', which was not a good sign since this almost certainly discounted lymphoma. We would obviously have to wait further for a fuller diagnosis before knowing for certain.

I suggested that he went to see Anna to tell her himself. We would follow shortly. John had come to the hospital and so the three of us made our way back to the ward and were ushered into the nurse's restroom. There Asif was explaining the findings to Anna, Mitchell and Sister Pam, who was comforting the two of them.

The tests had shown that the tumour was malignant, but its exact nature was still not clear. Once they knew then Anna would have to undergo chemotherapy or radiotherapy to shrink it. Anna and Mitchell had already been told the news before we arrived and were still taking in the enormity of what was being said. They were both crying, but then turned to comfort us. To comfort us! Anna made us all get together, Mitchell, herself, John, Bob and me, hold each other and cry as one. And cry we did.

Sister Pam suggested she find a room in the private wing where we could be together for a while away from the ward. Mitchell's parents had arrived to visit and having been told the news took Mitchell for a walk to give Bob and myself a little time with Anna.

How vivid that scene remains in my mind. Anna sitting on a bed, her eyes red with crying, hugging us both and talking as openly as she had ever done, reversing the family roles. She began to reassure us that she was very capable of coping with whatever lay before her. Of all the family, she felt that she was the one who would cope with cancer the best.

'This thing will try and destroy not only me, but you as well. Don't let it. Talk to each other and keep communicating. And wherever this thing takes me I want quality of time and quality of life, but most of all I want to have fun.'

We talked of things strange, like our obsession with arranging our funerals. She made me promise that at her funeral, if it came to that, she should be dressed in her wedding dress with fresh anemones in her hair, whilst I had to wear my pink suit that I had worn on her wedding day. She reminded me that the gypsy could be right after all. I looked at her in astonishment.

'How do you know about that?' I asked.

'You told me years ago.' I could hardly believe that I'd revealed such a warning to her.

Bob and I were childhood sweethearts, going out with each other, on and off, since we were twelve. During one of the 'off' periods I had taken a fancy to one of my older brother's friends. He was tall and dark and handsome, a few years older than me, but I'd seen the course of true love and gone back to Bob. We were holidaying with my parents in Scarborough and Bob and I were wandering the back streets when we came across a fortune-teller's booth. For a laugh I left Bob outside in the street and went in to see what she could reveal about my future.

'There are two men in your life. One is dark and the other is blonde. But the blonde one will win through and you will be married. A big wedding. You will have three children, but one of them will die.'

As each phase of my life unfolded it followed the pattern the gypsy had set. By the time we had our three children our life was good. Bob's career in football had taken off and he was successful. Our three children were healthy and happy. It frightened me sometimes that our life together was so perfect and I was afraid that something would happen to destroy it. But as the children grew into adults I was relieved that the gypsy's warning had finally proved false.

Were we in a play? If so the reversal of roles was highly improbable and I grew angry at the nonsense that was paraded before us. It should have been me in the bed, reassuring my loved ones, me seeing the stare of consternation. It was difficult to comprehend, let alone accept.

We all returned to the ward, where life had taken on a different hue. The nursing staff were very sensitive to the situation and suggested they make up a bed in Anna's bay for Mitchell to stay the night. This was no time for them to be parted.

Bob and I left separately and once again I headed towards the M25. I turned on the radio to be greeted by REM singing 'Everybody Hurts'. The sentiment of the song reflected our lives to a millimetre. I didn't just cry, I screamed! All the way round. 'No! No! No!' My disbelief and distress were totally overwhelming. By the time I arrived home I had no screams left. Bob and I slept, clinging to each other, exhausted from emotion.

Anna had also started a diary that very day. Her first entry is:

> *Friday 18 February 1994*
>
> *Today I was told I had cancer – how weird! We've cried/ laughed/cried and cried. I thought I already knew – but I kept a little dream alive that they'd all get it wrong – I was wrong.*
>
> *Everyone's very protective of me and will do anything I ask. Nurses are excellent. Mitchell's staying the night. I'm not scared, it's just unreal – I can't believe it's happening to me. I wonder how people will react to me now?*

It was good to see Anna next morning looking cheerful, amused that Mitchell had been taken for a patient by the breakfast-trolley lady. Much of the night had been spent talking between the two of them and the nurses. But 'Black Saturday' was only just beginning.

Anxieties began to creep into the conversation and moods of those around. We still had no idea what form of treatment Anna would have. We had been warned that she could be moved to Mount Vernon for possible chemotherapy and radiotherapy. But until there was a positive diagnosis of the tumour no decision would be made. Suddenly the leaflets on cancer treatment became horribly relevant and we all read them avidly.

Friends and family came and went, all trying to be cheerful, but the atmosphere had begun to change. Anna and Mitchell took themselves off down the corridor, the two of them agitated in their mannerisms, leaving the rest of us to sit and exchange small talk. Anna returned alone and sat herself down at the jigsaw. I asked what was wrong. She replied in no uncertain terms that she was angry.

'Why?' I asked.

'Because I should be able to cope with things better than I am?'

'So what makes you think you're so special that you should be able to cope with it better than anyone else?' I shouted. Tears were not absent.

'Because I should! I shouldn't be feeling like this!'

'Then why not let your anger go?' tempted Bob, offering the raised palm of his hand. 'Go on Anna, hit it. Make a fist and hit it.'

Anna declined, not wanting to hurt her father, but his insistence challenged her daring and she let fly with venom, thumping her fist into his palm. Bob's face reflected his surprise and astonishment, but smiles and relief put an end to the outpouring of energy.

Mitchell, meanwhile, had taken his brother Nathan to the crying corner. His mood was becoming morose, his anger vented towards everything and anything. His lack of sleep over the past few days and the realisation of the seriousness of Anna's illness resulted in a confused and irrational mind. We were all of the opinion that he needed to get away from Anna and the hospital for a while to help him see things from a different perspective.

Bob and I had decided to leave Anna alone. We saw Mitchell and asked if he was OK. 'No, just feeling anger.' We told him he should try doing what Anna had done, by hitting her dad to relieve the tension. What we didn't realise was that Mitchell thought that Anna had hit Bob for real. He took himself straight up to the bay to remonstrate with her for lashing out at her father.

John and Robert had come over to lend their support as ever and realised that emotions were getting very much out of hand. We arrived back on the ward to find Robert trying to make Mitchell see reason, but not succeeding. The men went off downstairs for a walk leaving Anna to eat her supper whilst I sat on the bed reading. Anna was having difficulty feeding between the sobs, so I asked her if she wanted to tell me about it. 'Oh just leave me alone!' she yelled.

If ever she wanted to turn on my tap then she succeeded. What else could she have said? What else could I have done? She stoically sat there eating the food in which she had no interest, whilst I sat there looking at a magazine, the words of which were a complete blur. By rights we should have been sitting together with our arms round one another for support. But instead insular hurt wedged us firmly apart.

John and Robert had managed to persuade Mitchell that he needed sleep. He calmed down and went up to Anna. We decided to leave them alone for the evening.

The hardest thing I had to do was walk away from Anna's room. I couldn't bear to see her upset and confused. It was so easy when she was young and had a temperature. I knew how to look after her then. Tuck her up in bed with a hot water bottle and a hug. Now I had to walk away from her with my own feelings of rejection burning in my chest I began to sob in the corridor. I sobbed down the stairs, through reception and to the car park.

Bob took me in his arms and held me tight. 'Don't, don't. You know she's only taking it out on you because you're the nearest. She wouldn't do it to me – not Daddy, my Daddy.'

Those words brought a smile to my face. It had long been their little saying, ever since she had seen and loved *The Railway Children*. I knew what he was saying and it was true. Who else could Anna vent her feelings on? It was only *because* of our closeness that she felt she could act as she did.

But my despair was not diminished. It was bad enough that Anna and Mitchell should have to cope with the traumas they were facing at such a stage in their lives. It was worse that we seemed unable to help them in coping with it. Anna's diary:

Saturday 19 February 1994

Today was a bad day – we were unprepared for another well of emotion – but it came and hit us very hard. I freaked out. I got angry at not being able to control my emotions – this set off waves of anger from everyone – and we all fell out with each other. I didn't like it – the last thing that's needed now is bad feelings. I'm scared for Monday to come – whereas everyone else is wishing for it to come – I'm scared that hoping and praying I'll get better won't be enough. And yet I'm not afraid to die – I'm just scared of dying.

Mitchell's staying tonight – he's upset and we discussed how he'd feel if I died. He'd thought of suicide but decided that disappearing would be better!! Being together – alone – has been good – very good – it certainly helps you to appreciate each other.

Sunday 20 February 1999

Mitchell very angry again tonight – went back over yesterday's events – admits it's just because he's angry and not event itself! Confusing and upsetting – I don't need this on top of everything – and yet I want Mitchell to let it out to me – I can't win and neither can he.

After the emotional turmoil of Black Saturday the following days were a complete contrast. Anna and Mitchell became as calm as they were previously manic and my relief was huge. By Monday the jigsaw was completed, the magazines read and the games had long been abandoned. The waiting game had once more taken over. Mr Rees arrived to deliver the news that there were still no results. He had never known it before, that it was unique in his lifetime as a surgeon. Neither was there any explanation as to *why* there were no results. Anna had now been in Harefield Hospital for two weeks and we were still no further forward knowing what was wrong with her than when we started.

At 6.30 pm on Tuesday evening Mr Rees arrived into the room with his entourage. 'Well Anna, with your permission I want to do something about it tomorrow – I want to operate.'

Astonishment took over – we were truly gobsmacked. He explained that he wanted to take a large biopsy, relieve the windpipe and try to investigate. He didn't know what he was going to find or how he was going to proceed, but he would perform a thoracotomy, as had been the initial intention, and take things as he found them.

'But you're supposed to be going skiing tomorrow,' I said.

'That's now postponed till Thursday. I couldn't go on holiday leaving Anna as she is, so we're going to have a go.' On his way out Bob stopped him in the corridor. 'Is it that urgent?' he asked. Mr Rees looked him in the eye. 'If I didn't do it tomorrow I fear that she wouldn't be here when I got back.'

The fact that something positive was to be done relieved the tension for us all. It would be Anna's third anaesthetic in two weeks and a third attempt to get answers to all the questions.

At 9.00am next morning Bob and I accompanied Anna's bed to theatre. We gave her a big hug and a kiss and as she entered theatre she called back, 'Buy me a big present!' We tried shopping, we tried walking, we tried driving, but in the end we headed back to the hospital to be close at hand. Once more the League of Friends provided us with comfort and shelter.

Nearly four hours later we were talking to a very exhausted surgeon. 'Well I've got it!' he said with delight.

'What do you mean got it?' we asked.

'I've got it out. It's in a bucket — it's white and I don't know what it is, but I've got it. It took a bit of doing. I've never seen anything like it before in twenty years of thoracic surgery. We will send half of it to the Marsden and half to Mount Vernon. Her trachea is free and she can now breathe normally.'

'Is her trachea all right?'

'Yes, sometimes in situations like this the cartilage will rupture but I just pressed it out and it sprang back into shape beautifully.'

We were overjoyed. We shook him by the hand and thanked him profusely. Was he going back into theatre?

'No, I've left them to put her back together. I'm going to go and have a very stiff drink!' With that he left.

By this time the staff on duty had gathered at the nursing station and had been listening to the news. We turned round and they were all in tears. They hugged us and showed us just how touched they were by the news. The tea lady came past in floods of tears, reflecting everyone else's massive relief.

We rang Mitchell who was overjoyed and immediately began his journey in to Harefield and arrived well before Anna returned to the ward. As they wheeled her back I went to the side of her bed.

She opened her eyes as I said, 'He's got it all out Anna.'

'What all of it?' she asked.

'Yes all of it.'

'You're lying to me.'

'I promise you I'm not, they've got it all.' At that she went back to sleep.

It was decided, because of Anna's immediate needs that I stay the night and that Mitchell and Bob go home for some sleep. It helped me slip back into the role of mother so comfortably. This was how it was meant to be. The chair at the foot of her bed unfolded into a supportive footrest so I could be next to her all night. Neither of us was that comfortable so we talked on and off until 3.00am

Bob arrived 7.45am and suggested I go home for a while. I drove round the M25 in some sort of stupor unable to comprehend all that had taken place. I could feel my adrenaline pumping and my mind filled with the past six days. Emotions had been catapulted one way then another, our minds hardly managing to catch up with events.

A few days previously we had been in despair, not knowing what Anna's future held. Answers had been at a premium, then just as suddenly the whole situation had been turned on its head and Anna's future was seemingly secure. No sooner had we come to accept one situation than we were turned in the opposite direction to re-adapt our concepts.

During all of this the unknown still played the biggest part. How dangerous was this tumour, other than the immediate threat to her trachea, which had now been miraculously removed? Was this the total solution to the cancer? Would Anna require more treatment? What sort of cancer was it? How was it started? Would it come back?

I reached home and had a welcome shower. I changed into my keep-fit gear and headed for my aerobics class. In a strange kind of way I desperately needed the exercise to get rid of the enormous adrenaline surge that was with me. I grabbed a warm-up tape, put it into the stereo and made myself ready, only to be greeted by the familiar tones of Take That, Anna's favourite group. In a strange way it seemed to keep us in touch even though my mind was on the job in hand of teaching a class full of ladies.

The final week of Anna's stay in Harefield was in marked contrast to the first two weeks. Recovery was slow and painful but Anna's determination to get back her fitness meant that she practised her physiotherapy assiduously.

We learnt more about the operation from Asif, Mr Rees' registrar. He told us of his admiration for Mr Rees, how it had taken the surgeon fifty minutes to persuade the tumour away from any one part of her chest. Once he had a small hold he spent another hour prising it away from the trachea. It had been very difficult and time-consuming. The tumour had been wrapped round the aorta and the aortic arch as well as the trachea, but at no time did the initial attachment show itself. Where the tumour was coming from remained a mystery.

Harefield presented us all with a learning curve that took the family by surprise. Our minds had been partially educated in the ways of cancer but there was much that we had yet to understand – our own reactions for example. For Bob and myself it was a chance to claw back our parental function and be there to support and protect our child as we rode the roller-coaster that had driven the days. For Mitchell it was confusion and panic that his seemingly perfectly healthy wife was now facing an illness that could result in the worst scenario. For Anna it was more of a physical problem but she also had to juggle her parents' need to protect and her husband's love, with the emotional agitation that fed our concern and Mitchell's anger.

She wanted Mitchell near her, but didn't want to deal with the transference of his exasperation and confusion. She wanted her parents' support but didn't want to go back to being their little girl. She had to cope with the nightmares that crept into her mind and she had to try to keep a level head above the turmoil. But most of all she wanted to be back to normality.

Harefield was now a capsule in our lives.

Remission

February 1994 – September 1994

'Malignant Schwannoma. Soft tissue sarcoma. A malignant growth of the nerve sheath.' Thus read the results from Mount Vernon. Mr Rees explained that it was a very rare form of cancer and the recommended treatment was removal by surgery. He was delighted that the decision he'd taken was the correct one. The reason for the original confusion was that schwannomas grow with a sac around the tumour and therefore give the appearance, on a scan, of being a cyst. It was somewhat of a relief that at last they were able to put a name to the cause of all the trauma.

'It's gone now and you should be able to get on with your life without a problem,' explained Mr Rees.

'Why did I have it in the first place?' asked Anna.

'Absolutely nothing to do with lifestyle. Just bad luck. You should have no more problems now it's been removed. Now get on with the rest of your life by indulging in excess of everything. I don't want to see you for three months.'

So that was all right then. Suddenly, after six weeks of waiting for histology results, of being gradually informed that what they were really dealing with was cancer, of coming to terms with future medical treatments, of worrying about whether Anna would die and how long it would take, of coping with a major operation and the recuperation, suddenly Anna could go home, get on with her life and enjoy herself.

The confused messages began to scramble my brain. Hadn't we just spent two weeks at home since the operation coming to terms with the future? My own conception of cancer didn't recognise the facts that were being put before us. Couldn't malignant cells be spread through surgery, or travel to other parts of the body via the lymph system and the blood? My ignorance was causing anxiety deep inside the pit of my stomach. Mr Rees was suggesting that Anna was cured and there would be no need for any further treatment, just a return visit every three months for a check-up.

We had waited so long for an answer and yet, when it finally arrived, it solved nothing. It merely provoked more questions. I needed assurance that Anna would be screened by a cancer specialist, assured that all the cancer had been resected, and that any recurrence would be recognised immediately. Perhaps then the tension that ate away at my stomach would ease. Mr Rees understood my concerns and agreed to make Anna an appointment to see Mr Makepeace, a consultant oncologist at Mount Vernon Hospital.

Mr Makepeace was a very friendly, cheerful person, quietly spoken as though treating all information as confidential. Anna warmed to him immediately and felt that he was genuinely interested in her condition. He expressed his incredulity at having a patient with malignant schwannoma and told us that it was extremely rare. He reassured us that the treatment she had received from Mr Rees had been absolutely correct. However, he would be happier if she were to have four weeks of radiotherapy to act as a mopping-up exercise, just in case any stray cells had transferred themselves through the sac during the operation. Anna would begin the course in a month's time, giving the wound time to heal

Anna now had breathing space to get herself back to fitness and to come to terms with everything that she had just been through. She started on a very gentle programme of aerobics to improve her physical condition. She would have preferred swimming as an exercise but since her scar was causing problems with healing she was not allowed to put it near water. But her mental health was not so well attended and it began to take a battering. Thus her diary reads:

> *Wednesday 16 March 1994*
>
> *Watched 'Peak Practice' on TV- 30 year-old diagnosed Hodgkin's Lymphoma – started wishing it was what I had – at least they'd know what to do! Found myself getting a bit freaked/ scared about everything – wanted to talk to someone – but no one I knew! Maybe things are only just sinking in – I don't think I've had butterflies about it before. Feeling pissed off with it all when I think about it at the moment. Find I'm managing to forget all about it and then suddenly remember – and I get angry.*

It was important for all of us that life returned to normal as quickly as possible, but since Anna was not allowed to resume work we decided to concentrate on things domestic. So we planned a visit to the Ideal Home Exhibition with Jane, John's partner, as a fun day out. Anna and Jane were more like sisters. They had the same wacky sense of fun, shared secrets and enjoyed each other's company. It pleased Bob and me that our three children and their partners all got on so well together. John and Jane lived in Crouch End, just round the corner from Robert and Sarah so it was natural that they saw a lot of each other.

On arriving at Earls Court we threw ourselves into the exhibition like lambs to the slaughter trying to visit every stand that provided public participation – the personal massager, the water beds, the complimentary coffee and biscuit house, the kitchen appliances – managing to see much and make a nuisance of ourselves at the majority of the displays. We decided there was a tier system to our needs. Megs was looking at conservatories, Anna at loft conversions and Jane for garden gates.

But by lunchtime it was fairly obvious that our day had finished when Anna ended up in a heap on the floor unable to move another yard without rest or sustenance. Thus ended her hopeful return to normality and her recuperation continued in a more leisurely way.

Harefield will be remembered for many things, not least the way the family closed ranks in order to help Anna in her time of need. But naturally she and Mitchell wanted to get on with life in their own way and this included not always calling on others for support. I was aware that they were keen to show us that they could cope with the situation on their own and when it was time for her to have an MRI scan at Mount Vernon, prior to radiotherapy, Anna and Mitchell told us they would find their own way.

It was only later that she confessed to me the experience had been overwhelming and very frightening. Having filed away their previous experiences under 'accomplished', it came as a shock to be thrust into such an uncompromising environment as Mount Vernon. A large notice over the door declared 'Cancer Treatment Centre' and heralded the way forward towards other signs: 'Chemotherapy', 'Radiotherapy'. The boldness was repellent and panic overcame their brave adventurous spirit.

It was only when they were homeward bound that they sought solace in road signs and house names which reflected the people they loved. 'Home Farm' was the name of Nan Wilson's welcoming house, and Primrose Way reminded them of Nan's maiden name, and had a calming effect. Together they had taken on the challenge but realised that perhaps it was easier if the load was shared.

At the beginning of May Anna and I returned to Mount Vernon for the start of her treatment. We sat in the radiotherapy waiting area nervously taking in the scene around us. So many people. So much cancer. So few young faces.

She was led into a room to be marked up on her chest area, tattoos that would indicate the boundaries for the alignment of her treatment, a process that required her to be very still.

We then went in to see Mr Makepeace. He carefully revealed that unexpected items had been found on the MRI scan. Some 'abnormal tissue' had shown up where some of the tumour had been left behind in a cul-de-sac. He explained that it would have been impossible to see it during the operation, but with careful planning they hoped that the radiotherapy would be able to kill it off. It would entail six weeks of treatments instead of four, with time concentrated on a specific location as well as the general area.

The game was on once more. Having climbed the ladder so steadily we lurched and slid our way down the snake. It was now the beginning of May and the peaks and troughs that had been the pattern of our lives during the last three months seemed set to continue. We left Mount Vernon shellshocked and disbelieving, comforted only by Mr Makepeace's words that Dr Lyn, who was planning Anna's radiotherapy, was the very best and the most brilliant man for the job.

To combat the tedium of daily visits to Mount Vernon we would try to vary the days by taking different routes, making up whimsical stories about other patients and reawakening our interest in shopping. Mitchell and Bob would take Anna when work allowed and Robert and John accompanied her on other occasions.

Anna writes:

> *Friday 6 May 1994*
> *Now had 3 sessions of radiotherapy – really odd – lie on a hard table, get lined up with laser lights – everyone goes out and machine buzzes for 30 seconds – I chant in my head 'Kill it. Kill it!' constantly while it's on. Then moved under a table and another 30 seconds of buzzing.*
>
> *I could handle travelling to radiotherapy if they could tell me I was OK.*
>
> *Probably as scared as I've ever been right now – thoughts totally on 'Will I die?' 'How long have I got?' Nothings going to help at moment – I just know I don't want to die yet. Is it really happening to me? Sometimes I think it's not fair.*

After the first ten days I was beginning to get a little concerned that

Anna had not shown any sign of asking for counselling, something that I felt was going to be of great importance to her healing. There was a lot of information around the hospital encouraging people to make use of the Macmillan Centre, a fairly new building near the Cancer Centre where books could be browsed, coffee sipped and counsellors consulted.

I knew Anna was keen to know more about malignant schwannomas so I suggested we go to the library in the Centre. She agreed and into the quiet reverential atmosphere of the room we crept. A lady introduced herself and offered to be of help with anything we wanted. I said I thought Anna might like to have a talk with someone; Anna quite vehemently denied this. She just wanted information on her own cancer and where could she look?

We were invited to examine the many books and learned that Anna could have as much information as she wanted if she gave the details of her illness and name of her specialist. Material could then be brought over from the research centre for her to read. Before we left, the lady put her hand on Anna's arm and, with her head on one side, asked, 'And how are you coping with your cancer Anna?'

Anna hurriedly replied, 'Er, I don't really know.' We left.

I learnt much from this experience and, on reflection, it foreshadowed a situation that would last throughout the next four and a half years. Anna would always need to be in total charge of her illness and lead from the front. She certainly didn't want to talk to anyone who was going to be patronising or condescending.

Anna had managed to borrow one book, the only volume with a reference to malignant schwannoma. She read out the findings to me as we drove home; 'a cancer usually found in the spine or the brain.' It was about as much help as the current edition of *Hello!* magazine.

After eleven days of therapy Anna had to go back on the simulator for an hour for more planning. We took the opportunity to speak to Dr Lyn about her treatment.

We were keen to hear his opinion about the way forward, and it was difficult to take in all that he was saying. But that was down to our own apprehension clouding our understanding of what he was imparting rather than inexact explanation. He was able to give the information reading from his memory of notes and X-rays that he'd studied. We asked him how he felt treatment was going.

He was *fairly* confident that the radiotherapy was going to work, except that where the tumour lay was a very difficult area to get at;

not only was it in a cul-de-sac, it was sitting right next to the spine. Radiotherapy could not be directed at the spine itself because of the possible damage. Therefore the planning was absolutely crucial.

Anna asked what would happen if the radiotherapy didn't work. Would she be given chemotherapy? He explained that the cancer she had was so rare that no chemotherapy had been created to combat these sort of cells. They could always try new mixtures and it was possible that someone would hit on the right blend one day, but as far as the present was concerned, it was not a viable alternative.

What about another operation to remove the tumour? Dr Lyn felt this also was not an option since the tumour was in such an awkward place it would be too risky to attempt.

'So if radiotherapy doesn't work, what alternative do I have? Are you telling me that is it?' Anna asked.

Dr Lyn confirmed this, and we plunged deeper into the trough.

We reached Knebworth in near silence, stunned at the prospect of what we faced. Once home, the inevitable happened and the frustration and anger in Anna erupted in a cascade of tears and temper.

> *Tuesday 17 May 1994*
>
> *What hope is there? Death seems to get more and more likely. Can't feel positive when all I get is knocked back. Got flowers from Tracy and Gill – upsets me even more for some reason. Why can't we just get back to normal again – or even have a bit of good news for once? I'm certainly losing hope, and we probably haven't even started yet!*
>
> *Feel like I need more space – feeling very trapped and claustrophobic.*

I was very aware that under no circumstances would Anna want me to interfere, but I was concerned at her low morale after the consultation with Dr Lyn. I phoned Mr Makepeace's secretary, explained the situation and asked it would be possible for him to make a special effort to see Anna after her next treatment.

He did. He was gentle and kind and explained how brilliant Dr Lyn was in his field. He told her he was very confident that the radiotherapy would work and that even if it didn't they still had many other ways to attack the tumour. However, he did tell her that under no circumstances must she consider getting pregnant. She had to think of herself and put all thoughts of a family out of her mind for a long time.

Another silent journey home. It was becoming more and more difficult to talk to Anna. If I tried to introduce the topic of her illness she just brushed it aside and said, 'Oh I don't want to talk about it. It's too boring.' And yet I could see the anxiety that was building up inside her. I so wanted her to talk about her fears but she shut the door and threw away the key. It has been interesting to me since to read her diary of this time and learn of her inner feelings.

> *Wednesday 18 May 1994*
>
> *I'm sitting here in the lounge – lonely. Mitchell's gone to TLS party. I watched 'The Way we Were' Spoke to Rob and Sarah but still feel lonely. I don't actually want to be with anyone/see anyone – I would give anything in the world of mine (apart from my husband, cat and family) to be rid of this disease. It's not that I'm feeling ill – although I can't actually swallow much – just that it's thrown the whole world upside down and I don't know when it's gonna stop. What I want to do is run away, be by myself and make it go away.*

Bob and I took a break and decided to go to Christchurch for a few days to our house by the river. Here we could relax away from the routine of going to Mount Vernon every day. We received a phone call from John and Jane. 'How do you like the thought of becoming a grandma?' Jane was eight weeks pregnant and they were both a bit stunned by it. It wasn't planned but they were thrilled.

We put the phone down, holding our breath. Yes, it was great news. Yes, we wanted to be grandparents, but oh, how was Anna going to react to the news? Our feelings were so mixed and slightly emotional wondering what the next seven months would hold.

Anna was twenty-seven, married and had a good future to look forward to. Many of her friends were beginning to have their own families and she had often spoken of the time she would give birth to her first baby, of how she would like me there at the birth for support and how she felt it was perhaps wiser for Mitchell to be in the next room. Hospitals were not his favourite environment and blood and needles combined to bring on a state of panic.

Now that whole scenario would be played in front of Anna's eyes once more as she had to accept that others were having their families whilst she had to put it on hold. Her recovery was important and the effects of radiotherapy would stay in her body for a long time after treatment had finished, something that would be dangerous to a growing foetus.

Anna and Mitchell had decided to have a barbecue in the garden, asking John and Jane, Rob and Sarah to join them. Jane was very nervous that she had to tell Anna her news, wondering what the reaction would be. She found the task very emotional and tried to break it to Anna in the most gentle way possible.

Anna reacted with delight for John and Jane, confused by her feelings inside and trying her best not to show how she really felt. Her body became hyped and she spent the rest of the evening flying from one place to another, not allowing herself to dwell on her innermost thoughts.

Monday 7 June 1994

Mitchell off work all last week – went for bike ride and ended up having really open talk – stood on bridge over A1M and screamed and yelled – good therapy! Need more time to myself – trying to let Mum and Dad realise this I'm sure they do but they obviously will worry knowing that I'm upset. I've definitely got to take time out by myself to get everything sorted out. And although it's my choice to be by myself I still feel completely lonely and by myself (alone) – even when I'm with people. But when you feel such anger and hurt I think it's impossible to just hide it. I'm certainly going to try and hide it but my life is screwed up enough anyway. Why do I worry so much about how everyone else is feeling and still, with all I'm going through, try to take more on myself? There is no-one who I want to talk to fully about how I'm feeling. This is definitely going to stay with me and have an effect on me – probably for the rest of my life. How I feel now is quite scary – the loneliness – no-one really knowing how I feel – I could not even explain to someone how I feel even if I wanted to – there is no description – it's just a feeling of solitude/scariness/anger.

Dennis Potter died today – it seems like its weekly now that someone famous dies of cancer. You just wonder what the headlines would say if it was you! Despite all this I actually feel frighteningly calm.

Her final radiotherapy session was on 15 June and she was booked in for an MRI scan at the end of August. She went in to see her boss and discussed going back to work either September or October. Meanwhile we tried to get on with normality and she started swimming the following week, determined to get herself back to fitness.

The next month was taken over by the football World Cup in

the USA. Anna was happy to spend her time watching as her father worked, presenting the matches for the BBC. She had always loved football and was particularly proud of the work Bob did so her viewing was a necessary pleasure. By the middle of July we were all in need of a holiday

> *17th July 1994*
>
> *Mitchell knackered from work – pretty distant – not usual self – work + + + + . Hopefully holiday will help him. I'm a bit confused as to how I feel – in limbo (till September)*

So Anna, Mitchell, Bob and I went to Montserrat, a small island in the Caribbean, for ten days. It was glorious. It allowed us to be together in a relaxed and heavenly atmosphere where thoughts of cancer were the last thing on our minds. Anna could swim to her heart's content and at the end of the holiday she looked as healthy as she had ever done.

But feeling well brought about its own problems. She could do most things that she'd wanted to for the last few months but it didn't stop her mind from being tortured.

> *16th August 1994*
>
> *Lou and Kev had baby this am. Went to see her. And Sharon has Carla. Babies everywhere! God – I wish I had one. Found it really difficult today – I wanted to prove that I could do it too! Lesley Elliot (Patient) died whilst I was away. Holiday excellent – M back to normal. Get home ten minutes then back to work! Had big talk Sunday – made it better! Scan coming up 31/8/94 then OPA with Makepeace. 6/9/94. Scared stiff. Be back to work if everything OK otherwise – God only knows!*

On our return we had word that ITV were interested in signing Bob as their new number one football presenter. Bob had been with the BBC for 20 years and he was working out of contract, waiting for a meeting with the Head of Sport Jonathan Martin.

Bob was a BBC man through and through and never had thoughts of working for any other organisation, even though he felt he was taken for granted much of the time. He had presented everything in sport from *Olympic Games* to the *Marathon*, from the *Grand Prix* to *Grandstand*. He was the regular sports presenter on *Breakfast Television* and presented *Football Focus* every Saturday during the season. But when it came to the big football occasions such as the Cup Final, the European Championship and the World Cup, the chair would always be occupied by Des Lynam. Des was the BBC's number-one presenter, and quite rightly so, his unique, easy laidback style appealing to the majority of viewers. But Bob's speciality was always football. He'd played it, lived it and coached it. An opportunity to present programmes involving only football was one that he could not refuse so he listened attentively to what ITV had to offer.

By the end of August he had agreed to move over to the other side, despite a huge effort by the BBC to keep him, and his first assignment was an interview with his old team-mate and close friend, George Graham, now Arsenal manager at Highbury.

On the same day Anna had to attend a consultation with Mr Makepeace for the results of her MRI scan. Mitchell, Anna and I all felt sick with nerves as the nurse ushered us into the consultant's room where we waited for his arrival. It seemed to be an age before the door burst open revealing an ebullient Mr Makepeace, results in hand, declaring 'It's gone! I've looked at the scans and it's all gone!' We were all silent for a few seconds, not daring to believe what we had heard. But the smile on his face revealed more to us than his words. He was delighted to be the bringer of such tidings and we were grateful recipients. We hugged, we cried. We had no reason to disbelieve him. We left on a surge of adrenaline to find Bob. He had to share the joy. The four of us had endured this cancer for the last eight months and it was only right that he should be in on its demise.

It seemed an age getting from Mount Vernon to Highbury. We needed to tell him face to face. We needed to witness his joy. We rushed into the marble halls, past the revered bust of Herbert Chapman and over to the enquiry desk. 'Where's Bob Wilson doing the interview with Mr Graham?' We were directed to the sponsors' boxes that looked out over the clock end of the majestic stadium. I can't remember running with Anna at any time that year. But we were running now.

We burst open the door of the box where they were supposed to be to find Bob and George sitting on a ledge, about to begin the interview. The cameraman and sound recordist were startled by our entrance and thought we were three Arsenal fans that had infiltrated the security.

There was no doubt in our faces as to why we were there. Bob knew immediately. I went over to hug him and told him 'It's gone! The cancer's gone!' He went to Anna to seek confirmation. The four of us stood there holding each other in joy. The sponsor's box was soon full of people with tears streaming down their faces. George was as delighted as we were and immediately ordered a bottle of champagne.

Thus the interview began. It was not the best interview Bob had ever conducted. It was his first for ITV and it came only minutes after learning his daughter's life had been saved.

The Anna Years

Anna on her Christening Day, 1967

Anna, dwarfed by her father's Highbury goalmouth.

Family, 1970.

Mother and daughter at pre-FA Cup Final party, 1971.

The Wilsons, including Misty

'Threepwood', the family home

Junior school time

Family 1977

Teenage years

Anna and Mitchell
on her 21st birthday,
7 December, 1987

Mitchell echoing
Anna's hair

Nursing qualification

Diploma for Community Nursing,
University of Hertfordshire

Anna the nurse, at her happiest

Mitchell and Anna working on the
Bob Wilson Goalkeeping School

The Bride on her big day
26 September 1992

The happy couple at Knebworth Park

Mother of the Bride's pink wedding suit

Walk over Hengistbury Head, first signs of a problem with Anna's breathing January 1994

After diagnosis and first operation, Anna competing at Carrom in Covent Garden. Photograph by *Daily Telegraph*

Mitchell, Anna, Sarah, Jane, Louis, John and Robert

Reflections of Mortality

'We are just receiving news that the television presenter Jill Dando has been attacked and killed outside her home in Fulham.' Bob and I stared at the television, disbelieving the words we had both just heard. How could it happen? Not Jill. Why would anyone want to end Jill's life? It had to be a mistake. The afternoon saw us immersed in the reports and pictures that filtered through the various TV stations. The phone began to ring incessantly with friends passing on their sorrow and shock.

Jill Dando was a very dear friend of ours. Her murder by a gunman stunned not only those close to her, but the whole nation. If it did nothing else, it came as a reminder that life is cobweb-thin, spun together by circumstance and fate. She was yet another young, beautiful female whose life was ended before she'd had time to live through the joy that love had brought. Like Princess Diana before her, Jill had finally found the man who fulfilled her dreams and made her ecstatically happy.

Bob had spent eight years working alongside her on *Breakfast News* and he used to boast to friends that he always spent the night with two women – with me until 3.00am and with Jill from 4.00am They would spend time in makeup catching up on all the gossip and shared many of the misgivings about their insecurities. When Bob moved to ITV to become their principal football presenter, Jill also moved on to the news and the *Holiday Programme* and eventually became the number one female presenter at the BBC. We kept in close touch, meeting for meals and parties. She was always concerned for Anna and would phone for news of her progress. Jill's death occurred only four months after Anna's. Both girls were beautiful, both full of vitality, both in the prime of their life. Except that Anna was given five years to prepare.

September 1994 – December 1995

Like all of us back in 1995 Jill was thrilled at the news of Anna's remission and felt that all the pain and worry was finally behind us. Anna would now be able to go back to her old life and pick up the pieces that had been so hastily strewn around. She could forget all the fears that had crowded her mind and replace them with resolution and determination. She could return to work with a slightly modified attitude to her patients, having been on the receiving end for eight months. She could make her home a more beautiful place and she could concentrate on her marriage.

Anna had been the recipient of a warning shot across her bows and she could now look at her life in a different perspective. She could be happy and content that her brush with death had been just that and she'd been given another chance to appreciate every day that arrived.

The news of Anna's remission had filtered to the press and we were inundated with calls for interviews. But Anna was basically a very shy person and never one to seek the limelight. The thought of appearing on television filled her with dread. However, she did agree to do one interview with journalist Val Sampson called 'Relationships' for the *Daily Mail*.

We were pleased because it seemed a positive step from Anna. Her willingness to talk to a stranger was an apparent acceptance that her condition was finally on the mend. To all those that were close to her it appeared just that. But her diary tells a different story.

> *6 September 1994*
>
> *It's gone! Out patient's appointment with Makepeace today after MRI last week. Apparently it's gone! WOW! Went to Highbury and found Dad then got wrecked for rest of day. Now in bed – pretty wrecked (hence the writing). I'll write when I'm sober – but I feel good!*
>
> *14 September 1994*
>
> *Starting work Monday – went in today. Got home and talked to Mum – newspapers and TV programmes phoning up daily! I'm pissed off! Everyone around me is happy and saying 'You must be so happy' I'm not. My marriage is fucked – I'm scared about work – I feel fat and ugly and although I might be clear now, what are the chances of me surviving till old age? Not very high I'd say! First time I've cried properly for ages.*
>
> *Roy Castle died last week.*
>
> *2 October 1994*
>
> *Start work properly tomorrow. God I'm scared. Don't even know what of! Don't know if I want to be a nurse anymore! Mitchell and I – going up and down – one minute we're fine and next it's shit again – not really what's needed right now. Interviewed by Daily Mail – out on Tuesday – Dad and me. Didn't realise*

how hard it'd be talking about Dad to Val – got very emotional.
Want to get next few weeks over with and then see how things
go – I need it all to settle down soon!

12 October 1994

Now things really are out of control! Mitchell and I have been
discussing separating over last couple of weeks We're both
totally messed up because of this fucking disease – it does ruin
your whole life! Had to come home today because I couldn't
keep going. Sometimes I think it would be easier if I'd never had
the op and then at least everything would be over by now! Only
managing to really talk about it to Jane – usually meet once a
week. I keep spinning out totally and losing it altogether! Pure
anger inside of me. What a fucking shit life I've got.

Unknown to all except Mitchell and Jane, Anna was very screwed up about her life. Instead of giving her an appreciation of all that she had, her recovery had only served to raise questions about her future and about her own confidence. She never once let on to me that she was feeling this way, even though we had a very close relationship. She had to act as she was expected to act, as one just having been given back her life making the most of every day that came her way.

I only became aware of the problem when Mitchell told me that he and Anna had been talking about separating. I was shocked and unable to comprehend the fact that Anna had not confided in me. I had noticed that she had avoided being alone in a room with me, always busying herself and never allowing herself the luxury of having a mother-daughter talk. So on our Christmas shopping expedition to Lakeside, I confronted her with what Mitchell had told me. Unfortunately it also happened to be her birthday and what was supposed to be our fun day out turned into a day of tears. I was not used to Anna hiding things from me and I had hoped that talking about it would help But it merely made her feel she'd let me down, that she should have reacted differently to the situation, and should have been very grateful for being given a second chance. I had seen her fight her illness and face up to life with apparent determination. She didn't want to be a disappointment to me.

Looking back it is easy to see how it all happened. Reading her diary it is easy to understand her state of anxiety. She never felt the need of counselling or of unburdening. She felt she could cope without letting anyone else into her mind. What should have been a new appreciation of life became a time of mental pain and distress where brooding intensified the nagging doubts.

Mitchell too found it hard to come to terms with all that had happened. His reaction to the situation was to throw himself deeper into his work, getting home late and sinking into a silent world of his own. They tried to talk. They tried to sort out their differences but they were finding it hard.

Our first grandchild was born on 15th January. Louis Robert Abbott Wilson brought light to our lives. Anna was thrilled to be an aunty and she visited John and Jane with their new baby in the Royal Free Hospital. John took a lovely video of her holding Louis, looking so proud with not a hint of envy to be seen.

Louis was four days old when his other grandmother came to see him. After visiting her daughter, Caroline and David stopped off at our home to have some supper with us and celebrate the birth of our mutual grandson. We had just started eating when the phone rang.

I heard a very distressed Anna at the other end of the phone. 'Mum, Mitchell's left me!'

'Do you want me to come over?'

'Yes please.'

I excused myself, explaining the delicacy of the situation, and made my way over to Knebworth. Even though she had encouraged the split, Anna was distraught when the threats finally stopped. She still loved Mitchell, but hated what both he and she had become. She was frustrated that she could find no way of helping Mitchell out of his moods.

We talked like we hadn't talked for months. She finally opened up her heart and laid it before me. The relief was visible and she vowed to get on with her life with a totally different attitude. Tomorrow we would start redecorating the cottage. We went out and bought lining paper, paste, a wallpaper table and all the equipment needed for DIY decorating. If she was making a fresh start she might as well begin with her home.

23rd January 1995

Mitchell's now been gone for 5 days – feels like 3 months. Met up with him on Saturday (for 1 hour only!) Probably made it even worse! I'm trying to get on with everything – but it's difficult. Don't know how I feel – whether I'd have him back or not. One minute I'd give everything to have him back – and then I remember what it's really like. I really do think this could be it.

The separation lasted two weeks. Less if you count the amount of times Mitchell called on Anna in the evenings. He never used his own key but always knocked on the door like any other person. They talked for hours, on the phone and face to face. The separation had finally forced them to open up to each other, which in turn brought them back together.

At last their life took on an air of normality. Anna was happy in her marriage and her work, but she never really believed that the cancer had left her. She was worried by rib pain and a certain amount of breathlessness, although she tried to pass it off as being all in the mind. By April she was worried enough to get in touch with Mr Makepeace who arranged for her to have an MRI scan, which showed that the rib area looked fine, but not the original site. A bone scan and a PET scan were booked to try and identify if any other areas were affected.

> *24 May 1995*
>
> *Apparently changes seen on films – not completely sure what it is but EVERYTHING'S now flipped again. Dr Lyn explained that if it is tumour then operation only option. No more radiotherapy and chemo won't work! Good eh! Probably 10 times more scared this time – or so it feels – maybe I forgot what it's really like! Quite strange really – 2 months ago Mitchell and I discussed re babies. Now (yet again) the decisions been made for me.*
>
> *2nd June 1995*
>
> *Went for results of bone scan. Problem shown up on 12th vertebrae -? boney mets!! This can't be happening to me can it? I honestly don't believe it's true. M & I discussed us again last night – I know I've become withdrawn – and so has he – we're not talking and everything's breaking up again. Now in bed – not tired – don't know what to do. I've really got to get things sorted and make an effort – I feel I've stopped and given up and can't be bothered with anything.*

This was the last time Anna wrote in her diary. She could no longer bear to pen the reflection of her life.

On 23 June, Bob, Mitchell, Anna and I went for the consultation with Mr Makepeace for results of the PET scan. It showed three areas of malignancy. He felt there was nothing else he could offer by way of treatment so he wanted to refer her to Professor Souhami at The Middlesex Hospital. He was an excellent doctor and more experienced in Anna's type of cancer.

Anna was devastated. We had a two-week holiday booked in Portugal and were due to fly in two days' time with John, Jane and Louis. Mitchell was originally only coming out for the second week, but Anna said she couldn't bear to be separated from him. We changed his ticket.

It was not the easiest of holidays. The setting was perfect, the villa ideal. We had our own swimming pool where Anna could spend so much time immersed in cooling water. But tension distorted perceptions and the only person unaffected by this was baby Louis. He would gurgle and play to his hearts content oblivious of Anna's turmoil.

Professor Bob Souhami came to be adored by Anna. His manner was efficient but sensitive, gentle but rational. His outlook mirrored the youth that surrounded his every step, as privileged students followed in his wake. He gained Anna's confidence quickly and soon had her trust.

Further CT scans had revealed two tumours on the pleura, one on her rib cage and a one in the original neck area. The surgery option was proving difficult since Professor Souhami had approached many thoracic surgeons with her scans, all of whom told him that the tumour in the neck was in such a delicate position, they would not take the risk. The alternative was to try chemotherapy and experiment with various drugs to see if there was any effect. But whatever, the professor wanted to wait a while and monitor the growth of the tumours that they had identified.

The uncertainties trailed across the months and by September Anna had once more given up work. She was not well enough to carry out the lifting and carrying that was part of her district nursing, let alone be faced with images of her own destiny.

But her attitude to the life that she had was changed over a period of a few weeks by two incidents. The first happened as she was driving back from a shopping trip to Sainsbury's, passing the front entrance of the Lister Hospital. A young man was standing on the nearside pavement and as the fire engine, which Anna was following, drew near, he began to run and threw himself in front of it. Consequently his body was crushed under the wheels and was ejected in front of Anna's car in a very mangled state. She managed to stop, but then sat transfixed by the scene before her, at the lifeless body that was, a few seconds ago, full of movement, at the victim whose life had only just reached adulthood and at the vicious finality of his choice of death. She found herself unable to move, unable to react to the trigger of medical need, instinctively realising there was nothing she could do.

The firemen, all of whom were in a very obvious state of shock, ran to the rear of the vehicle and on seeing the state of the body, covered it with a sheet. They then taped off the area and began to wave the stationary traffic on, including Anna. When we heard of the incident Bob and I went straight over to Knebworth to be with her since she sounded in a very distressed state. She was stunned and bewildered by the events that she had seen and described the accident to us in great detail. She was angered by the reaction of the firemen, that they had no thought for her, the one person who had witnessed the scene and that they had waved her on without a care. She surmised that they too must have been in shock and so therefore never realised the effect it might have on someone travelling behind them.

On the local evening news that night they asked that any witnesses to the accident should phone the police to help in their enquiries. She gave a statement but, thankfully, never had to appear in court. The Inquest found that the young man had committed suicide, having gone missing from the Psychiatric Unit of the Lister Hospital.

The second incident happened on 12 November when Anna and Mitchell received a phone call from their friend John Renayne. He told them that Alison, his partner, had been rushed to hospital so could they meet him there. John, Alison, Mitchell and Anna had been friends for some time, having moved into the same area a few years earlier. Alison worked as a social worker and John as a financial adviser and they found that they had much in common with Anna and Mitchell.

Alison, who had seemed fit and healthy, had been ironing when she collapsed and was rushed to the Lister Hospital. Anna and Mitchell arrived at Casualty and found John. He told them that Alison had died but that the cause was unknown. They were devastated and confused and spent the next few weeks giving John the support that he needed. The post-mortem did not reveal why she died so there would have to be an inquest, but that would not be until sometime the following year.

Anna had been sure in her own mind that she would die before any of her friends so Alison's death and the suicide of the young man put everything in an entirely different perspective. The reflections of mortality that had danced before her eyes gave her renewed vision.

Anna still had a life, one that she intended to cherish, and one that was there to be enjoyed and appreciated. The realisation that any other person could die before her made her less introspective and a little more determined to get on with the life that she had.

Anna's own illness had become a big issue and she would spend hours on the internet looking for information on malignant schwannoma, for signs that some clinic or other in another part of the world had found a cure. However, the findings made depressing reading and she soon gave up her quest.

Whilst Professor Souhami had been deciding on the way forward Anna had been experiencing more and more pain and an increase in breathlessness. By the end of November scans and tests revealed that the neck and lung tumours had grown and it was decided that she should go to a surgeon for a second opinion. Mr Peter Goldstraw of the Royal Brompton Hospital was the only thoracic surgeon who was prepared to look at Anna to see if her problems were within his realm and an appointment was made for 14th December.

My own diary reads:

> *Thursday 14 December 1995*
> *At last I feel as if we have turned a corner. At last someone is prepared to take a gamble and do something positive to help Anna beat her cancer.*

The Royal Brompton Hospital is the National Hospital for the Chest and Heart and is situated in South Kensington − very close to all the designer shops! Although the corridors and waiting areas seemed cramped and utilitarian, the friendly ambience helped to calm our tension. We didn't know whether we were coming as errand boys to deliver the scans and X-rays that had been packed up by the Middlesex, whether Mr Goldstraw would need time to study the pictures whilst we were there or whether he would be able to give us any answers in the time that we had with him.

After going over Anna's history Mr Goldstraw asked her to go into the cubicle so that he might look at her 'scars'. She was immediately followed by the two nurses and two visiting doctors whilst Mitchell and I were left to imagine the scene behind the wall.

When we were finally reunited Mr Goldstraw explained that he had been in touch with all her previous doctors and was aware that she had received the maximum amount of radiation possible to the neck area and that there was no known chemotherapy available to treat the condition. He then said that he wanted to arrange for surgery as soon as possible and that it was a shame that Christmas was in the way. We must have looked shocked and explained that we had come in the expectation of his saying that surgery wasn't an option either.

'But there's no alternative. We *have* to operate. I don't know *how* but we have to do it. If Anna was older then we might not consider it, but she's young and very fit so there's no reason why she shouldn't make a full recovery.'

Within fifteen minutes of this consultation a CT scan, bone scan and a PET scan had been booked for the following week and a bed had been reserved for the middle to end of January. We were totally astonished! Never had we found such efficiency and such a positive approach. Neither did Mr Goldstraw show any sign of apprehension at the task ahead. He didn't know how he was going to perform the surgery, whether it would be one operation or two, but he was positive in his attitude.

'I like surgeons,' said Mitchell, 'They've got balls!'

We took ourselves off to the nearest coffee house to digest all that we had heard. It was a typical South Kensington meeting-place and we all decided that this was a very upmarket snack bar and with Harrods only half a mile away Anna would be in for some very classy presents.

It was towards that great emporium that we wandered, looking in all the windows along the way. Harrods looked resplendent in its Christmas regalia and the infectious atmosphere of the season helped lift our spirits. We had set out that morning with apprehension fearful of more bad news. But now our hearts were cheered and our future seemed much brighter. We could look forward to Christmas and New Year knowing that 1996 offered renewed hope that Anna would be given assistance to fight the disease in her new determined way.

The Enemy Within

January – July 1996

Journalist Roger Omond entered Anna's life on 20 January 1996. They had much in common yet were so much at odds. They shared experiences in time and place but never compared their lot. They shared a room, but never shared their thoughts. They shared similar fates but challenged them differently. Before coming face to face, Roger's presence loomed large in Anna's life – all because of an article he'd written in *The Guardian*.

Roger was one of the first of a breed of journalists who began to share their inner thoughts and fears whilst battling against cancer. It was unfortunate that he happened to write about his imminent admission to the Royal Brompton Hospital at a time when Anna was about to do the same. His article was neither comforting nor reassuring, particularly since he was returning for similar treatment to Anna's.

Two years later when 'cancer journalism' had become more fashionable, Anna found particular comfort in reading others' words. Ruth Picardie's books *Before I say Goodbye* and John Diamond's *Even Cowards Get Cancer* were both published on the back of newspaper columns through which they chronicled the difficulties they had encountered with the effects of the disease. The two writers were able to translate the feelings of a sufferer into basic prose, digging deep beneath any false exterior moulded for society's sake and telling how it really is.

Ruth, a mother of two beautiful children and thirty-two-year-old wife managed to mirror much of what was in Anna's head, unexpressed. So accurately did she echo many of my daughter's feelings, putting into words the thoughts that Anna felt she could never share with anyone, that it helped her reconcile the various demons that beset her day in and day out.

But Roger Omond wrote at a time just before Anna was about to enter the Royal Brompton Hospital for major surgery to her lungs and ribs; she was feeling uncertain, vulnerable and frightened, her cancer having returned in rather more areas than had been expected

Mitchell, Bob and I had accompanied Anna to a consultation with Mr Goldstraw on 4 January 1996. The results of her various scans had shown more activity. The problem Anna had been experiencing with her ribs turned out to be tumour that had penetrated her ribcage. The surgeon relayed the news in as gentle a way possible. 'It looks as though there are now four areas of concern.'

'Four!' said Mitchell, 'Oh we've done four before. We thought you were going to say eight or ten.' Mr Goldstraw was not yet in tune with Mitchell's humour so looked at him quizzically.

The surgery would have to resemble the first operation, though not as high on her back, and come further forward under her breast. He would have to take away some of her ribs at the front, which would be replaced by plastic, remove the tumours on the pleura and then try to excise the tumour from her neck. It would be 'adventurous surgery'. If he were unsuccessful in achieving the final stage he would attempt further surgery through the front of her neck two or three days after the first operation

Although he knew there were definitely four areas of concern that had shown up on the scans it was possible that he might find more. 'These cancers are devious little chaps,' he said. The good news was that everything was confined to the right-hand side of her chest. A bed would be reserved for her in intensive care where she would be nursed after the operation. She was to be admitted on 25 January.

On 20 January during a telephone conversation, Anna asked me if I'd seen the *Weekend Guardian*. 'Well I shouldn't read it if I were you — and certainly don't let Dad see it.' I went straight out and bought a copy.

Roger Omond had written a four-page article cataloguing his medical history, including the disastrous consequences of having a plastic shield inserted into his back after the removal of cancerous ribs. An infection had set up around the plastic causing him to have further surgery for its removal. A fistula (an open hole) had formed in his back and other problems arose as a consequence of his treatment. The case similarity didn't end with the fact that Anna was to face the same surgery in the same hospital. It appeared that his consultant was almost certainly Mr Goldstraw:

> *'Medical opinion was that, two and a half years after the last cancer operation, the chances of secondaries appearing had diminished greatly. But the surgeon's words before the first operation kept returning: "These cancers are devious little chaps."'*

The quotation was familiar to our ears. We had remarked on the choice of words when we heard it at Anna's last consultation. On reflection, had I encountered the piece as an uninformed reader I would have found it educational and moving but considering the situation we were in it appeared distasteful and unnecessary.

My anger was stirred that a journalist could express such a pessimistic view without thought of who might be reading his words. I had to let him know how I felt.

Dear Mr Omond

My mother-in-law, a wise Scottish lady whose optimistic personality infected all those with whom she came into contact, had an annoying habit of following every tragic tale with the phrase; 'Everything will turn out for the best.' Looking back over the years one can trace patterns that test her theory to the full.

She herself lost two sons in the Second World War aged 19 and 20 and yet never once was she heard to lay blame or ask for sympathy. Instead she would be positive believing that the loss of Jock and Billy had only heightened her and her husband's love for the rest of the family.

I read your article this weekend with great interest hoping to find a spark of inspiration from someone that had looked fate in the eye and risen to its challenge. My disappointment was overwhelming.

I have questioned time and again the possible motives you might have had for documenting your unfortunate medical history. Had you merely wanted to get the whole sorry saga out of your brain and onto paper then why wasn't the article placed into a drawer only to be taken out by professionals seeking research?

Was it meant to be instructional for the medical profession? In that case a text-book would surely have been the better choice. But why a weekend magazine? Did you have any thought as to who might be reading such an article?

My daughter of 29 who contracted cancer two years ago alerted me to the article. After surgery and radiotherapy initially cleared her, her cancer has returned to the lungs, neck and rib cage.

This Thursday she is entering the Brompton Hospital for surgery to remove tumours from the soft tissue and to remove part of the chest wall, which will be replaced by a plastic plate.

I will leave you to imagine her reaction and ours, on reading your diary of woe.

For the past two years she has faced continuing problems similar to those of your own, but never once has she ever questioned

'Why me?' Always she has looked to the future with real optimism. Hope springs eternal as far as Anna is concerned. Part of her inspiration remains that germ of hope passed down to her by her grandmother.

I do hope your own health problems improve dramatically and that you can enjoy a brighter future.

Yours sincerely

Megs Wilson

On 25 January the four of us reported to Elizabeth Ward and were shown to a side room, which overlooked Chelsea, the Kings Road and the hospital car park. Anna was pleased that she had a room to herself from where she could wave as we left her at night. The privacy meant a lot to her, particularly having a father so easily recognised. We could relax and be at ease with her without the worry of others watching our every move.

She wanted Mitchell to be near at night so we rented a small flat, within walking distance, where he might live for the duration of her stay. It consisted of a twin-bedded room, a bathroom fit for one of the seven dwarfs, a sitting area and a kitchen. It would prove to be invaluable as a base for all the family.

Mid-afternoon Mr Goldstraw arrived with entourage and spent all of eight minutes confirming his intentions. 'The whole operation should take about three hours.' I asked him if he knew a Roger Omond. 'Oh, yes. Mr Omond is on the ward now.' I expressed our concern at *The Guardian* article and its effect on Anna as she faced the same surgery. He hadn't read the article but reassured her that her own cancer was totally different from Mr Omond's.

We then became worried that we might meet Roger Omond and that he in turn would recognise us as the senders of the letter. How should we react? How would he react? Anna was not a lover of confrontation and she became nervous at the thought.

The staff nurse later told us that Mr Goldstraw had visited the journalist and said, 'I hear you've been upsetting one of my young patients. Well for that I've decided not to give you any anaesthetic tomorrow.'

We had been told that Anna was third on the list and would be going down at 11.00am, Bob and I collected Mitchell from the flat early in the morning and arrived to find that Anna had already been given her pre-med. Mr Goldstraw liked his patients ready early in case an operation beforehand was cancelled.

Once the Temazepam started to take effect Anna veered between happy and high, sleepy and relaxed. The operating time approached, as did our anticipation, and passed us by in mock amusement. By 12.30pm Anna's party mood was beginning to fade as the wait intensified. By 1.00pm she was back to normality and anxiety was taking hold.

The day before had been long. This was going to prove eternal.

The tension in Anna's room was palpable and despite our asking for another pre-med it seemed that the anaesthetist was too busy elsewhere. At 1.45pm the nurse arrived with another Temazepam, but this time the party mood didn't materialise and Anna became morose. Our time was spent once more amusing ourselves watching the world outside, the car park being the main source of entertainment.

Four fire engines arrived in the front forecourt ready to fight the raging fire in the hospital, only to be told that a false alarm had been triggered. One engine decided to reverse out and did a magnificent job of missing all the cars on either side, but demolished the concrete and metal pole that normally propped up the car park barrier.

At 2.45pm the porters finally came for Anna! She waved a cheery goodbye as she was wheeled out of the room, relieved to be finally on her way. Mitchell stayed with her until they reached theatre then returned to us. We hugged each other to help us through the pain.

The three hours at the apartment were long, but by 6.00pm we strode off back to the Brompton to await Anna's return to Intensive Care. The Elizabeth Ward staff nurse phoned down to theatre to be told that Anna was still being operated on and it would be another hour and a half. We were slightly taken aback, but not totally surprised, so decided to get in the car and 'cruise'. We tried eating, but went off the idea after a couple of mouthfuls.

We returned at 7.45pm only to be told that she was still in theatre and would be another hour and a half. The shock was quite stifling and it took all three of us a little while to come to terms with the fact that this was encouraging. It meant that they were trying to get everything out in one go. We returned to the flat and asked that the ward phone us when she was out.

The contrast between the stifling warmth of the wards and the biting cold outside was intense. However, the flat offered a much milder temperature, the single glazing allowing the icy blasts to penetrate the room.

Snow was once again falling, reminiscent of our days at Harefield. Two years had passed since we first learned of Anna's cancer, yet the weather and the prognosis were unchanged. Here she was facing another thoracotomy to try and rid her of the enemy within. But this time they appeared to be marching in legions.

Robert had come over to the flat on his way home from work and was happy to sit around. John said he and his guitar would make their way to be with Mitchell overnight. The outside world became irrelevant and we waited for the phone to ring.

At 9.15pm we got the call. Only the sound of our hurried footsteps disturbed the quiet of the hospital corridors as we made our way to the hushed entrance of the Theatre and Intensive Care Units. The seemingly diminutive figure of Mr Goldstraw, still wearing his theatre 'blues' and looking extremely tired, ushered us into a small comfortable room inviting us to sit down.

'I've managed to get to all the target areas. That means no second operation. The tumour at the front has penetrated the lung so I had to cut that out. The tumour on the pleura at the back had penetrated the ribs so I had to cut out that area and replace with plastic here, and at the front where we expected.

'The neck area had a lot of lumpy tumour and I had to cut right down to the nerve and take part of it away. I also had to remove a small part of the tip of the lung and as much of the pleura as I could. Unfortunately it was more extensive than we thought and in all there must have been about twelve or thirteen tumours. It just shows that with all the sophistication of modern scans we still couldn't detect them.

'With malignant schwannoma the tumour is usually sited in one place but I've never seen one like this and I feel that the tumours have been spread from the initial surgery. It's very difficult to avoid this. Who knows, I could have done the same myself. We have flushed everything through with tap water to kill off any stray cells. Tap water is lethal to cancer cells.' We asked of the chances of recurrence. 'I took away all the tumours I could see with my naked eye. I cannot give you a guarantee. Recurrence is very possible. You can go and see her in recovery when you're ready.'

He gave us his full attention, answering the questions we could think to ask and giving us the information he thought we needed. We were used to him talking to Anna, looking her straight in the eye and telling her how it was. Now *we* were the front line battling with the raw facts, trying to comprehend the implications, relieved to have finally reached this point. We tried to show our gratitude thanking him profusely, but off he went with a wave of his hand in a rather matter-of-fact way. Just another day's work done.

We waited outside the recovery unit until we were shown in to see Anna, no more than two at a time. The nurse explained that although she was asleep she might well be aware of us if we spoke to her. Mitchell and I walked into the room. It was rather like entering Kennedy Space Center, with monitors, pipes, tubes, and lights set into the clinical aura of stainless steel, accompanied by the rhythmical hum of moving machines. I glanced at the patient in the first bed and saw a familiar face beneath the oxygen mask. It was the same face that had looked out from the *Weekend Guardian* last week. Roger Omond's surgery had taken place just before Anna's and the two of them lay in Recovery with only a bed between them. We passed on to the third bay where Anna lay, unaware of the ironical situation.

The ventilator entering her mouth on the right-hand side had taken over her breathing causing her body to tremble slightly. Mitchell moved to her side and, clearly emotionally relieved to see her, spoke softly and kissed her. Her eyes tried to open as recognition filtered through, responding to our assurances that everything was OK. She looked pale yet still beautiful, her blonde curly hair framing her motionless face. The relief at finally seeing her after all this time was transparent and both Mitchell and I shed a tear. I left to allow Bob in whilst Mitchell continued to reassure Anna that all was well. At that moment she opened her eyes, just enough to see Mitchell putting up his thumb. She responded, trying to raise her own in reply. Mitchell was blown away! We said our goodbyes and left the recovery room. Mitchell's relief at seeing Anna and having her respond to his gesture was overwhelming and he cried unashamedly.

It wasn't until 11.15am the next day that we saw her again. Patience, a wonderful African nurse, invited me to go down with her to fetch Anna, who was now off the ventilator. She managed a smile when she saw me: then, with oxygen mask securely in place, she was wheeled out into the corridor and towards the lift. As the doors opened Mitchell and Robert were standing there unaware that it was Anna in the bed — but she had seen them. 'Bugger off, this is my lift!' the hoarse voice said through the mask. We couldn't believe that someone so doped up could be quite so assertive. They obeyed and used the other lift.

She was taken into the High Dependency Unit to be nursed with care and attention during the post-operative period. Lines and tubes were coming from her everywhere. She had a central line directly into her neck, which fed three tubes to the veins leading to the heart. She had wires coming from various parts of her body monitoring her heart and temperature, an epidural which fed pain-relieving drugs directly into her spine, two drips feeding fluid and nutrition into her arms, a catheter to empty her bladder when necessary and two tubes acting as drains coming from her chest cavity to remove any excess fluid and air from around the lung. Antibiotics were fed intravenously and oxygen through her facemask. Nurses danced attention on her to make her as comfortable as possible and most of the time Anna slept. But her discomfort became obvious throughout the day as she complained of a painful bottom and sore hip. We all took it in turns to sit with her.

The High Dependency Unit contained six beds and was situated directly opposite the nursing station on Elizabeth Ward. For most of that day Anna was the only patient until Roger Omond was brought up later that afternoon. He was more conscious than Anna and was positioned directly opposite so that when both were awake they would look directly at one another. I became nervous and uncomfortable about having sent him the letter. He was obviously a very sick man and I began to wish I had resisted the urge to write to him. I had no desire to make either his or Anna's recuperation any more stressful than it already was.

Despite her periods of drowsiness and discomfort, Anna soon recognised her companion and threw a look of panic towards me. I tried to reassure her that I didn't think he would link the letter with us and told her not to worry unduly about it.

By the next morning both occupiers of HDU were able to converse with their visitors, albeit through oxygen masks. Roger Omond's wife stayed with him most of the day talking him through the list of friends that had rung home wanting to know how he was, whilst I stayed beside Anna trying to make her as comfortable as possible. By the afternoon her temperature was rising rapidly, so sleep became her saviour, her breathing laboured and loud. She had asked that I stay the night and sit by the bed as I had at Harefield. It would be a comfort for us both.

At 9.00pm concern began to grow over Roger's condition. His heartbeat had quickened and his breathing became shorter and more difficult, despite efforts from the medical staff to oxygenate and nebulise him. At 9.30pm a decision was taken to send Roger down to ITU to stabilise him, leaving Anna and myself the only occupants of the HDU. A delightful Irish nurse, came over and suggested there was no reason why I couldn't sleep in the bed next to Anna since there were no other patients due into the unit. Unfortunately conditions were not conducive to sleeping since medications had to be administered very frequently and we had snatches of sleep only throughout the night.

By the time Mitchell arrived the next morning Anna looked a different girl. She was washed, clothed and sitting in a chair looking brighter, her smile not far from breaking. So good in fact that she was moved back to the side-ward, with privacy, a TV and the view on to the car park and the Kings Road.

Mr Goldstraw arrived with entourage. He thought she looked good and gave her an abridged version of the operation and its findings, not giving too much away whilst not deliberately hiding anything. Her voice, he explained, would be affected for probably six weeks since they'd had to cut into a nerve near the voice box.

'Oh and by the way, whilst we were stitching one of the patches, a needle snapped and fell into your body somewhere. There's no cause for concern. It's just that someone might pick it up on an X-ray at some time.'

He left as quickly as he'd arrived. Anna appeared happy with the consultation and didn't start the cross-questioning that I'd expected. As I wandered down Kings Road that afternoon, looking for a suitable present for her, I became terribly anxious that Mr Goldstraw had not told her everything. How would she react when she found out how many tumours there were? He'd only mentioned the four areas to her and made it all sound so routine. My stomach began to churn, my chest tightened and panic spread over my body. I'd come through all this and now the anxiety started again.

Trying to open a conversation around the matter I asked if she had been surprised by anything Goldstraw had said. 'Yes, my voice – and the needle.'

'Not the second patch on your back?' I asked.

'Oh yes, that as well.'

I waited, wondering if she was going to ask questions and she said, 'I do know about the eight other tumours you know. Mitchell told me.' I looked at her and she began to cry. I went over to hug her. It was the first sign of emotion that she had shown since the operation.

The following day her discomfort was extreme. She declared it to be the worst day of her life and really couldn't care about anything. The epidural had been removed and balancing her drugs to ease the pain became difficult.

It was whilst I was looking after grandson Louis in the downstairs lobby area that I was suddenly aware of someone smiling. I returned the greeting realising it was Mrs Omond.

'How's Anna doing?' she asked.

'She's fine,' I said. 'And Roger?'

'I'm afraid it's not looking good. Of course I've only just realised who you are.'

'Oh the letter,' I suggested, embarrassed at her discovery. 'I'm sorry about that but you have to understand the circumstances and the situation that led to my writing,' I offered by way of explanation.

'Of course,' she said, 'totally understandable. I just can't believe the irony of the whole thing, them being in the same ward together. I have only just received it.'

These last words took a little time to register with me.

'Has Roger not seen it?'

'Oh no, Roger's not seen it.'

My conscience was eased as I pictured Roger staring straight ahead at Anna and myself in the High Dependency Unit. 'I'm afraid it was something of the mother-hen in me,' I stumblingly explained.

'Oh no my dear, not mother-hen, lioness!'

My mane grew thicker and my tail swished at the thought of my cub lying upstairs in bed, so upset by her depressive day.

Louis meanwhile was amusing himself running between the elderly lady who insisted he take some of her smoked salmon-sandwich, and the newspaper rack outside the hospital shop. Both items, he insisted, belonged on the floor and he took great delight in throwing both salmon sandwich and twelve *Daily Mirrors* into the paths of oncoming footsteps. It was consoling to know that here was at least one person as yet untouched by the injustices that life is capable of committing.

Over the next couple of days Anna's condition improved although the pain at the base of her spine made sleeping difficult and she kept running a temperature. By Thursday, the seventh day post-operative, Anna was looking well and was hoping to be sent home.

'If you're eating, sleeping, walking, talking, drinking and shitting, and your temperature is normal,' said the senior registrar, 'then you fulfil the criteria for going home.'

Just before the consultant's round was due to begin Anna's temperature rose again to 37.2. Mr Goldstraw swept in.

'My goodness look at you amongst all these flowers. I guess you love the attention. Now, lots of exercise, walking, walking and more walking until your lung feels as though it's going to burst and you're sweating and out of breath. Everything I could see Anna, I removed. I've looked at the pleura and the last findings were very encouraging. Any questions? '

Anna stayed silent. Mr Goldstraw looked across at us.

'Did you feel that the pleura had been a feeding ground for the tumours?' I asked

'Without a doubt and that's why I removed it.'

'Will it make any difference being without it?' Anna finally asked. He explained that it acted as a lubricant between the lungs and the ribs. 'You may be able to feel the lungs against your ribs a little but other than that, nothing. Anything else?'

Anna produced a list. She started at number one. 'Bottom,' said Anna.

'Right, everybody out. Give the lady some privacy. She doesn't want you lot looking at her bottom.'

With that the six doctors that were trailing Goldstraw shuffled out the door, as did Bob who had been waiting in the corner.

Goldstraw came to the conclusion that the sacroiliac had been strained during the operation and hoped it would soon get better.

'Now you go home,' he said, ignoring the temperature chart. 'Come and see me at outpatients on 29 February. Now I've written to Souhami, and I've written to Reece and I've written to Mr Makepeace … ,' He was still talking halfway down the corridor.

Anna burst into tears of relief that she was to go home to Knebworth. She and Mitchell clung to each other. Tonight she would be sleeping in her own bed.

She came over to me, hugged me tight and, with tears streaming down her cheeks said, 'Thank you for being the best nurse in the world.' I failed! I held her tight and made her scream in pain.

She hugged Bob and thanked him for everything. Then it was all hands as Bob and Mitchell sped off to clear the flat whilst Anna and I packed up her room which had begun to look more like a florist's shop by the day.

Within minutes of her reaching home Mitchell had the fire lit, the candles flickering and the kettle on. Anna snuggled down into her chair, cushions all around her whilst her beloved cat Bella checked her out. Her anxieties lessened as she relaxed in the place that she loved most in the world.

Three weeks after her operation Anna was tired and still suffering pain in her hips and her back. Her side was extremely sore, but what hurt her more than anything else was the news that Take That, the pop group, were to split up. She and Jane had followed the band for the past couple of years, rediscovering their youth by going to the concerts in London. Their adolescence had been revisited as they joined girls half their age in the rituals of the fans.

But what disturbed us more than that was the appearance of Roger Omond's obituary in *The Guardian*. It was written by his close friend Donald Woods and chronicled Roger's life as an anti-apartheid journalist in South Africa.

> *Throughout that time when my family and I were the targets of threats and reprisals because of our friendship with Steve Biko, Roger and Mary Omond were our constant allies and friends, eventually carrying a vital message more than 150 miles at risk of police roadblocks to help us set up our escape from South Africa.*
>
> *They followed soon after and we had a reunion in London, as planned, where we toasted our entry into exile.*
>
> *Roger now began to produce not only articles but books, often after a full subbing stint. But typically his style tended in the main to stay inhibited – until he found he had lung cancer requiring radical surgery. He ditched his inhibitions and his writing flowered as never before as he produced the powerful pieces for the Guardian about his various operations and their effects. It seemed to me some of the strongest stuff I'd ever read by someone in terminal illness.*
>
> *When my wife and I went to see Roger in the intensive care unit at Brompton Hospital last week he seemed deeply unconscious, yet when we talked to him and asked if he knew we were there he opened his eyes and nodded slightly, and although we were elated at the brief communication we knew it was our last with him.*

Roger's death brought everything into sharp focus and we were intensely saddened by the news. Anna was home and recuperating. Roger would never again have that luxury. I felt deep sorrow for Mary Omond and wrote to her.

14 February 1996

Dear Mary,

Forgive my familiarity, I feel from our brief meetings that we shared so much in common, and thus an understanding of each other's situation. It was with deep regret that we read of Roger's death. You may remember our meeting in the foyer of the Brompton Hospital when you spoke of the irony that Anna and Roger should be sharing the HD unit together.

And it was in that unit where I witnessed for myself the brave fight that Roger was indeed having. I was sitting with Anna when they made the decision to take him back to intensive to try to stabilise his heart.

Despite all the efforts of those around him I was impressed that Roger stayed calm throughout. His acceptance of the situation was, I know, the result of the constant medical care he was receiving. But his enquiring mind was always asking for information.

I just wanted to say thank you to you for making my decision to write to Roger a little more comfortable – your understanding was appreciated and yes, I could always see the journalist at work in him, despite his exhaustion.

It must have been truly comforting to have your cheery demeanour by his side.

Roger will be a huge loss to you and to the causes that you both held dear. But his writings will serve as his testament to life and the memories you have will hopefully help you through your darkest hours.

Anna is making good progress and joins me in sending condolences to you.

With very warm wishes to you, our thoughts and our prayers.

Yours

Megs Wilson

Perhaps it was Roger's death that gave Anna the fresh impetus to try and regain the fitness she had lost. Although we had never spoken he had left an indelible mark on our lives, one that would never be forgotten. It helped to focus our minds on the narrowness of the tightrope on which we walk. Thankfully, Anna's balance had been restored.

During the spring Anna and I spent a lot of time together, swimming, going to the gym and shopping, the latter being therapeutic for her mind and recuperative for her lungs. She became relaxed and happy, relieved that life still held enjoyment. She and Mitchell settled back into as normal a life as possible, enjoying each other's company, pleased to be together at home.

On 13 April I received a letter in unfamiliar handwriting and was surprised by the contents. Mary Omond was spending Easter in Greece where she was beginning to get some strength.

> *Dear Megs*
>
> *Both your letters — the first to Roger and then the one to me after he died — are here with me now, when I'm just beginning to get some emotional steam up and have the time, at last, to write to thank you for your strong connecting. It was an extraordinary coming together at the Brompton — Roger and Anna in the HDU and our chance meeting downstairs on the morning your letter of 21 January was forwarded. I'm very glad we did get a chance to talk and to find common ground between our vantages.*
>
> *I'm here for a breather and also to celebrate Greek Easter before returning to London to start a new job in May. Life after Roger is taking some getting used to and I still grope for bearings.*
>
> *Thoughts of you and of Anna and of her convalescence in the spring. I imagine her sitting in the garden, getting stronger in the sunshine, with such a lot to live for. I wish her and you — and your family — my heartfelt rooting for well-being. Viva!*
>
> *With best wishes.*
>
> *Yours*
>
> *Mary Omond.*

The circle was complete.

It was good to have a period of calm and we were amazed at Anna's recovery and resilience. Although she was not able to return to nursing, she wanted to be occupied, so began to help me in the administration of the goalkeeping schools that Bob and I ran. Being such a meticulous person and having a gift for understanding and working computers, she soon had my office more organised than it had ever been — or been since. She kept everything in order and up to date, creating hand-out sheets, updating the income and expenditure and generally managing the courses.

Although we tried to push the implications of her illness into the background, they still hovered near us, menacing clouds looming on the horizon in threatening mode. I desperately wanted her to get on with life, but having been so close to her for such a long time it was difficult to let go. Anna would get annoyed if I phoned her at home too frequently, suspecting that I was making sure all was well. Her manner would be terse and short, enough for me to understand that she wanted her space. I tried to be sparing with my calls but would often find some lame excuse to phone.

But spring became summer, as near normality as it had been for years. We were able to enjoy the luxury of warm days and balmy nights, the smell of fresh air and the freedom to roam.

There was no end to the football season that year. Euro '96 made sure of that. Bob spent the month travelling up and down the country presenting programmes from all the major stadiums in England. He would have two weeks to rest before pre-season training started again. His role as the Arsenal goalkeeping coach had given him the luxury of staying close to the professional game whilst still working in the media. He was never happier than when he was out on the field coaching his keepers. It was a role made for his obsession with goalkeeping. It provided him with job satisfaction and the joy of seeing his protégé keep goal for England. In Euro '96 David Seaman had become the country's hero, performing miracles in front of the home supporters.

During those two precious weeks, Bob and I went to Christchurch for a break. We would spend time on the boat, and on the beaches, reading and relaxing. Anna was due to have a consultation with Goldstraw but she'd told us there was no point in travelling up to London. She and Mitchell would be fine by themselves. We were to forget about everything and chill out!

It was 5.00am I woke up in a cold sweat, frightened by what I had just dreamed.

Anna, Mitchell and I had gone to see the consultant – but of course he was a total stranger – and Anna was telling him that she had not been well, had been coughing frequently and had expelled some small hard bits. She asked the doctor if they were fragments of tumour. He told us we had to see the 'South African', so we went along to another consulting room, but before entering I realised that I had left my handbag. I went to fetch it and by the time I had returned Anna was being held down by three nurses who were trying to insert a suppository.

She looked over her shoulder at me, a pained expression etched on her face and it was at that point that we both realised that the cancer had returned. Her eyes were pleading with me to help her but at that moment one of the nurses pushed a sleeping tablet into her mouth, followed by a mouth guard, as used during operations.

I couldn't get the dream out of my head; it was so clear in its detail. The desperate look on Anna's face continued to haunt me all morning. Towards lunchtime the phone rang and Anna's voice greeted me, noticeably quieter than usual.

'Are you all right?' I asked.

'Yes, I'm fine.'

'Thank goodness for that,' I said, relieved.

'Why?'

I recounted the dream in all its detail. There was a period of silence on the other end of the phone.

'I don't believe what you've just told me. I *have* been unwell. I've had pressure in my neck and that awful headache like I had when we went to Manchester. And I had to stay on the settee one day I felt so awful. But the weirdest thing is that I *did* cough up a hard bit and I *did* wonder if it was a piece of tumour. We were coming home from Mitchell's party for Trigger (a new work project) and I coughed up this bloody substance and as I wiped it on the taxi window I realised it had a hard bit in the middle. That's when it crossed my mind that it might be a piece of tumour. Jane and Robert knew I was not well but I'd warned them not to let you know because I knew you'd want to come to the Brompton on Thursday.'

'It just goes to show that we are joined by a little bit more than blood.' I said. 'I hope you cleaned the window.'

'By the way,' she said, 'did you get a message from me about some chocolate?'

'No, I didn't. Why?'

'Well Mitchell went out to the pub and I tried telepathy in the hopes of him bringing me back some chocolate but he never got it. I just wondered if it had got to you instead.'

'Sorry Anna, I never got it, but if it comes my way I'll let you know. And yes, I do want to come to the Brompton on Thursday.'

Don't Look Back In Anger

Thirty years previously, on the afternoon of 6 December 1966, I was suddenly aware that my body was slipping into a routine it had only once performed before. An overpowering urge had taken hold and I was washing down walls, ironing radiator-dried clothes and preparing my house for an event eagerly anticipated over the previous nine months.

The first wave of a contraction stopped me in my tracks – and I suddenly remembered what was to come.

The memory of my labour in giving birth to my first baby John, sixteen months earlier, had certainly gone fuzzy round the edges. Nature has its own editing suite where it deletes all the inappropriate recollections of birth and leaves an acceptable version. It had been hard and lonely. Bob was in Jamaica on a pre-season tour with the Arsenal. I was due to have John just before Bob left, but since I was two weeks late I'd missed the window of opportunity to have my husband holding my hand at the arrival of our first-born. Instead I was to find myself crawling round the labour ward on hands and knees, crying my eyes out, frightened and distressed.

The North Middlesex Maternity Annexe prided itself on its history of once being the home of Gracie Fields. It was a magnificent place situated towards the top of The Bishops Avenue, Finchley, generally known as 'millionaires' row'. The house stood proudly in huge grounds that once hosted only the best parties for the most famous of people. The rest of the houses on the avenue were homes for the rich, mainly wealthy Arabs, with high walls, electric gates and burglar alarms. I arrived in the middle of the night, accompanied by a kind neighbour, was shown to the labour ward and left for the next fourteen hours to get on with it. There was no solicitous nurse comforting me, telling me I was doing well, no birth partner, no friend.

Just an assertive Sister demanding, 'Mrs Wilson! What do you think you're doing?' When I tried to tell her I was in pain, she just tut-tutted and helped me back on the bed. 'Goodness me, you've got a long way to go yet. Pull yourself together and try to relax.'

It had all seemed so easy at psychoprophylaxis classes. 'Breathe in, breathe out, allow the pain to flow over you, relax!' Except there was no bloody pain in rehearsal.

At three fingers dilated I was taken into the labour room and left to endure the final stages totally by myself. I screamed as I felt this sudden urge come over me. It worked! The Sister came rushing through the door.

'Mrs Wilson! Oh for heaven's sake, it's here!'

John made his entry on a rush of breaking waters having no thought for my understretched loins. The absence of any professional encouragement or control over the final stages of labour forced my insides to tear like a burst paper bag.

'Oh you've got a boy!' He was plonked on my chest and I waited for the wave of joy to fill my chest. I felt empty and alone.

'Now Mrs Wilson, we'll take you down to the ward and then bring you back to stitch you up after supper. It's fish and chips. All right?'

All right! All right! I had just gone through what is supposed to be the most rewarding moment of a woman's life and been left wanting, I had been torn this way and that, I had been deprived of my kith and kin and they offered me fish and chips!

At visiting time my dear mother arrived, so proud that her daughter had produced the first grandchild. I was in floods of tears.

'They never said it was like that·in the books,' I sobbed. I now know how she smiled inwardly yet comforted me with the pride and love only a mother can give.

That night I cuddled my son John. He was beautiful, he was all mine and the feeling of love was quite overwhelming.

Sixteen months later when the contractions confirmed that my second baby was on its way into the world, I was thankful that this time it would be different. My husband was at home, so was the midwife and I was in control. We sat all evening by the fire which helped to warm the December night and when the contractions became a little uncomfortable, the three of us went up to the familiar bedroom that had been prepared for the arrival of the baby. No hospital, no loneliness and no fear.

This time it was just as the text-books would have you believe. The pain was always bearable and I was encouraged and comforted and calmed. Anna was born at 2.00am on 7 December 1966, the year England had won the World Cup. She slithered into the world to be caught by a very alert midwife who instantly noticed that the cord was wrapped tightly round the baby's neck. She reacted quickly to the situation, hooking her finger between neck and umbilical and looping it over the tiny head. The pressure on Anna's neck was released and her windpipe opened up to allow breath into her tiny body. She was 6 lb 12 oz.

'What's a strapping girl like you doing giving birth to a little thing like this?' the midwife asked with a smile. My new-born baby girl lay on my welcoming chest, and we bonded instantly.

We hadn't chosen a name. Inger had been a favourite for a long time, but somehow it didn't match the tiny frame that was our new daughter. John came running into the bedroom that morning to look for his new sister. Suddenly he seemed so grown-up, so tall, no longer the baby.

'What shall we call her?' we asked him.

He tried to say his cousin Joanna's name, it being the first female face that came to mind. 'Anna,' he said quite clearly. It was perfect. Short, unfussy, yet so feminine.

By the time her second brother was born she was two and a half, had blonde tightly curled hair and a face like a cherub. Her maternal instincts arrived early and her need to mother Robert was quite a help to me. Three children under four was quite a handful but the way Anna entertained the new baby meant that Robert was often getting more attention than I could possibly give.

Anna Louise Wilson was a sixties baby. She could have been a wild child had she not been so shy. Her love of fun and laughter was always tempered a little by what others might say. Yet she admired those who were without thought for authority and followed them carefully. She enjoyed the friendship of girlfriends at school but hated the gang-like cliques that demanded her affiliation. She wanted to be accepted and needed to conform but was unable to follow if the lifestyle was unsavoury. Her very closest friends were those who shared her carefree style, her need to laugh and her sensitivity to others.

The influences on her later life could all be traced back to music she had heard as a youngster. Of all the pop groups that she could have followed during her youth, she chose the Beatles, whose songs she had heard so often as a baby from her parents' record collection. We were great fans.

She loved films, 'White Christmas' being a particular favourite, having cuddled up to me one December night after coming downstairs feeling unwell and being captivated by the wholesome theme of the musical. But it was Marilyn Monroe who was to be her idol. She adored everything about her and collected many books and photographs of the tragic star. She loved her films, adored her looks, admired her persona and possibly saw in Marilyn the same vulnerability that she felt in herself.

There was always music playing in the Wilson family cars. We have fond memories of summer holidays in Norfolk, driving through the countryside in a white Triumph Stag, hood down, John, Anna and Robert on the back seat, and all of us singing 'Saturday, Saturday,' along with Elton John at the top of our voices. Without exception, we all like music. Without exception we like music with a great beat and we like it loud.

Much later in life, whilst John was at college in Bournemouth, the whole family was able to rock together once more. John and his friends had formed a band, one that was going to take the world by storm. They were good and they were called Writing Degree Zero. Bob and I quite enjoyed being groupies for a while, following the band to such salubrious places as The Rock Garden and The Mean Fiddler in London.

We had hoped to celebrate John's twenty-first by taking him and his friends out for a meal but were told that if we wanted to be with him at his crossing into confirmed adulthood, we would have to attend the gig they were playing that night. Anna, Mitchell and Rob had travelled down to Bournemouth and then on to the venue following John's instructions. We arrived at a pub; outside were a hundred and ten motor bikes. We looked at each other, took a big breath and entered the noisy atmosphere as though we belonged. But the absence of black leather adorning any of us immediately indicated to the biker throngs that we were not there for the company. We apologetically squeezed our way through to the 'stage' end of the building and waited for the evening's entertainment. It was not the way I had envisaged celebrating my first-born's 21st, but once the band had got into their routine, and we were able to sing along and groove to the now familiar numbers, we had a truly brilliant time.

It was at Bournemouth that John met Jane. They were on the same course studying English and Media. John lived in various houses during his three years away, always with the same group of lads, and always in a property with damp, peeling wallpaper, ripped lino, missing stairs and snails. Such delicacies as washed linen never seemed in evidence and the kitchen sink was a receptacle where constant piles of unwashed pots waited for the next portion of food.

Robert and John had been most unbrotherly during their

adolescent period at home, but once John had moved away Robert would go and stay weekends with John and his friends, finding another side to his brother that he admired.

The relationship between our three children has always been close. John was the pioneer for them all, the first to go to school, to Cubs, to college. By the time Anna was ploughing her way through life's surprises we, as parents, were a little more relaxed. And Robert managed to bring himself up without the tensions that had accompanied the preliminary paths of the other two mainly because he had Anna as a substitute mother, allowing her to dress him in the most outrageous costumes clothes and call him 'Susannah'.

As they became more established with their partners all six of them would enjoy time together, influencing each other's taste in music and learning to appreciate a wider range of styles.

Anna's eclectic tastes ranged from Take That, The Carpenters, Oasis, George Michael, Barbra Streisand, Ocean Colour Scene, The Jam, to Robbie Williams.

July – August 1996

After the phone call at Christchurch when I recounted my dream, Anna's illness came rushing back to the forefront of our minds. We had all been trying to ignore the signs, pretending that she was fine and that the uncertainties in our minds would gradually fade as she improved. I travelled up to London and went to the Brompton for the Thursday appointment with Anna and Mitchell. We felt safer in a crowd and could each try to ease the tension of the situation for the others by trying to be frivolous and casual.

It is unwise to become ill during the months of July and August, seemingly the time when all senior medical professionals take their holidays. Mr Goldstraw was absent but in his place was another senior registrar who had been to see Anna once or twice in hospital. He was concerned about the blood she had coughed up but felt that the logical explanation was a clot left over from the operation that she hadn't been able to expel, being unable to cough normally. The removal of the nerve that affected her voice also restricted the ability to cough deeply. The length of time the clot had been in her lungs would explain the 'hard bit in the middle'.

He took her into a cubicle to examine her. When she emerged a few minutes later she looked shocked. The registrar had felt round her throat and pressed at a very tender point. She felt the place for herself and found a large lump sitting in the hollow of her neck.

'It could be a recurrence or it could be a gland that's up after the cold that you've had. I can see something on the X-ray but I'm unsure if it is something new or scar tissue from the operation.'

She was taken to the scanner, which allowed Mitchell and I to talk of the future, a future which had now been brought sharply into focus. The lump might well be harmless, it could be gone in a week, it could be benign, it could be innocent. But nonetheless it prompted Mitchell into talk of giving up his work at the Creative Store, abandoning computers, the medium in which he was a natural, and allowing Anna to do whatever she wanted to do in life. The bigger picture was beginning to emerge and Mitchell wanted to respond appropriately.

Anna came out blinking in the sunlight, cheerier than when she had gone in. She had decided that since it was three weeks to the appointment with Goldstraw she would put the whole thing out of her mind until then. She was not even going to phone for the results. They went off down the Kings Road determined not to let the day's findings get the better of them, resolved to put on a face for the world that said, 'We're fine'.

Professor Souhami, her oncologist at the Middlesex Hospital, had received the scans and was absolutely certain that the lump was a malignant lymph gland and that it was indeed a recurrence. He was aware that Anna was very wheezy and that her cough and voice were somewhat worse than he had heard a few weeks ago. But he was puzzled as to why the lymph tumour affected her breathing so much.

However, by the time Mr Goldstraw returned from holiday our hopes were high that he would be holding all the keys to unlock the puzzle of Anna's increasingly frightening symptoms. By the time the four of us had reached his clinic she could hardly walk across the room without being completely out of breath. She couldn't speak three words without gasping for air.

'It's not leaving you alone is it Anna?' His first words to her spoke volumes. He could see her distress; he could tell there was a problem. He was shocked at her condition.

'We've been told there's no blockage of the windpipe and can't understand why she's so bad,' we explained.

'Of course there's a blockage,' he said. 'There's yet another tumour in Anna's chest and it's blocking the trachea further down. You can see it on the CT scan.'

We were rocked and shocked to the core. We knew something was wrong, maybe the lungs, maybe a gathering of phlegm, but it had not entered our heads that there could be yet another tumour. Anna became tearful; I felt my own head fill with emotion. Bob and Mitchell stared straight ahead, unable to take in the enormity of what had just been revealed.

'We will have to admit you immediately and operate tomorrow. I have to clear the airway so that you can breathe – it's quite important Anna,' the last remark an attempt to lighten the load. 'I may have to insert a stent to hold the trachea open and once this is in place it will be there for the rest of your life. We may have to make a small incision in your throat from which a small T-tube will emerge.'

We made our way up to Elizabeth Ward and were shown to a side-room, where we could be on our own and share our feelings of disbelief. There was much hugging and a few tears, shared between ourselves and then dismissed. Mitchell went downstairs to make a few phone calls. I put my arms round Anna who was still crying.

'Are you frightened?' I asked.

She nodded. 'I'm so worried about Mitchell. You've got Dad but he's got no one.' I tried to assure her that Mitchell would be fine and that we would always be there for him.

At that moment the door burst open and there stood Mitchell, holding the strings of purple, orange and white helium balloons in one hand, a bunch of sunflowers in the other, a pile of magazines under his arm. Laughter squeezed its way back in.

Goldstraw arrived with entourage on his rounds. 'Are you still breathing?' he asked with an impish grin. 'See you tomorrow.'

'Any idea what time?' Anna asked, hoping to be first.

'It could be morning, afternoon, evening or the middle of the night.' And off he swept.

She was ready by 6.30am, dressed in her white operating gown, prepared for a long wait. The family arrived on cue willing to dance attention on her so that time would disappear. But as John, Jane and Louis arrived, so did the porter and she was wheeled past us giving us the royal wave. We all dispersed to seek refreshment or buy pressies.

The shops on the Kings Road, Mecca of fashion at the height of the sixties scene, were a godsend and it was always easy to find a small gift to cheer her up. I walked back into her room and wait for her return only to find Anna sitting up in bed, pyjamas on, declaring 'About bloody time. Where is everybody?'

'Say that again!' I said. I couldn't believe it was the same person that had gone to theatre two hours ago. No wheezing, no gasps for air, no coughing – and no stent. Anna looked radiant. The first thing she had done on coming round was to feel her throat to see if the tube was there. She was highly relieved.

We had to wait another three days before Anna could have a scan and see the results of the operation. In swept the Pied Piper, entourage sticking close to his heels, smiling as he saw Anna's expectant face.

'Has the wheezing gone?' he smiled. 'What we found was that the tumour in your chest had been pressing so hard against the windpipe that it had perforated the trachea and burst through like a raspberry. As we expected the biopsy confirmed that it was a malignant schwannoma. Now since radiotherapy hasn't proved to be a success and since we are told that chemotherapy is not a good option, I feel we have to open you up once more and get the tumour out and remove the damaged part of the trachea. The malignant part will be cut out and the trachea will be shortened. We cannot put any tube in to extend the windpipe since nothing can replace the trachea'.

A strange feeling of elation enveloped the three of us – he was willing to have another go and operate. We all had been convinced that the surgeon Goldstraw was going to hand Anna back to the medical man, Souhami, telling him he could do no more.

'Until we have the MRI scans we are not totally sure whether the two tumours are linked or separate. I tend to feel that they have nothing to do with each other and that they have resulted from the primary tumour since they are both outside the range of the two operations that you had, but on the boundaries of each. You will have to see a head and neck surgeon about the lymph gland since it is outside my speciality.'

We asked if the two tumours could be removed in one combined procedure but he felt that would be too adventurous an operation. He would speak with the other surgeon and discuss the implications of the case. Meanwhile she was not to worry unduly about the time factor. If she had any more breathless symptoms another bronchoscopy would be performed and the tumour lasered away again – although this could not be done indefinitely.

Mitchell suggested that Anna might end up as a hunch back as a result of the shortened windpipe at which Goldstraw laughed and swept out of the room. An MRI scan was booked for Thursday and in the meantime she could go home.

Sometimes a day comes along when you wonder just who's pushing the buttons. Anna arrived at our house on our way to the Brompton for the scan. Her freezer had defrosted on the kitchen floor – the door had been left open. She then spilt orange juice all over the fridge and ruined the food, and the ceiling in the lounge had begun to bow and threaten to fall in. Her back had been excruciatingly painful all week and by the time she'd arrived at our house Mitchell had rung to say the Brompton was trying to get in touch – the MRI scanner had stopped working. She would have to go to Mount Vernon the next day.

Jane went with Anna whilst we looked after Louis. We thought it would be good for the two girls to indulge themselves and wander round the shops at Watford afterwards, but Anna couldn't manage it. Her back pain was beginning to dominate her life, and she was gradually increasing her dosage of morphine and Voltarol.

But Oasis was coming to Knebworth Park, to sing in the biggest outdoor concert ever staged in the country over the whole of the weekend. It was something to get excited about, something to deflect Anna from the relentless march of her illness.

Two hundred and fifty thousand people each day were due to converge on Knebworth Park the weekend of 10–11 August. It was as though Anna and Mitchell were welcoming the world to their back garden, to the park at the top of their road, where they had had spent many hours walking, talking, flying kites and lying in the grass; where they were married in the church and where they spent the first night of their honeymoon in Knebworth House.

Gun Lane was a convenient spot for their friends to meet before and after the events of the weekend. Anna and Mitchell laid on food and drink and a space to sleep for those in need. She had been looking forward to the weekend with slight trepidation, wondering if she would be able to cope with the pain that was now a part of her life, and the coughing problems that were now troubling her. But we needn't have worried. The excitement of the whole event gave her an adrenaline rush that put her on to another plane. Knebworth Park had become the centre of the music universe for two days and Anna and her friends were part of it.

Her dancing was limited to upper body movements and the shaking of her hair. Her singing sounded just like the many others that had been straining their vocal chords for forty-eight hours, and her smile was as radiant as it had ever been. For two days the reality of her situation retreated and Oasis transported her from the routine of hospitals and tests.

The concert had provided its own oasis allowing an air of normality to enter Anna and Mitchell's life. Laughter and enjoyment were priorities for them both and they were determined that even though disease had invaded Anna's body, they would do all within their power to stop the invasion of their life together.

New bone scans revealed further secondaries at the top left-hand side of her spine and at the base of her back where she had been having so much pain. Chemotherapy had never been an option as malignant schwannoma was a non-chemo-sensitive tumour. However, Professor Souhami felt there was nothing lost in trying a course in order to shrink the tumours thereby making Anna more comfortable.

'In the meantime, Anna, I'd be grateful if you would have no more crises!'

Robert and Sarah were intensely concerned. I felt very little – numb but certainly not emotional. Bob was very emotional and found himself crying uncontrollably – very unlike him. John and Jane both felt numb and Robert was intensely concerned. Anna decided a sports car would help, preferably red. However, she realised that the mortgage was perhaps a touch more important.

Three days later it was Bob Wilson's Goalkeeping School time. It had been in existence for 13 years and during that time hundreds of aspiring goalkeepers aged between six and sixty had passed through the capable hands of our coaching staff.

Anna and my sister Liz had always helped me run the courses on the administration side, dealing with the bookings, organising the groups, the residential arrangements, the equipment, the registration and the final presentations. Bob was in charge of the 'active' side, leading the group activities and giving individual coaching to each and every student. Robert had become one of our coaches working alongside a loyal staff who knew the 'Bob Wilson' method inside and out and looked forward to meeting up during the school holidays.

It was Bob's way of putting something back into the game at grass-roots level and he was at his best when teaching the art of goalkeeping to fellow keepers. The students became part of our extended family for the time that they were there, enjoying the attention to goalkeeping detail that was not always available at their own clubs.

It was strange not having Anna there to help in the run-up to the late August course but it was lovely to welcome all the staff to our home the night before we were due to start. They were eager to obtain all the information needed for the next day's intake, familiarising themselves with names old and new.

At 9.00pm the phone rang; it was Mitchell. 'Megs, I'm at the Lister Hospital with Anna. Don't panic. She's being well looked after. She's been coughing up blood for some time and decided to get herself in as quickly as possible. There's no need for you to come to the hospital yet until we know what's happening. They might want her to go to the Brompton. I'll phone in a while. She sends her love'

Bob was in the middle of a protracted story but my sister Liz had been watching my reaction to the phone call. Our busiest time was always the first day as the students arrived.

'Do you think you and Anita can register one hundred and twenty-seven boys tomorrow without me?' I quickly asked.

'No problem,' said Liz.

Mitchell phoned back to say they were sending Anna to the Brompton by ambulance. They would phone me when they were leaving so that I could make the hour's journey by car. Anna had insisted he go home and to wait for my call from the hospital.

I had a bath and changed into comfortable clothes that I could spend the night in. I grabbed makeup, washing bag, towel and book and set off as soon as the call came to say Anna had left.

My car journey took me through Notting Hill and it was carnival night. People in jovial mood thronged the pavements and I had to wind my way through diversions to get to the Brompton, worried sick about what this next crisis was going to bring.

On my arrival at the hospital Anna was already tucked up in bed eager to tell me about her adventure. She had been at home and suddenly coughed up what she thought was a huge load of phlegm only to discover fresh blood. By the time she had filled two cereal bowls she thought it perhaps prudent to get to the hospital. Nikki the duty nurse in Accident and Emergency, was a good friend of Anna's and she was instructed to accompany her in the ambulance.

They had travelled from Stevenage to London on a blue light and at high speeds, being driven down the Edgware Road, often on the wrong side. She was very excited by the fact that in all her nursing career, this was the first time she had ever been in an ambulance with a blue flashing light. She talked me through the whole experience describing in great detail the daring sensation of speeding through the traffic, whilst cars lorries and buses pulled out of the way to let them through.

'And how's the bleeding?' I asked, concerned for the danger that she had been in.

'Oh, it's stopped!'

In her excitement she had almost forgotten the reason she was now lying in a hospital bed.

The next day the duty doctor told Anna that he felt that the crisis was over. If the tumour had perforated an artery or vein there would have been a recurrence of the bleeding. She was advised to stay in over the weekend, just in case, and would be allowed home on Monday. She was bored but safe and had plenty of visitors to help the time pass. Monday was a bank holiday so the traffic was light and the return journey was almost as quick as her emergency ride. Calm was once more restored and we were left to wonder just how many more times we would play snakes and ladders with her health.

Need For A Steed

I remember waking up early one Christmas morning. I must have been all of nine years old and so excited to discover my stocking that Santa had filled. After taking out the usual nuts, pennies, apple and orange, I discovered a leather harness. It was tan in colour and had that wonderful smell that only new leather can emit. Deliriously I screamed with delight that my parents had bought me the one thing that would make all my dreams come true – a horse. I sat practising fastening the halter to my imaginary horse and couldn't wait to be taken to the stables to be introduced to my new pet. The hours I spent down there mucking out paid for the rides that I so loved. And now I would have a horse of my own.

I could hear strange sounds coming from my brother's room signalling that he too had opened his stocking and had obviously found a musical instrument of some sort. His feeble attempts to play and my misguided delight had alerted my parents who lay in bed giggling at our reactions to their surprises. They nearly fell out of bed when they heard me call out to my brother Peter that I had been given a horse for Christmas.

It was only when they guided me to the kitchen that the real purpose of the harness became clear. There in a basket was the dearest white puppy with a large black patch on his back. The harness was too big just yet but in a few weeks' time when he was old enough and big enough I would be able to take him walks.

I got over the disappointment, thanks to the charm of Patch, and my parents always said that I *could* have a horse, but not until I was eighteen. How could they know that by then the male gender would have entered my life?

Consequently I was not at all surprised when Anna, aged 10, showed the same signs and symptoms of the love for horses. She enjoyed riding and tried to persuade us to buy one of her own. We went round to the local stables and it was explained how she would have to get up at five-thirty every morning to muck out the pony, groom and feed it before she set off for school. She had a long think and decided that the wiser option was a longer sleep – she too would wait until she was eighteen.

It was an activity that we enjoyed together except that one day, whilst on holiday, the horse she was riding swerved to avoid a puddle and threw Anna to the ground. She broke her arm rather badly and spent the rest of the holiday time travelling to and from the hospital. It made her nervous of riding but gradually her confidence returned. And later on in her life it would serve as relaxation in the time spent recuperating between cancer treatments. We would go to Knebworth and ride the outer circuit of the park, up through the avenues of trees and across the expanse of grass, nudging the curious deer, skirting the church and the barns and back towards the stables past the majestic house. The horses knew the route and once we had turned for home would be eager to take us back to their base.

We would be ready for the gallop, reining in the horses for as long as we could before I would say, 'Are you ready?' and off we would fly up the hill towards the church, laughing at the daring of our speed and thankful for the freedom we were enjoying.

It was an activity that, because of the presence of secondaries in her bones, we had to shelve. The chance of her falling off or injuring herself was too dangerous.

September 1996 – March 1997

On 2 September 1996 Anna began her chemotherapy. We had embarked on a totally new experience. A different area of the hospital, new faces, unfamiliar nurses and an altered routine. She was to receive her treatment as an outpatient at the chemotherapy day unit of the Middlesex Hospital.

The preamble to the final administration of the chemicals was long and tortuous with more tests and even longer waits for results. She was finally shown into a pleasant room overlooking the tree-lined street that divided the hospital buildings. Anna's designated nurse sat opposite and explained the procedure and the possible after-effects of the drug she was about to administer. She then set about inserting the cannula into Anna's wrist and in order to make polite conversation asked what Anna did for a living.

'I'm a nurse.'

The simple everyday task of inserting the needle suddenly became very difficult for the poor girl but after a couple of tries she was satisfied with the result. A saline drip was standing next to the chair and this was inserted into the cannula and the pump switched on. The nurse explained that it was important to clean the vein before any of the chemicals were introduced. After five minutes this was then changed and a syringe full of an anti-emetic was injected followed by the bag of chemotherapy, which hooked on to the steel holder. This contained the drug carboplatin and looked exactly the same as the saline had done – a clear liquid.

As I watched the chemo drip, drip through the tube and then into Anna's arm it took on a huge significance. This was the chemical that was going to destroy Anna's cells. Not just the cancer cells, but also the healthy cells. The information booklet had clearly stated that after this treatment the patient would be sterile and periods would more than likely stop. Wow! Even though she had probably been made sterile long ago by all the scans and X-rays that she'd had over the previous two and a half years, this somehow seemed far more decisive. She had always wanted children. If she could have been a mother at four she would have made a good one, but when the time came to marry Mitchell they decided to wait until they were more secure in their financial situation. Now, seemingly, the decision had been taken out of her hands.

It took approximately an hour for all the liquid to be transfused, then the saline was introduced again and the cannula withdrawn. Anna was dispatched with her anti-nausea pills, tablets to line her stomach, and steroids. She was to return in a month for a repeat dose, carboplatin being a long-acting chemotherapy. She was glad to be on her way home.

We hoped the summer of crises was now behind us and that autumn would provide the mellow calm much needed by us all. The next week found Anna unable to lift her head off the settee save to be sick in the bucket that Mitchell had at the ready. Her back pain was excruciating and her wheezing was making a reappearance.

Ten days on and she felt well enough to attend her cousin Jo's lunchtime birthday party. She spent three hours from 8.00am trying on every item of clothing she possessed, determined to look radiant. At 11.00am she was satisfied, hair beautiful, makeup immaculate, clothes just right. Then she decided to reach for a handbag in the top cupboard of her wardrobe. Wearing her high boots, she clambered on to the bed, reached up, grasped the bag then lost her balance and crashed onto the bedside table.

She waited ten seconds to see what was hurting imagining her plastic ribs to be displaced, but was delighted to find she was unharmed. Smiles turned to anger though when she looked at her trouser leg to find it was torn! Anger turned to frustration and then to tears as she kicked the doors and thumped the walls. Mitchell did his best to calm her down but failed. Repressed fury and weeks of frustration came pouring out in torrents and they finally set off for the party in silence, Anna's makeup now tear-stained and her face set.

The long journey helped calm her down and she was able to once more look as though she was in complete control. Her determination to appear as normal as possible was always at the front of Anna's mind. She hated being treated differently just because she was ill and couldn't understand why people's body language and attitude had changed towards her. She shunned patronising sympathy, abhorred undue attention, and longed to be treated as normal.

At the party she was painfully aware of the sideways glances, the contrived approaches and knowing looks that came her way from strangers who knew of her situation. Only the children felt able to greet Anna and Mitchell in a natural way without any hidden agendas.

We are known as a very close family and whenever there's a party it's bound to be wild and emotional. Once Anna had made her entrance and coped with the inquisitive looks, the family helped her enjoy her time as only the family can. The party animal in Anna was released and she was able to forget her impending seclusion.

There was no change in the size of the lymph gland despite the chemotherapy and Anna's wheezing was becoming a problem again. Professor Souhami advised her to get in touch with Mr Goldstraw to arrange another bronchoscopy to clear the obstructing tumour.

Anna was admitted to the Brompton that week and was taken to theatre at 8.45pm Her breathing was getting worse by the minute, sounding rather like a boiling kettle. It was quite frightening just how quickly the air passage blocked once the tumour began its journey through the wall of the windpipe and across the trachea. By 10.30pm she was back on the ward and breathing freely.

It had taken only five weeks for the tumour to grow back and although it was good to know that it was easily removed, our concern was for how many times this might happen in the future.

For the following month Anna had respite from pain and discomfort and by the time we saw Professor Souhami the lymph gland had reduced in size. Necklaces that had previously been difficult to fasten now fitted with ease. The Prof said that if there was the same amount of reduction after the next session of chemo then he would consider giving her a large blast of the carboplatin. He had been unsure whether the chemo would have any effect but he was delighted with the results. We were quietly thrilled that this was the first positive sign that we had been given and accepted the next session of chemo with gratitude.

As Christmas approached the thought of shopping filled Anna with alarm. Although she loved it so much she couldn't imagine just how it would be possible. She could only walk for short distances before having to rest, the pain in her hips and back making it just too difficult. We were determined not to be deprived of an activity that we loved so much so a solution was sought.

We hired a stretch limo and invited Jane, Louis, Sarah and my sister Liz to join us on a Christmas shopping trip around all the London stores. We did Harrods, Selfridges, Debenhams, Dickins & Jones and Liberty. We had lunch in Harvey Nichols and we were collected and deposited at the front of every store, our chauffeur arriving at our command. Shopping was piled into the boot and refreshments were on hand inside our luxury capsule. It was perfect, not spending too long in any one shop and being wafted from door to door like superstars. We laughed, we sang, we compared purchases and we talked – and talked.

We decided that from now on it was the only way to do Christmas shopping. Little did we realise then that this day would be the inspiration for many future special days.

Anna's thirtieth birthday was approaching and we had gone to great lengths to keep the party secret from her and thought we'd succeeded, but didn't know that she'd received a card from one of the relatives wishing her a happy birthday and saying how sorry they were not to be at the party. She was upset that someone should be so tactless but didn't let on that she knew.

It *was* a surprise as she had no idea of just *how* many friends and family we'd asked along to a local restaurant, which we'd taken over for Sunday lunch. Family had come from all parts of the country and they were amazed to see just how well the birthday girl looked.

The remarkable thing about Anna was that she always gave the appearance of being the fittest person around. Her Raphaelesque hair framed a face with strong features, a wide engaging smile and dazzling teeth. In a huge crowd it was always easy to spot the girl with the blonde curly hair. She was unmistakable.

As she arrived her cousin Philip began playing the bagpipes, a sound to stir all the family's emotions. The Scottish heritage that had been handed down from Bob's parents, Nan and Grandpa Wilson, was something of which we were all proud and the skirl of the pipes brought the hankies flurrying to the fore. The surprise worked and Anna was so thrilled to see that everyone had made an effort help her get through her thirtieth year. Even my dad and my step-mum Amy had travelled down the motorway from Derbyshire to be there at the age of eighty-nine!

The party moved from restaurant to home where the celebrations continued late into the night and it thrilled Anna that she had reached a birthday that at one time looked in doubt.

By Christmas week the tumour in the trachea was making her breathing difficult again so Mr Goldstraw operated to give her clearance during the holiday period. This was the fourth time in as many months, her chemotherapy following the same pattern, but by the end of January she was once more back in the Brompton so that she could again have her breathing eased. Mr Goldstraw was concerned at the frequency of the growth and that this time he had removed a large blood clot that was also blocking the trachea.

The New Year saw Mitchell with a change of career and a renewed commitment, which we all felt would be a re-focus for his life. He had done his share of consultations and so on our next medical visit to London there was just Anna and me.

We went to the Middlesex for our appointment with Professor Souhami. He explained that Mr Goldstraw had recommended that Anna have some very specific radiotherapy to the inside of the trachea, called brachytherapy, to try to alleviate the problem of the continued perforation. Anna questioned the safety of such a move knowing how much radiation she'd had previously but he assured her that by going in with a bronchoscope the spine would be protected from any damaging rays. The radiotherapy would be applied very specifically to the localised area and hopefully prevent the tumour's growth across the airway. He also wanted her to have radiotherapy to the lower part of her spine since the latest scans had shown there to be a problem around the sacroiliac.

The professor was always friendly and considerate. His affection for Anna was obvious as soon as we walked into a consultation. He took her into the examination room and slipped back out to talk to me.

'How is she really? The trouble with Anna is that she is always so sparky and it's difficult to know just exactly how she is.'

I explained that she did put on a bright face for everyone, but that she had had a particularly bad six weeks. She seemed to be having more bad days than good.

I asked him for his opinion and he said, 'Well I feel that all these things are being caused by the illness, which is beginning to get a hold.'

He returned to Anna to examine all the areas of concern, including a new lump that had appeared on her back. He stayed talking to her for another ten minutes sitting on the bed next to her.

'You seem a bit down,' he said.

'I'm pissed off,' Anna told him in her blunt outspoken manner. He talked through all her problems, listening with a sympathetic ear and telling her gently that the illness was taking hold. And all the time Anna was sitting there in just her knickers.

He got up slowly, glancing down onto the bed. 'Oh, I've been sitting on your clothes – and you haven't got dressed!' he said, only then noticing her semi-nakedness.

Meanwhile, no chemotherapy whilst this next treatment was taking place. She was delighted!

We were beginning to look for more and more ways to deflect the attention away from the meandering menace that was slowly making its way through her body. The cancer was making its bed where it was most comfortable and there seemed to be little that could be done to divert it.

But Anna insisted that it wasn't a problem and that she just had to get on with it. As long as she had Bella the cat, her husband and a good laugh every day then she was content. She would be annoyed if I phoned too often, showed too much concern or became overprotective. She needed life to be normal and treated as normal disliking any reminder that the situation had changed. She was determined that any restrictions would be minimal and that her illness be put to the bottom of the pile.

The dream of having a horse of her own had never really left her and her love of freedom and speed still burned inside her. But since riding had become impossible because of her pain and the brittle nature of her bones, she had turned her attention to another way of satisfying her need to feel the wind in her hair.

One quiet restful afternoon, the sound of a roaring engine split the peace and sent Bob and myself running to our front door, wondering if Formula One had changed course and swept through our driveway. The hooves that had once galloped beneath Anna's frame had been substituted for alloy wheels and the chestnut fur and flowing mane, for flaming red steel. Her face was filled with the thrill of a gallop and her eyes sparkled at the daring of her steed.

An MGF sat snorting outside our house, chafing at the bit to be off on yet another chase, steered by the gentle hands of its eager jockey.

'Are you coming for a ride?' She beamed at her father. It was a demonstration model that she had on loan for the day and she was impatient to put it through its paces. Bob, always a sports-car nut, didn't need to be invited twice and was into the passenger seat like a seasoned enthusiast. The three-point turn completed, they were off on yet another circuit of the course.

I sensed that the beloved VW, her pride and joy when new, had now served its purpose and would soon be replaced by the racier model. As soon as they returned the calculations were done, the economics discussed and reasoning went out of the window. Why would she want a large boot when she could only carry a small amount of shopping from Tesco? Why would she need to have room for more than one other person? Why shouldn't she have what she really wanted, if it was affordable?

We had to agree; depending on the price offered in exchange for the VW, we could think of no sensible reason why she shouldn't go ahead and look for an MGF. Her search didn't take long and within a few days we were invited down to the local dealer to inspect what they had on offer. In the window sat her dream with only 4000 miles on the clock. There were four other cars that were available but for one reason or another could not be Anna's for another two weeks.

'But I might not be capable of driving then!' she impishly remarked, playing the sympathy card. Her slight exaggeration could be forgiven but it was an insight as to just how vulnerable she felt her active life to be.

As we sat in the showroom, the salesman said he could have the car ready in a couple of days.

'I'll only have it if it can be ready tomorrow,' said Anna teasingly.

'Done', said the salesman. It was hard for Anna to contain her excitement. She now had the task of taking her VW home and clearing it out ready to say goodbye.

But first thing next morning she had an appointment with Professor Souhami. We were ushered into a room by his senior registrar, Mark Napier, who explained that everything had been arranged for the brachytherapy to take place next week. Meanwhile the Professor was making a point of seeing all his patients before he left! In six weeks' time he would be taking up a new appointment as the Dean of the University of London Hospitals so the next appointment would be her last. A great honour for him and a great loss for us.

Had it been an ordinary day I think Anna would have gone into a deep depression knowing that Souhami was leaving. She had come to look upon him as a friend, someone who would talk to her straight, who could joke with her about her cancer without offence and read her mood as she walked into his consulting room. I think he, in turn, had become very fond of her. He liked her spark, her cheekiness and her determination.

But this was MGF day. We had to collect the car at 3.00pm. We were there at 2.45pm. She spent an hour being shown the finer points of the car before she whisked me back to Threepwood in her red machine. She was so appreciative of our own enthusiasm and thanked us profusely.

There was no need for thanks. The joy on her face will last in our hearts for-ever.

Candle In The Wind

February – October 1997

How many paper hearts does it take to cover a ceiling? Thirty-seven if your room is the size of Anna's and Mitchell's. And how long does it take to make them all before sticking them up with sellotape? Apparently most of the night whilst Anna slept. It was so much more original than a Valentine card and so much more personal.

Although she was nervous about her hospital visit the originality of the gesture had cheered her and we were further amused once we got on to the ward where bouquets of red roses, sunflowers and single blooms were being delivered for various nurses in the unit. The entertainment helped ease her tension as she was given her sedation ready for the bronchoscopy.

The tumour in Anna's throat was giving cause for concern and it was decided to begin the brachytherapy as soon as possible. Before they could perform the internal radiotherapy she would have to report to the Middlesex Hospital and, under sedation have photographs and measurements taken of the tumour.

She remembered nothing afterwards but was soon in possession of a Polaroid photograph of the tumour that had perforated her trachea. It looked like a large bulbous eruption of varying colour and filled the centre of the picture. At last she was face to face with the enemy, powerless to defend herself and only her curiosity satisfied. Now that they had the picture and the measurements, the hospital could prepare to attack the area with the isotope from inside the trachea. The procedure would take place in about a week's time.

She arrived home to find another Valentine card and hurriedly tore it open. It was from Dennis and Jan, close family friends who lived in Christchurch. Inside the card was a gift of a flight on Concorde to Paris, lunch and a sightseeing tour, then home on Eurostar – first class! She was stunned by their generosity and decided that she and Mitchell would make the journey to Christchurch at the end of the week to thank them personally.

Bob and I had already travelled down to our weekend retreat when the sound of the red MGF heralded their arrival just after sunset. We looked out to see Anna and Mitchell in the car with the hood down, Anna sitting at the wheel wearing shades and a Grace Kelly chiffon scarf draped casually round her head – excellent in Monte Carlo but a little chilly in the English winter. It had been a beautiful day, but this was February and whatever warmth there had been in the sun, it wasn't enough to keep the body from freezing over on a journey of two hours. Consequently when they got out of the car all they could think of was a hot bath. They had been determined to keep the hood down all the way and agreed that it had been an exhilarating experience. We had a lovely weekend, relaxed and happy, Anna able to thank Dennis and Jan personally for their wonderful present.

The next time she saw Professor Souhami she told him of the constant pain in her ribs, both hips and in her sacroiliac. He gently explained that all her pain was down to the spread of her cancer but that radiotherapy on all the areas would ease the discomfort.

'How's morale?' he asked.

'Fine,' I said. 'Ask her about her new car! MGF!' She promised him a ride but he declined with a smile, explaining that he felt his heart wouldn't stand the pace.

He assured her that Mr Whelan, the doctor who was taking over from him was the ideal person for Anna since he was a specialist in sarcomas. He was a very nice man and would be perfect for Anna – particularly since she was so bossy!

Her radiotherapy began the following week, and would now include her sacroiliac, her right hip and the back right rib area. The hope was that the pain she had been experiencing would be reduced by the treatment.

If anything could take her mind off her situation the day's visit to Paris by Concorde might be just the thing. What we had never told Dennis and Jan was that the two modes of transport Anna feared were flying and travelling in tunnels underwater so the flight and the journey back on Eurostar would be an interesting exercise! We really didn't know how she was going to take it but as time drew near she began to get excited. The trip was planned for 22 March and the departure would be captured on video by Mum.

What I hadn't done was to find out which runway was being used for take-off that day. London Heathrow is extremely large. I had enquired as to the best vantage point for seeing the planes ascend. I was directed to Queens Building but the essential signs disappeared and after half an hour of driving from one end of the airport to the other, I became lost. As I was sitting in the traffic jam I was suddenly aware of a huge noise that was getting louder and louder. People had stopped, others waved their arms in the air and I realised that it was the unmistakable sound of Concorde taking off. I could neither see it on the runway nor watch it in the air. All I could hear was the deep thunderous roar and feel the vibrations through the car. My choice of words was neither ladylike nor fitting for an educated woman, but they were a great release for my frustration.

Anna and Mitchell were totally exhilarated by the actual flight. However, Anna's expletives on take-off and landing matched my own verbalisations and gave great amusement to all on board. Their day in Paris was romantic and truly memorable affording them quality time together, something sadly missing in their everyday lives. They broke away from the rest of the party, choosing to visit the sights on their own catching up with the others at the station to board the Eurostar for their first-class return home. For a day the routine of illness and treatment was put aside and they were able to be a normal couple enjoying an exciting day together.

The Paris trip was the start of a period of calm, the radiotherapy helping ease the pain. But it was also the closing of a chapter in Anna's life for she had to say goodbye to Professor Souhami. It was not easy, and as she and Mitchell gave the Prof champagne and letters from us all, they were each as tearful as the other. Leaving his clinic was one of the saddest times she would experience since she was losing her doctor, her psychiatrist, her confidant and her friend.

But for one slight blip, life was returning to as normal as it had been for some time. Bella had been with them for six years. When she came to them she had been an abused cat and, naturally, extremely timid but soon came to love the company of humans running to greet visitors entering the house. During the day their bedroom was hers where she lay either on the bed or in the airing cupboard. At night she would creep inside the bedclothes to lie between Anna and Mitchell. She was the baby of the house and was loved to distraction.

Anna phoned me and my heart sank at the sound of her sobbing. 'Are you all right?' I asked anxiously.

'No I'm not.'

It was the phone call I had been dreading. I quickly prepared myself for the next crisis in Anna's illness when she said, 'Bella's died!' She was distraught. I was relieved.

They had rushed to the vet with the cat when they realised something was wrong and left her in capable hands. They returned that evening to be told that she either had a heart condition, or a tumour; they had found fluid on the lungs, hence the tube coming from the cat's chest. The vet handed them the box so that they could take Bella home to be nursed, but one glance inside and Anna knew immediately that she was already dead. They decided to leave her there to be cremated and made their way home beside themselves with grief. Their substitute child had been taken from them and it was very painful.

On the morning of Sunday 31 August Bob and I woke early, turned on the television and were bemused by the programmes being broadcast. Presenters with shocked expressions were unusually moved by the story they were reporting. Diana, Princess of Wales had been killed overnight in a car crash in Paris and every station had cancelled the planned morning's schedule to focus on the news the whole world could not believe.

We were riveted to our screen, unable to move away in case we missed a snippet of information that might give us another clue as to the details of the tragedy. Little did we realise that the same scenario was being played out in millions of homes throughout the country.

I phoned and woke Anna, needing to share the dreadful news. She in turn woke Mitchell and they too found it hard to leave the television all day, addicted to the scores of reports coming from each and every station. That week there was very little else on the television screen except the Diana story. London became the centre of the universe as preparations for her funeral took place amid worldwide interest. The day before the ceremony, I decided to make my pilgrimage and walk the route that would be Diana's last.

I made my way to Kensington Palace Gardens and was stunned at the sight of the hundreds of bouquets left in front of the palace gates, at the overpowering smell of lilies and candles that permeated the air and the silence that accompanied the thousands of people who had come to pay their respects. I then followed the route the hearse would take all the way to Westminster Abbey. I had no idea why I should want to do it - perhaps to be part of history.

The finality of Diana's death once more brought the continuance of Anna's life fully into focus and we all learned to appreciate the fact that every single day we had together was truly precious.

Her ability to take everything that was being thrown at her was quite extraordinary. She would not allow anyone to show emotion or sympathy and she was insistent on keeping her own inner feelings firmly shut behind solid doors. 'Once I open them then the tears will begin to flow and I don't think they would ever stop.'

I had a phone call during the evening to say she had a project for me. Could I do some research on wheelchairs? I knew how hard it was for Anna to even talk about the subject let alone admit that she had finally accepted the necessity. I tried to sound matter-of-fact and told her I thought it very sensible on a practical level and that it was a very brave move. She tried to keep the conversation as light as she could, but I could hear the sobs beneath her words.

On 11 September she began her new course of chemotherapy in the hopes that this would attack the tumours that seemed to be continuing to form in her bones and the morphine medication was increased

It took a day before the sickness set in and by the third day she was so exhausted she spent the time resting. Her voice disappeared from the strain of vomiting but when I phoned in the afternoon she was very happy. She told me she had decided to smoke a joint to see if it helped. Immediately it had stopped her from feeling sick and her pain had eased! I took the news in a matter-of-fact way, as I felt the mother of a mature daughter should. She was doing her best to educate us in the medicinal properties of cannabis which was obviously having the desired effect. We approved, after all, anything that made the situation better was extremely welcome.

By the beginning of October Anna was feeling like her old self again. Her walking improved and her pain had eased. She and Mitchell had been out and bought two kittens to celebrate their wedding anniversary. Jack and Stoli were typical of their genders and reflected the characters of their new owners. Jack, the male, was spiky-furred and mischievous, Stoli, the female, delicate and loving.

On the whole, the year 1997 had been a good one despite the continuing spread of the disease through her bones. Her breathing had been untroubled, thanks to the brachytherapy and she had been able to enjoy quality time with Mitchell, the family and her friends.

Her body still longed for children but her mind had to exclude the likelihood. She was able to practice her maternal instincts on Louis and her friends' children, all of whom she adored, whilst Jack and Stoli were totally smothered with love.

The whole country was still in shock from the news of Princess Diana's death, the tragedy of a sudden loss and the effect it would have on her two boys permeating everyday life. But for Anna, it brought her own life into greater focus and allowed her to appreciate the comfort of just being alive.

Two Boiled Eggs

October 1997 – April 1998

'You can't wear that, it's a skirt!' Louis was nearly three and even he could understand that there were differing dress codes for men and women. He had been helping his grandpa open up birthday presents – grandpa's birthday presents. First there had been some long white socks, suitable to wear with shorts for summer golf. Then elasticated garters with bright red flashes, reminiscent of the sort worn by scouts – Bob looked at me quizzically, unable to see the connection to himself. The next present was a large pin, the sort used to hold nappies together, at which time the penny began to drop. And finally the skirt – short, pleated and made of tartan cloth.

Bob's family were Scottish, his father being an Ayrshire farmer's son and his mother a Presbyterian minister's daughter from Glasgow. His parents had moved to England when Pop Wilson secured a job in Widnes, consequently their six children were all born in England but with passionate Scottish heritage.

I had been excited at buying Bob a kilt plus all the regalia and, as he opened the sporran I could see he was delighted too. We all demanded he put on the outfit and model it before the whole family. They had arrived to help Bob celebrate his fifty-sixth birthday, John and Jane, Louis, Robert and Sarah, Anna and Mitchell. It was heartwarming when we gathered, it felt natural and safe.

Anna was continuing to receive the carboplatin chemotherapy every three or four weeks and it seemed to be doing its job. The pain in her legs had eased and she had a few good days between the bad. But what had shown up on the latest scans was a hole in her right hip where the bone had disintegrated. I tried to make light of it by suggesting that this was obviously the reason why she had lost weight recently. She managed a wry smile.

But trouble was never far away and she began to complain of intense pain inside her chest which she described as a crushing feeling. There was also a new swelling on the back right hand side of her ribs, a raised area the shape and size of the hollow of a hand which the CT scans showed quite clearly. Mr Whelan explained, 'Unfortunately there's also another tumour on the inside of the ribcage next to the lung, sitting on the spine. It's this that is giving you the intense pain you've been experiencing. The main nerves in the top half of your body come down your spine and then round your rib cage. The tumour sits at the exact spot where the nerves emerge from the spine.'

The normal course of action would be to apply radiotherapy to banish them and alleviate pain, but the area had already been radiated, this thwarted plans for any further treatment.

It was decided to step up her morphine from four to six times a day and change the chemotherapy. They had two options. The first, doxorubicin, could be administered in fifteen minutes and it was possible that she would lose her hair. They could offer her a cold cap to wear for 4 hours before the chemo was administered giving her a ninety-eight per cent chance of saving her hair.

The second would mean a stay in hospital of three to four days and the certainty of losing her hair.

'Not bloody likely!' exclaimed Anna. The very thought of going into hospital sent alarm bells ringing in her ears. Mr Whelan pointed out all the implications of the two chemotherapies, there being very little difference in the effectiveness of one over the other. She opted for doxorubicin, a very toxic chemical that would almost certainly cause hair loss but allow her to go home to bed! It was booked to start in one week's time, but this was the middle of November and Christmas shopping still had to be tackled!

Last year it was a stretch limo – this year it was a hired wheelchair. I really hadn't passed my test but was determined to prove that I was the best wheelchair pusher in town. Leaving the car park and heading for the double-doors to the shopping centre, I decided to show off my skills and quickened my pace as I commentated on the race that we had supposedly joined. What I didn't realise was that the piece of track we were crossing was an actual road; round the corner came a lorry heading straight for us.

I pulled on the brakes and shuddered to a halt instantly, nearly hurtling my charge in the process. We laughed at the imagined headlines. 'Mother catapults daughter under wheels of lorry.'

She coped brilliantly making light of her situation, just thrilled to be able to begin buying her presents. In fact she found it so easy that she had me pushing her round Lakeside shopping centre for six hours! I kept asking her if she was OK. 'I'm fine, not a bit tired!' I couldn't let on for a moment that exhaustion was about to finish me off!

'It was so good to go shopping with you again Mum.'

Those words swelled my heart. Our times together had consisted of consultations, X-rays, chemotherapy, radiotherapy and waiting for results. Our quality time at Lakeside was worth more than I could have imagined.

When chemo day came she tried wearing the ice cap, but lasted only twenty minutes of the recommended four hours. The pain it gave her on top of her head was unbearable so she told them to go ahead and administer the toxins.

As we left the clinic she was obviously stressed about how quickly she would lose her hair so we went straight to Selfridges and bought two wigs. After trying them on she was surprised to see how well short hair suited her and her mood calmed knowing that, when the time came, she had a good substitute.

This was the beginning of a devastating sickness that was to be with Anna until April, five months when her weight plummeted and Mitchell's devotion was tested to the full. Anna became very vulnerable, frightened and weak, and those solid doors began to creak open and let out her imprisoned emotions.

She vomited constantly through the last week of November and the first week of December, but miraculously it eased towards her birthday and on the sixth she was at last allowed a good day. All the family gathered at Brookmans Park for roast chicken, mashed potatoes and veg – Anna's favourite and we had a ball. Dennis and Jan had sent a Harrods hamper and whilst Mitchell and Anna began unwrapping the goodies, Louis took great delight in karate-chopping the polystyrene packaging until the whole room was filled with snow.

The next day she was thirty-one. She cried. She spoke to John on the phone. She cried. It snowed. She cried. Her best friend Louise came round and for the first time they cried together. She had always given us the feeling that she could cope with her illness on her own but finally she was beginning to let us in and share it with her.

Three days later I got a phone call. 'Are you doing anything this afternoon Mum? Could you come over with your scissors?' Her hair was coming out in lumps and it was time to cut it off.

Hair that framed her face, that sat on her shoulders and tumbled down her back; corkscrews of gold that singled her out from a crowded room, that created envy, comment and identity – it all had to go.

I cut off the bulk in one swift movement knowing I would keep the handful of hair for ever. She handed me the razor and demanded

I shave close to her head. She looked in the mirror at the result. It was stunning, her eyes and cheekbones now dominating her face for the first time since she was a baby. She may have lost her hair, but she was lucky to still have her beauty.

Mitchell sat in the chair Anna had vacated and handed me the scissors.

'No Mitchell! I love your long hair!' she cried. He looked very much like the conventional images of Jesus, hair parted and falling to his shoulders, beard prominent.

'This is the reason I've been growing it, so I can lose mine at the same time.' I cut it and Anna shaved his scalp. They stood in front of the mirror and laughed at the result, looking like two boiled eggs.

Nausea and sickness dominated the run-up to Christmas. Her anti-emetic tablets ceased to work since they were being expelled in the vomit with her painkillers and any liquid that she had tried to drink. Only an injection by her GP helped to stop the malign cycle that had taken over.

The bucket was her best friend and Mitchell became her nurse and since he hadn't been into work for some time his boss had arrived to see him. He offered Mitchell three options; continue to work, work-part time or finish and be paid off. Opting for the latter, Mitchell reasoned that whilst he worked, he only took time off when Anna was ill. If he was not working he could then be with Anna and enjoy the good days, when they came.

Christmas Day was one of them and once more the family closed ranks and selfishly revelled in the joys of present giving. When all the wrapping paper littered the floor and the bows were no longer holding together the secrets of the presents, and laughter and surprise had filled the room Robert came forward with a large flat rectangular parcel and presented it to Bob and me. I could feel his eyes on us in anticipation of our reaction. Under the wrapping paper was a photograph frame which held a portrait of Anna taken the previous October when her hair was at its most glorious. The black-and-white picture showed Anna's personality to perfection, her vitality and vibrancy transforming the monochrome image into a veritable blaze of hues and colours. I looked across at her, now shorn of her glory, looking pale and tired from sickness and we smiled through our tears.

The New Year reminded us that it was now nearly four years since cancer had invaded our lives. How familiar we had become with its devious personality, its cynical moods and malevolent ways.

It no longer surprised or shocked us, but irritated and disappointed our expectations. It entwined itself in our consciousness and never allowed us to forget its presence for one moment.

January had not yet departed when another boulder fell into the rocky road along which Anna and Mitchell steered. Jack and Stoli had become a worry to Anna as they chased around the house, Stoli not quite accomplishing the art of using the cat litter. Jack would follow Mitchell everywhere, even into the loft where the computer equipment sustained his sanity and his freelance work. If Mitchell went out of the front door, Jack would wait patiently for his return.

It was a neighbour who knocked on the door to ask if they owned a black cat. There was one lying under his car and it was unclear how he had met his death. Anna was consumed with guilt for shouting at Jack the night before and Mitchell was beginning to believe that he must be very wicked having the things he loved taken away so.

The breathlessness that had warned us last time that the tumour was growing across Anna's trachea was once more apparent. It was only a year since she had undergone the last excision and once more she found herself fighting for breath. Mitchell admitted to us that he was finding sleep difficult, convinced he was going to wake up one morning to find her dead beside him.

She was admitted to the Middlesex where brachytherapy was performed to remove the tumour which was sitting halfway across the trachea, and which restored her breathing to normal.

We arrived home to be greeted by Mitchell, Stoli, Robert and Sarah. She was relieved to walk back in to her precious home. She teasingly put her arms round me and said, 'Now Mum, I want you to promise me that I'll never have to go into hospital again.'

It was getting more and more difficult to alleviate the constant discomfort. I would spend time massaging her feet, her hands, and her head, whilst Mitchell did the round of daily chores at which he had become so adept. When she was well enough, Bob would take her to the cinema in the afternoon where they and four other people would sit watching the latest offering.

One of Anna's favourite films as a young girl was the musical, *Fiddler on the Roof.* There is a scene when Topol's newly married daughter and her husband rush her father and every family member back to their home to see the new 'arrival' – a sewing machine. The excitement at their new acquisition leads to much dancing, singing and celebration.

Similarly we were summoned to their home to admire the made-to-measure wheelchair – and the ensuing scenes were not that dissimilar. We admired the colour – red – the ease of braking, the cushions and the wheels. Mitchell demonstrated his talent at wheelchair dancing, lifting up the front axle, leaning back and spinning round. We touched it, polished it, manoeuvred it and collapsed it and agreed that if ever you wanted a wheelchair, this would be the one.

Mitchell found it hard seeing Anna so ill. The realisation had come to him that she was approaching a crisis. He had married Anna because he loved her and because she was the only one he wanted to spend the rest of his life with. And that wasn't going to happen. Now he had to come to terms with the fact that his wife was going to die and that he would eventually be without her.

'All that we are going through now, and all that we struggle to do only has one ending - we will lose Anna and that seems so unfair. I feel so sad. I don't know which way to turn or what to do. Anna thinks that I have my dream situation in working from home and can't understand why I'm not happy with it. We are together so much and yet I feel so lonely. When Anna goes to bed I sit here on my own for hours. I can't go out at night because I don't want to leave her and yet all my friends are working during the day.'

Robert and Sarah began to make a habit of spending the weekends at Knebworth, sensitive to Mitchell's situation and wanting to help in any way they could. The four of them got on so well that it distracted them from reality and helped lift everyone's spirits. Anna's day began to revolve round how many times she was sick, how much pain she was in and what television programmes could amuse her most. Visits to the cinema had come to an end and shopping was no longer pleasant. Any movement was painful and she spent much of the time sitting at home in her blue armchair.

As the cancer spread further through her bones, her ribs, hips and spine were feeling much of the effect. Acupuncture, acupressure, TENS machines and hot water bottles were all tried in an effort to ease the searing pain coming from the sciatic nerve and travelling down her legs to her toes. Her dark moods were difficult to lift – pain and sickness were beginning to dominate her life.

The palliative care team at the Middlesex had been called in to see if they could solve the problems. They were concerned that the more they increased the doses of morphine, the more nauseous she became.

They wanted her to try a new synthetic morphine that had been available in this country for only the past six months. It had come over from America and so far had proved successful in other patients who seemed to have sensitivity to morphine. It had appeared to have no side-effects such as sickness and constipation.

Almost overnight the vomiting stopped. It was like a miracle. For six months her life had been dominated by the proximity to a bucket. Her weight had dropped, her energy was depleted and her moods would waver from anodyne to acid. It had been difficult enough coping with the pain, but the sickness made it almost unbearable. Now, if they could increase the dose of the morphine substitute to alleviate the pain, she could perhaps be spared on both counts and concentrate on living as normal a life as possible.

But unbeknown to us, the brachytherapy that had been administered in February was no longer effective in holding back the tumour in the trachea and Anna's breathing became very hoarse and laboured. She was required to measure her peak flow, the rate at which breath is expelled through the airway and to report if there was a significant change. In the space of a week it had dropped from 352 to 200 and it was easy to hear that there was a problem.

To her delight it was decided she should return to the Brompton Hospital to see Mr Goldstraw. It was Easter and she was lucky that he had just returned from holiday. We drove to the hospital car park.

The attendant came over as I wound down the window. 'Oh, you're obviously going for treatment,' he said, looking at Anna. 'How long will you be?' I told him we would be there all day and he showed me to a space. 'How old is your daughter, only I'm assuming you're going to the children's ward.'

Anna looked aghast. 'I'm thirty!' she said knocking off a year so as not to embarrass him too much.

'Oh, I'm sorry,' he said. 'You can have your parking for free if you're on the children's ward but I'm afraid I'll have to charge you.'

Our laughter reflected our relief at being back in the surroundings she trusted most. Here she felt safe. She was confident that whatever happened the staff would always be there to put her interests first. The familiar corridors and wards allayed her fears and she was relaxed about entering the side-room overlooking the Kings Road that she had last occupied over a year ago.

Football Crazy

April – July 1998

'Good luck, play well, have a good game, keep them out,' were the words Bob always heard as he left to play for Arsenal as their first-team goalkeeper. Three young children would line up at the front door to wave their father goodbye as he left to travel to the match. Football had been our life and we were fortunate that after retiring as a player Bob was able to transfer his experience to the television screen as a presenter, first for the BBC and then later for ITV.

He also became the first specialised goalkeeping coach in the English League working with the Arsenal goalkeepers from 1974, and was able to practise the two professions alongside one another. His recent transfer to ITV as their main football presenter enabled him to give up the early mornings and the multitude of other sports programmes to concentrate on presenting live matches from the UK and from around the world. The day Anna was admitted back into the Brompton, Bob was due to present the live semi-final of the Champions League from the studio on the south bank of the Thames. He was near enough to pop in to see her at the hospital before his rehearsals and he too was buoyed up by her return to familiar ground.

Mr Goldstraw swept into the room on his afternoon rounds, accompanied by Sister. He looked like a young Marlon Brando in 'Julius Caesar.' His hair was flattened from the pressure of wearing his surgical cap, his blues indicating that theatre work was still in progress.

'Oh I like your hair – it suits your face!' he said setting the tone. He had been so used to seeing Anna with her shock of blonde curls that her baldness came as a surprise. 'Now what's been happening to you?'

Anna summarised the past year and told him her concerns at hearing whispers that he was considering inserting a stent, a small metal tube, into her trachea to keep the airway open.

'I don't really want to insert a stent today,' he reassured her. 'I want to see the situation and review it after I have unblocked your airway. We'll soon get you breathing again. Have you any other pain?'

She told him about the sciatic nerve being affected by the bony metastases in her hips.

'Any more areas?' he asked.

'No that's about it,' said Anna cheerfully.

'Except for the tumour on your spine, the one on your back and the various ones on your ribs,' I added.

'Thank you. It's important we know that for when we handle you in theatre. I'll see you soon.' And with that he swept out of the door.

Anna was relieved she was not to have the stent inserted just yet. She was ready for her operation and was even looking forward to going to theatre. By 4.15pm the porters had come for her and Mitchell and I waved a cheery goodbye outside theatre, then set off for the nearest café for a cup of tea.

She came back at 6.30pm and it was lovely to see her smiling face and hear her breathing clearly with no sign of the rasping. I immediately rang Bob at the TV studio so that he could go on air knowing that she was OK.

The next day Mr Goldstraw divulged his findings. He drew a diagram showing that the last radiotherapy had damaged the trachea and had made it swell permanently. Thus her breathing tube was much narrower so that when the tumour broke through it blocked the airway more quickly. He had removed the blockage and his intention next time was to insert a Y-shaped stent at the weakest area, which was at the point where the trachea divided into two bronchi to service both lungs. This would have to be looked at every six weeks so he wanted Anna to get in touch with him as soon as her breathing started to fail.

She returned home with renewed vigour. Her appetite went from nil to ravenous in five days and she managed to devour seven cartons of ice-cream in a week. The effects of the synthetic morphine on her sickness were quite dramatic - she seemed to be more comfortable with her pain and her quality of life was returning.

Her interest in football had never waned, no matter how ill she felt and both she and Mitchell were becoming so excited at the successful season Arsenal were having. The club were in the FA Cup Final and battling for top spot in the Premier league with Manchester United and it was looking as though the coveted 'double' — the winning of both competitions — was a real possibility.

The last time it had been achieved by Arsenal was in 1971 when Bob had been the team's goalkeeper. Collecting his medal at Wembley had been the proudest moment of his professional career and for his family, an achievement that was rare in its accomplishment.

Anna missed going to the matches, mingling with the crowds and cheering on her heroes. She had become an armchair fan, following the fortunes of her favourite club on any television channel she could find. Robert would try to tempt Mitchell into going to the games, but he felt far more comfortable staying with Anna, keeping her company and the house in order. He had recently painted the spare room and returned from a shopping trip to Habitat with duvet, curtains and pillows in an effort to make the second bedroom habitable. Robert and Sarah now had comfortable accommodation when they stayed.

Our next visit for chemotherapy was cancelled before it began. Because of the continued growth of the tumours, the doctors were obviously uncertain it would be of any benefit and Anna's blood tests revealed that her platelet count was very low. It was explained that platelets were the agent which helped the blood to clot. The hip bone, being the largest bone in the body and also the largest supplier of bone marrow, had been attacked by both the treatment and the cancer and therefore its manufacture of platelets had been halted. If she were to have any more chemotherapy it could cause her to haemorrhage.

Three days later Arsenal faced Everton at their home ground of Highbury, in the final game of the season where a win would secure the Premier League title. Bob had taken his place with the rest of the coaching staff at the edge of the pitch, anxious that this should be the first of the brace of games that would bring the double to Highbury once more. He was nervous for the team, and for David Seaman, the Arsenal and England goalkeeper he had now coached for six years.

Anna and Mitchell were glued to the TV at home whilst John, Robert and I shouted ourselves hoarse in the East stand at Highbury where we had followed Arsenal's fortunes for over thirty years. We were rewarded for our efforts by a 4-0 win for Arsenal, breaking the record by winning ten Premier League games in a row. What scenes there were on the Highbury pitch as the players jogged and danced their way round the ground as the fans saluted them in celebrations! David Seaman and the other goalkeepers had dragged Bob on to join in with them and he waved his way round the pitch experiencing the cheers of the crowd as he had once done as a player.

As I pushed and shoved my way from the stadium into the street, having been separated from everyone, I felt emotional. There was joy all round, singing, dancing, chanting, beer flying. The crowds jammed the roads immediately outside Highbury as players threw shirts, shorts and other unwanted kit through the dressing-room windows to the mob outside. I felt totally isolated from it all. Here were people delirious with happiness and, as I pushed my way through the thronged street back to the car, I was torn between profound sadness that Anna could not be here to enjoy the victory, and delight that success had once more come to Arsenal.

Winning the Premier League had given Anna and Mitchell something to focus on and the following week saw their house strewn with red and white bunting in readiness for the cup final. They were happy to watch the match on television, particularly since they would be able to watch Bob on ITV presenting the six hour programme all day from Wembley. What she had not divulged was that her peak flow had suddenly dropped to 180 and breathing had become difficult. She had rung the Brompton who had told her to come in as soon as she felt she needed to. However, the cup final had, in her book, to take precedence.

On 16 May 1998, Arsenal beat Newcastle 2-0 and the team climbed the steps of Wembley to receive their trophy - they were 'double' winners once again. Whilst Anna and Mitchell went off to the pub to celebrate, Bob and I went to Sopwell House Hotel where the club were celebrating the victory. The players were tired but happy and enjoying their success together at a wonderful party. We felt privileged to be there once more, remembering the first Arsenal 'double' celebration twenty-seven years previously.

We made our way home just in time to see *Match of the Day* on BBC, which showed highlights of the cup final. Towards the end of the programme there was an interview with David Seaman, who said, 'It's great, not only for us, but for all the other people, people like my coach Bob Wilson, who has been telling me all week that he's the only Arsenal goalkeeper to have won the double.' Then holding up the medal, 'This is for him, but I'd like to dedicate this match to his daughter Anna.'

Bob was thrilled that David had spoken so publicly about their closeness as coach and player and delighted he should remember Anna at such a time. We assumed Anna was asleep after her visit to the pub so we didn't phone. What we didn't know was that she was watching the programme in bed and heard the interview. She sat there by herself, Mitchell still out with his mates, saying, 'That's me, that's me on *Match of the Day*!' Thinking we were still at the celebrations and wanting to share her moment of glory, she phoned Sarah, the only other person who might have seen it.

'Did you see it!' she asked excitedly.

'What are you talking about?' said Sarah. Anna's moment of glory had gone unnoticed as Sarah had been watching a film on another channel.

Every four years the footballing world looks forward to the FIFA World Cup finals and this year the host nation was France. The tournament was due to start on 10 June and Bob would be leaving us for five weeks whilst he presented ITV's coverage from twenty-two different locations from Paris to Nice, Marseille to Bordeaux. This was to be the pinnacle of his career and we were very proud that he had been rewarded for all his hard work over the years by becoming ITV's voice of football.

We had a farewell meal at home and had decorated the dining room with football jerseys and balloons in team colours, 'England' table linen and flags representing England and Scotland, the two home teams that had qualified.

Anna had brought a card for Bob telling him he was 'the best' and to have a wonderful World Cup. When it was time to depart they hugged each other, both in tears. 'I promise I won't be ill, Dad,' she whispered. It was hard for Bob to leave knowing just how bad she had become and he asked that I not keep anything from him whilst he was away.

Only four days later she was back in hospital, just three weeks after the last operation to clear the airway. Mr Goldstraw felt that because of the brief interval between the tumour's growth and the fact that her platelet level was so badly down he would insert the stent. We agreed not to tell Bob. The rest of that day was spent watching the football on TV. Three games a day was a luxury and a great way to pass the time in hospital.

Her platelet count was down to eighteen and they had to be especially vigilant that she didn't have a haemorrhage, particularly with the surgery being so close to her lungs.

She was wheeled back into the high dependency ward two and a half hours later, looking very frightened behind her oxygen mask. Something was obviously wrong with her but it was difficult for her to talk. Once the nurse had left she said in a whisper, 'Something happened!'

When she had come round in the recovery room, she must have been lying there for five minutes when she found breathing becoming more difficult. She began to worry that the stent was now blocking her airway and finally, when she found that she could no longer take a breath she tried to alert the nurse with her arm. Her limbs were still paralysed and she could move no part of her body. She then tried to mouth to the nurse, 'I can't breathe' and began banging her head on the pillow to alert her.

The nurse realised what was happening and called for the anaesthetist who immediately injected Anna to reverse the effect of the paralysing drug used in the operation, allowing her to breathe. In all Anna said the whole thing lasted about forty seconds, going on four hours. She had been so frightened by the experience that in those few seconds she wondered just how long it was going to take for her to die. Would she be put to sleep before she died? Who would take over for the World Cup in Bob's place?

'I think I've wet myself...,' she whispered, shocked at such a reaction. The nurse, who was aware there had been a problem, helped to restore her dignity.

'...and can I watch the football?' She was soon in front of the television watching her dad present the evening's game from France. Normality had returned. She was discharged to enjoy England's opening match in the luxury of her own home. They beat Tunisia 2-0 but only because Anna was holding one of David Seaman's shirts that her dad had managed to procure for her.

Her appetite diminished and she was having problems with mucus in her lungs which she was finding difficult to expectorate. But she was cheered when Bob was allowed to fly home for a day. They gave each other a big hug. We spent the day talking and dealing with some of the more practical things – cutting his hair, washing his laundry and getting him to sign letters.

Before he left Anna told him about her recovery experience. She wept as she retold the story and her fear was evident. But he was happy to have seen for himself that she was well after the stent insertion.

On 30 June England faced Argentina in the second round, a match ITV were covering. Such was the fevered excitement in England that the country ground to a halt to watch the contest, attracting a record television audience of twenty-six million viewers. It seemed the whole country was holding its breath hoping that England would be victorious and make their way through to the quarter-finals. However, fate intervened. David Beckham was sent off and elimination on penalties followed. Gloom descended on a nation.

The World Cup Final on 12 July saw France become world

champions, beating Brazil 3-0. The final goal was scored by Emmanuel Petit with an assist by Patrick Vieira, the two Arsenal players, who slightly compensated for England's earlier exit.

Bob was relieved to be home again having spent five weeks away travelling to twenty-two cities on as many flights. Anna had been called back for more radiotherapy to her back, which previously hadn't been advised because of the long-term damage to her spine. When Anna queried this, the doctor danced around the explanation, but finally had to admit that with her, 'long-term' was not now an issue. The aim was to give Anna quality of life.

We travelled to the Middlesex next day and took our places in the waiting area. Cancer respects neither wealth, race nor creed. There are those willing to talk to anyone and everyone about the complications of their own case, out loud and to the rest of the waiting area. Some prefer to remain silent, others are frightened, confused, broken. They all wait to be called to the radiotherapy machine for their few seconds or minutes being zapped by the rays. In their groins, breasts, testicles, lungs, faces. Some walk jauntily when called, facing their fate without fear. Some shuffle with difficulty. Some hide their faces conscious of their disfigurement.

We owe much to football – our livelihood, our friendships and much more. It has brought us joy and despair, fulfilment and desolation, camaraderie and solitude. It has brought us material wealth and loyalty of spirit. It has allowed us to compete at the highest level and forced us to accept defeat against the lowliest of opponents. It has taught us to accept failure and enjoy success. Through Bob's talent and hard work, we as a family have experienced a life full of colour and vitality and been advantaged beyond our dreams. But most of all the game has given all of the family a stamp across their foreheads: 'Arsenal and football supporter for life.'

Anna the Invincible

July – October 1998

The tenuous hold that Anna had on life came to test our reserves pretty severely over the next three months. We never appreciated just how poorly she had become, or how serious her condition was until we were driven to the edge to look down into the abyss. A phone call from Mitchell warned us that she was unwell with a temperature

'Don't be silly Mum, it's only a bit of flu.' It surprised me that as a nurse she could not see, or refused to acknowledge, the implications of her illness

She was admitted to the Brompton where the blood tests showed that Anna had a very bad infection of the lung. She was put on intravenous antibiotics and told that once her temperature was down she would undergo another operation to have the stent cleaned and changed, since there appeared to be no air going into her right lung. The bronchus was almost certainly blocked, possibly by phlegm that had become immovable by her weakened ability to cough.

To Anna's distress, Mr Goldstraw was away. However, she was unable to show her disapproval since her temperature had induced sleep to help her body combat the infection.

Bob shot off to the dentist hoping that he could have his treatment and be back for Anna's return. Mitchell and I waited in her room, drinking tea, reading articles aloud, and looking at the clock. At 1.30pm we decided to ask if they knew why she was so long. We had surmised that the first half hour had been spent transfusing platelets into her. The nurse told us that she was still in theatre, that they were having difficulty re-positioning the stent. We were concerned but not unduly. I set off for another cup of tea.

I was met by Mr Goldstraw's two junior doctors, still dressed in their operating blues and who had been assisting Mr Laddas. I smiled and said, 'Hi! Everything ok?' They stopped and said,

'It's been very difficult. We need to talk to you.'

We went to Anna's room where Mitchell was waiting and along the way the senior nurse had been asked to join us. My heart began to beat much faster. Mitchell looked up and I raised my eyebrows indicating the entourage behind me. They closed the door quietly and we waited.

'The operation has been very difficult.'

Mitchell immediately interjected, 'Is she all right? Can we see her?'

'Yes, she's all right and yes you'll be able to see her. When Mr Laddas went in to clear the stent he did not find sputum blocking the airway, but tumour. As he tried to clear the tumour it broke up and caused a problem with bleeding. He realised he was going to have a bigger problem when he removed the stent. He was right. Blood, clots and tumour rushed into Anna's lungs. It took some time to clear. The stent is now in place and she is on a ventilator. She may be on it for forty-eight hours until she can breathe by herself.'

Mitchell repeated, 'Will we be able to see her? Can I hold her?'

He said he would let us know when. They walked out of the room and I immediately burst into tears. Mitchell calmly put his arms round me and held me close. He was under control. I was out of control.

Mr Laddas then arrived, with the team. 'Last night Anna could have died of pneumonia. She could have died today. It was a very difficult operation. I had zero time. There were blood and clots and tumour gushing into her lungs. When I stopped the bleeding I looked at the lung and there was thick pus at the bottom. It was very infected. I managed to put the stent back so now we are giving her platelets. She is on a ventilator and we will bring her back gently. We do not know how much damage has been done until we try to let her breathe on her own.'

Once more Mitchell asked if he would be able to hold her. 'You can see her in about an hour. She will be ventilated, but once we have her breathing again and she is well enough, you will be able to take her home.' We both shook George Laddas by the hand and thanked him for what he had done.

We tried to fill the time by walking – through the park, down unknown roads, into shops, strange and familiar, to the party store, the nursery and arrived at the 'Paint it Yourself Pottery Shop'. Should we go in and see what we could produce? No, the situation was bizarre enough.

We could waste time no longer and returned to Anna's room where soon the familiar footsteps signalled Bob's arrival. He listened and was concerned having guessed that all was not well.

We were led into the recovery room. Strange to think that the last time we were here was two years ago after Anna's thoracotomy operation, the memory of that day still vivid. This time she was at the far end of the room. She lay still, the ventilator tube leading from her mouth into the machine that was breathing for her. Three bags of plasma lay on her bed to be infused after the platelets had finished. Wires led from all parts of her body to the machines behind her that played out the rhythm of her pulse.

The nurse in charge was very cheery and optimistic. She would take Anna off the ventilator only when she could see that Anna could use her lungs unaided. Once she was brought round we would be allowed back in to see her.

We decided to go and eat. Bob and I ordered, but Mitchell wasn't hungry. We all began to express the same concerns. How would she be when they brought her round? How much damage had been done to her lungs? What if we had spoken our last words to her? Nightmare imaginings crowded our normally rational minds.

Our food arrived and Mitchell decided to go for a walk by himself. He would see us on the ward. I played with my food. Bob pushed his round the plate. Mitchell returned, unable to walk anywhere. We made our way to the ward and waited.

'Anna's off the ventilator. You can go down and see her.'

Her oxygen mask covered her face but her eyes were relaxed and smiling. 'How's your tooth Dad? Did you go to the dentist? You were late Mum!'

'You look stoned!' said Mitchell.

'I am stoned,' said Anna mischievously. How could we have thought that Anna would do anything other than sit up in bed waiting to hold court?

The machines blinked and whirred around her. A computer at the bottom of her bed was being watched carefully and plasma was being pumped through her veins at speed. Her breathing sounded very rough and bubbly, as though she had swallowed all the bathwater.

She was brought up to the High Dependency Unit for close observation and was soon ready to greet Rob and Sarah, who had been filled in with all the details in the visitors' room.

'Hi Rob!' Anna croaked. 'Have you heard this joke about David Beckham?' She then told him an extremely rude joke, which completely creased him up

It became Anna's 'I nearly died' experience which she continued to joke about at every opportunity, trying desperately to lighten the situation for all concerned. 'You know, what you've got to remember is that it's far harder for you than it is for me. I'm asleep and know nothing, whilst you are pacing around wondering what's going to happen.' I was not sure whether that was any consolation.

Mr Laddas told her she was walking a very fine line. He had found another tumour on the other side of the trachea and that she should come back for another bronchoscopy in four weeks' time. For once she was in no hurry to leave the confines of the hospital, thankful to have the skill and patience of the nurses to comfort her.

The near death experience made Anna realise just how vulnerable she was, how easy it was to go from 'well' to 'poorly'. She returned home where she became more open with the family, talking to Mitchell, John, Robert and Sarah about how aware she was of her fragile hold on life.

She jokingly made remarks about her funeral, suggesting who should be there and who not, and how much she would want to be part of it. Mitchell suggested we have the funeral before she died so that she didn't miss out.

August had arrived bringing Mr Goldstraw home and a welcome outpatient consultation. 'Well Anna, how long did you manage to go before the stent blocked?'

'Five weeks,' she told him.

'Well congratulations! You've just broken the record for the shortest time it has ever taken for a stent to block. The quickest before you was at seven weeks. OK, so we'll see you at four weekly intervals. As it's now a fortnight since the last op I'll see you in two weeks' time.'

Unchecked by the side effects of chemotherapy, Anna's curly hair had begun to grow quite thickly, but darker than ever before. She hated looking so different so I suggested we try lightening it with highlights. I'd buy a home kit and have a go. It took me an hour to pull all the tufts of hair through the holes in the plastic cap with a crochet hook. I painted on the bleach and waited the recommended time.

As I pulled off the cap Anna looked like a hedgehog, blonde spikes sticking out from her head in sharp two-inch points. We washed, combed and dried her hair and laughed hysterically at the results. We tried toning the highlights down, but they turned orange. So it was back to the scissors! *Short* and shorn, was fine.

A fortnight later and sitting on her bed during his pre-theatre rounds, Mr Goldstraw explained that this time he had a new stent to insert. It was much wider at the lung end and more solid round the trachea. It was made in Germany and he hoped that it would stay inserted for a few months and simply be checked every four weeks by bronchoscopy. Anna asked if it would take any longer to insert.

'I don't know, it's the first time I've ever used one!' They laughed together at the pioneering spirit emerging from her situation.

Plasma, blood and platelets had become her friends, giving her the protection needed to prevent haemorrhaging during operations. The new stent was in place, leaving her with a very sore throat but a good clear passage to her lungs. Mr Goldstraw was confident of its effectiveness in holding back the tumour and she was allowed home to her husband and cat.

Late August and early September brought a period of calm and Anna was able to take pleasure in the warmth of an English late-summer sun, enjoying the house and the garden that brought her so much satisfaction. Her hair was pretty and she began to sport a healthy-looking tan. She was troubled by her inability to clear sputum and phlegm by herself so regular massage and physiotherapy on her back helped her bring any loose matter, which was always thick and bloodstained, up into her mouth.

By mid-September she returned to the Brompton where a bronchoscopy revealed that the stent was still firmly in place. Mr Goldstraw was delighted and didn't want to see her for three whole months. But only two days later she was coughing up fresh blood and plenty of it. She returned to the ward for a couple of days to have more platelets and antibiotics to help clear an underlying infection that had been detected in her blood tests, then returned home to continue her gradual recovery.

John had been contacted by the BBC, who wanted to pay tribute to Bob by making him the subject of a *This Is Your Life* programme. Twice John had told them that it was not possible, Anna was far too ill to take part and the family wouldn't want it at this particularly hard time. However, Anna learned of this and said that it was unfair that her dad should be denied such a tribute just because she was ill. I should get in touch and tell them we would agree to the programme.

We were all naturally worried about Anna's situation but felt that if she insisted we go ahead, it might just give her something to look forward to in her bleak world of drugs, injections and anaesthetics.

We chose a day when Bob was in Germany to contact Sue and Kate, the programme's producers. We decided to meet at home since it was easier to find photos, watch videos and discuss the people in Bob's life. Anna drove herself over in Mitchell's car, her own MGF being too low and too hard on the bumps for her to be comfortable. It was a joy to see her driving once more, something she hadn't been able to do for weeks.

She really enjoyed the planning and became excited at the thought of the shock on Bob's face as he was 'caught' by Michael Aspel, the presenter. Sue and Kate assured her that should the unthinkable happen and she became ill, the programme could be deferred at any point in time, right up to the recording. It had happened before and it was not a problem.

Kate and Sue left and Anna and I spent the next two hours pouring over old albums, laughing at forgotten fashions and remembering holidays and events captured in so many photographs.

The response from old friends and colleagues was astonishing. George Best agreed to make a tribute video to be shown on the programme, as did American singer Johnny Mathis, a good friend of many years. Most of the 1971 double team would be there and Arsene Wenger, the current Arsenal manager, had also said yes. Bob's Loughborough College friends were coming, Mike Turvey from America plus Nigel Seale and John Leavold. Bert Trautmann, Manchester City goalkeeper of the fifties era and Bob's all-time hero, had also agreed to appear. We were all very excited at the thought of Bob's reaction to being surprised and meeting so many colleagues that had been a big part of his life.

John was very worried that the press would pick up on the fact that Anna was so ill, and, knowing her fierce determination to protect her privacy, he couldn't see why she had agreed to the programme going ahead.

'Do you think I want to go on national television looking like this? I want Dad to have this tribute paid to him. He deserves it and I want him to know how much other people respect him.'

It was only then that John realised just how serious Anna was about the programme. The press had tried several times to publicise Anna's state of health, the latest attempt being in May whilst she was at home. A *News of the World* reporter had arrived on their doorstep. He at first pretended he was asking about an abandoned car round the corner from their house. Mitchell overheard and came to the door. The guy then said, 'Are you Anna and Mitchell?' When they answered in the affirmative he admitted who he was and that he'd been sent to see how Anna was.

Mitchell told him she was fine and they were both looking forward to Arsenal doing the double. I was furious and, as I was in Christchurch, called our answerphone at home. There were ten messages from various newspapers asking us to phone them. ITV had also left a message warning us that a freelance journalist was going round the papers with a story about Anna. We also learned that a reporter had staked out our own house all day waiting for us to return. Fortunately Anna's appearance at the door was enough to satisfy him that there was no story. Anna felt that if there was no mention of her illness on *This Is Your Life* there would be nothing to print and if she wasn't sitting there on stage there would be no programme. It would only go ahead if she was well enough.

Ten days later I got a call. 'Mum, I need to go to the Brompton.' If Anna volunteered herself to the hospital it had to be serious. She and Mitchell had not slept properly for the last three nights, Anna fearful for her breathing. She looked dreadful and had difficulty walking and talking. We got her in the car plus wheelchair and sufficient nightclothes for a prolonged stay. We realised she would not be coming home after just a couple of days.

Tests at the hospital revealed her pulse to be 140, her temperature 39.2, her blood levels low and her white count high. The nursing staff showed great concern. 'No I'm fine, this is just normal,' Anna told them. Her struggles with breathing, mobility and eating had become an everyday way of life. X-rays revealed a bad infection around the stent area so she was given antibiotics, platelets and a blood transfusion in order to stabilise her condition.

I phoned the *This is Your Life* team to warn them that Anna was in hospital but asked them to go ahead with all the planning. The programme recording date had been set for 1 November, which was only fifteen days away, but we had been in similar situations before and I was more than confident that Anna would be fine.

Mitchell had arrived and her dark mood had instantly lifted. He had commandeered her wheelchair and was sitting beneath the wall mounted TV monitor. When anyone passed the door he pretended to try and switch it on to see how many passing people offered to help him. Anna laughed at his boldness and stupidity. He turned in the wheelchair and went out of the room, into the corridor and began speeding up and down past her door. His antics, all designed to cheer Anna up, had the desired effect. He stayed late into the night, caught the train home, but began to feel unwell during the journey.

He phoned the next day to say he had a raging sore throat and a high temperature so he was advised to stay at home for fear of passing on further infection to Anna. Mr Goldstraw meanwhile wanted to operate and felt he might have to remove the stent once more so needed Anna to be given more platelets. She would be on his list the next day. Just as she was feeling down Sister Claire arrived at Anna's door with the most beautiful bouquet of cream lilies and purple flowers wrapped in purple paper – her favourite colour. The card read 'Missing you madly.(My temperature is higher than yours) Mx.'

Robert had called to see his sister. He and Sarah were going up to Hull the next day to be the main witnesses at the wedding of their friends Mark and Jen. Robert was very upset by Anna's condition and didn't want to leave but she persuaded him that they must go and she promised that she'd be fine.

She had a bad night and was distressed, missing Mitchell and feeling extremely low. When we arrived next morning her breathing was very bad and she could no longer cough at all. We were worried about her state and how her body would cope with an operation. I went to see Sister Claire to ask her just how bad she thought Anna was.

'Anna is a very poorly girl. Mitchell must come in. It is far more important that he is here to help her. She's on such a heavy dose of antibiotics that it should kill any infection she might catch from him.' The staff knew the difference Mitchell made to Anna, how her face lit up as he walked in her door and how he could make her laugh in the darkest of times.

I read the message loud and clear. They were obviously concerned at Anna's condition. Her temperature was still high and she was showing no signs of recovery. I phoned Mitchell and told him to come in. We didn't tell Anna in case he didn't arrive before she was taken down to theatre. She was getting anxious about the operation, feeling very unwell but was able to sleep. Bob spent most of his time looking out of the window just hoping that Mitchell would make it.

An apparition appeared at the door of her room, complete with face mask. Anna, visibly cheered but exhausted, managed to stay awake for the rest of the afternoon happy in the knowledge that Mitchell was there.

It wasn't until 5.00pm that the porters came to take her down. She had been filled with platelets her count needing to be fifty to operate. We said a swift goodbye as Mitchell accompanied her down to theatre. Within a minute he was back in the room to warn us that she was on her way back. A phone call had been received as they were passing the nursing station to say that her platelet count had dropped to twenty-two on the last test. She couldn't go down until more platelets of her tissue type had been found. It would be another two hours before they arrived from Colindale where they were banked.

She was distraught as they brought her back into the room and protested that she had been there four days, why hadn't anyone got the platelets in earlier? It was explained that platelets couldn't be ordered until they were definitely needed since they had to be used straight away. Since her count had been fifty in the morning they assumed it would have still been at that level in the afternoon. Her spleen must have been taking all the platelets. The operation couldn't proceed until they knew three more bags were at the hospital. I sat by her bed and tried to calm her down.

'Stroke my head Mum,' she said.

It worked. She calmed and fell into a sleep. But I could feel how hot she was. She was distressed and needed a lot of comforting. By seven o'clock she began to shake alarmingly. From being hot and having the fan on she had become cold and shivery. I went out to find a blanket and a nurse, who took her temperature. Since it had risen to 39.4 the nurse phoned down to Mr Goldstraw who was in theatre. Mr Goldstraw came rushing into the room. He knelt down beside her and looked at her fingers, blue even though she was on full oxygen and said, 'Speak to me Anna.'

She whispered haltingly, 'I just want to be able to breathe.'

'Anna, we're between the Devil and the deep blue sea, but you give me no alternative. I'm going to operate. I want you down in theatre now.'

I told him jokingly that he'd have been in trouble if he hadn't operated today and he replied, 'It's easy to say yes, but it's sometimes much more difficult to say no.' He explained that he would do whatever he had to but that she would be ventilated overnight to give her a rest.

With that he and the others were gone and Anna was whisked out of the ward, guarded by Bob, Mitchell and myself. We were not letting her out of our sight until the last possible moment. Along the corridors, down in the lift and then the goodbyes outside the theatre doors. We all kissed her and were equally aware that whatever we said might well be our last words to her.

'Take care darling … God bless … I love you … see you soon.' It was all so inadequate.

We made our way back to her room, now bare without her bed and we each took up a seat. We talked long and hard about the realities of the situation, what we wanted for her, what the possibilities were and what we might expect. She was in pain, and unable to breath. We had just seen her as near to death as she had ever been. The helpless body I had held at the side of the bed was not long for this world. She was suffocating. Hardly a breath was passing her lips. The chances of her pulling through seemed very slim.

We drank tea and waited. We looked out of the window at the horizon beyond Chelsea which was suddenly ablaze with the most amazing electric storm. Flashes of lightning chased each other across the sky turning the darkness into daylight. We laughed and decided Anna must be putting up a bloody good fight.

At 8.45pm, only an hour and three quarters since she'd been taken down, Adrian, Goldstraw's junior doctor, arrived with a nurse. His demeanour said everything.

'I'm sorry but the operation was even worse than the last bad one. When he got in Mr Goldstraw found there was a blood clot sitting in the centre of her trachea. The tumour had grown round the top and bottom of the stent thus blocking her airway. He had no alternative but to take the stent out. There was huge bleeding. We thought we had lost her twice. As soon as we pumped one lung the other filled and as soon as we pumped that the other filled again. The only thing we could do was to ram in another stent in the hopes of stopping the haemorrhaging. She's ventilated but there is damage to the lungs. I'm afraid it's very serious.'

Mitchell asked, 'Can we see her? Can I hold her? Will I be able to take her home?'

'Yes, you'll be able to see her eventually. Just now she's still bleeding.'

'How serious is it?' asked Bob.

'Very serious. I'm afraid there's very little chance of her surviving the night. I'm sorry, but I have to ask you this next question. In the event of a cardiac arrest, how vigorously do you want us to attempt resuscitation?

It was so unreal yet we had been prepared. But we knew what Anna would want us to say. Her quality of life was so poor and she was having to battle harder and harder with very little reserves. She had always said that if she were to go she would prefer it to be after an anaesthetic, in the theatre at the Brompton.

We agreed there should be no resuscitation. We were numb and sat there speechless. We phoned the family to let them know the situation. Robert and Sarah were with Mark and Jen, the night before the wedding. I apologised to Jenny, but I said I thought they should return. She was very understanding since she had lost her own brother recently. Robert was calm and he promised me not to speed on the motorways.

Mitchell phoned his mum and dad who insisted they come straight to the hospital. We were pleased to be having such support and decided to wait in the hospital's reception area. John arrived, having picked up a message on his pager and was utterly devastated when we told him the news. Mitchell's brother Nathan arrived followed by Paulene and Colin, Mitchell's parents. We hugged and cried and talked of Anna, of how wonderful she had been all this time and what an inspiration to us all.

At 10.00pm, Adrian came down, still in his theatre blues, to say that miraculously the haemorrhaging had stopped, she was being taken into intensive care and that we should be able to go and see her. Someone would come for us. As we sat in reception our mood changed from deep depression to more of a party atmosphere. Those in the hospital that were working nights were all rooting for Anna and the receptionists said it was a good sign if she was still OK.

As it passed midnight the lack of any communication began to worry us and by 1.30am we feared something had gone wrong. Robert and Sarah had arrived at 1.15am much to our relief, and we were all anxious to have news. Finally we were told she was in intensive care and that we could visit her.

It was hard to believe that her body had been taken through such stress levels. She looked calm, a little puffed around the face, with her arms stretched above her head, the ventilator reaching down into her lungs keeping her breathing. Relief at finding her still warm was overwhelming. There was no struggle for breath, her chest rising and falling in even time with the machine. In turn the rest of the family visited and stayed by her side for some time before returning to the hospital foyer.

Duvets, pillow and blankets were brought so that Robert, John, Sarah and Mitchell could bed down on the benches whilst Paulene, Colin and Nathan said their goodbyes.

The nurses had moved two beds into Anna's room side by side. Bob and I knew we had to rest in case sleep paid us a visit. But reality's harsh despair only brought thoughts that so far had been banned from our minds. Anna the invincible was now hanging on by the finest of threads and we were being forced to consider her death.

'How can we live without Anna?' I heard myself cry through tears. We had been prepared to stay on this roller-coaster ride for as long as it took, but it had taken such a toll on us all. My mind continued to deal with reality and I realised that if Anna died tonight, her funeral could only be ten days away. I pictured myself in the pulpit talking about her, dressed in the pink suit that I wore at her wedding. Panic began to seize me. 'I'll never get into it, I'm at least half a stone heavier and it will be too cold!'

'It's hopeless isn't it?' said Bob and we got up and began to tidy her room, packing away her belongings so that it could be prepared for someone else. It was 5.15am and we decided to visit her again. She looked calmer and even more beautiful. Her arms lay across her body and she looked rested and at ease. There had been no change all night and she was stable.

We made our way down to the foyer and sat and watched the youngsters. Unknown to us they had been with Anna most of the night and had only just gone to sleep. Shift workers came and went and the nursing staff began to arrive each asking for news of Anna.

By 7.30am we were all up and ready for some breakfast. Bob was desperate for the toilet so we said we would wait, but Mitchell decided we should all hide so that when Bob returned he would be annoyed at our disappearance. Like little children we huddled behind a huge brick pillar, giggling at the thought of Bob arriving at the scene to discover that we'd left him behind.

'You know, it's not like this in the films. When the daughter of the family is on a ventilator you never get the relatives playing hide and seek!' said John. It was bizarre, but then Anna would have loved it. Bob reacted as predicted and we all had a good laugh at his expense.

Sitting round the breakfast table in the refectory we were quiet, each with our own thoughts, when Anna's physiotherapist came hurrying across the room with a smile on her face.

'You're not going to believe it but Anna's opened her eyes. She's still ventilated but she's waving to everyone!'

We were speechless. How were we meant to feel? All night our hearts and minds had been steeled for the bad news. Now it seemed that Anna was defying predictions once more.

She smiled at us as we entered and she pointed to the clock on the wall, querying the time. We explained that they wanted her to have a good night's sleep so kept her ventilated. She made it quite clear how uncomfortable the tube was in her mouth and the doctor promised that they would remove it during the morning when they were happy that she could comfortably breathe on her own.

We reported back to the troops and it was hard to know where our emotions were. The roller-coaster ride had reached the bottom and it was beginning to climb back up again. How steep would it be this time? How much effort would it take for Anna to recover and what quality of life would she have?

However, the physio soon came to find us. Anna was asking where we were.

Back in Intensive Care the curtains round Anna's bed were drawn; from behind them came loud music puncturing the pressurised atmosphere. We entered the curtained area to find Anna sitting up in bed watching MTV on a portable television, magazines by her side.

'Why didn't you come and sit with me? I was bored. Amanda brought all this in for me.' Bob and I smiled across at the physio and our eyes met in bewilderment. Anna inspected the central line that fed into her main artery and the intravenous lines into her feet. 'It's a bit over the top isn't it?'

We explained that Mitchell had gone home to change. 'By train?' she asked. 'No, John, Robert and Sarah have taken him home.' Details began to sink in and her eyes began to well up as realisation dawned that the whole family had been there overnight.

By 2.00pm she was wheeled up to the High Dependency Unit on Elizabeth Ward, where she protested. 'Can't I go back to my own room?'

Sister Claire relented and agreed. Fortunately I had unpacked all her belongings and arranged them exactly as they were before she had left for her op. I went downstairs to buy Coke and water but by the time I had returned she had deteriorated very quickly. Her temperature had risen and she was not comfortable. Amanda called me to look at her X-rays. The one taken in the morning showed the right lung with some air in it but the one taken at midday showed that it had collapsed. She explained that Anna was going to have to work very hard to clear the other lung of the blood that was still in there.

She slept for much of the day but in between kept requesting snippets of information. Was there anyone else there last night? Who stayed the whole night? Who came to see her on the ventilator? By this method she pieced together the whole story, information about the operation, how we'd been given the news and what sort of party we'd had through the night. She was quiet but pleased that there'd been a few laughs along the way.

Mitchell, Robert and Sarah arrived to take over the afternoon shift and stayed with her through the night. It gave them an opportunity to voice their concerns. Mitchell told Anna how she should stop fighting for him. All he wanted was for her to be comfortable and out of pain. Anna told them that she never wanted to go there again – so near the edge. She was always worried about Mitchell and what would happen to him. Robert answered her that it wasn't just Mitchell that would need the family support, the family would need Mitchell.

Mr Goldstraw strode into her room. 'By the looks of you, you've recovered from this operation far more quickly than I have.' He went through the procedure with her once more and was wonderfully optimistic, telling her he would always be willing to find a means of keeping her airway open.

For the next few days she was happy to recover in hospital in no hurry to get home. She felt safe and she needed to rest but most of all she craved company. She had been frightened by the enormity of the trauma and she wasn't comfortable unless someone was with her all of the time. So from that moment on it was decided that each night we would take in it in turns to sleep in her room. She spent her time looking at the larger picture, trying to make sense of it all, coming to terms with the never ending ride.

'What good could possibly come out of all of this Anna?' I asked, posing Nan Wilson's theory that 'everything will all turn out for the best.'

'You'll do something Mum, something related to all of this, I know you will'

'But what on earth am I going to do without you?'

I caught myself by surprise in my acceptance of her frailty.

'Mum, I'll always be with you just remember that. I'll always be there … and by the way, we are still going ahead with *This Is Your Life* aren't we?'

Time for smiles and optimism after first signs of recovery; photographed by the *Daily Mail*

Another special treat from Dennis and Jan Roach on a visit to Christchurch

Anna, caught perfectly

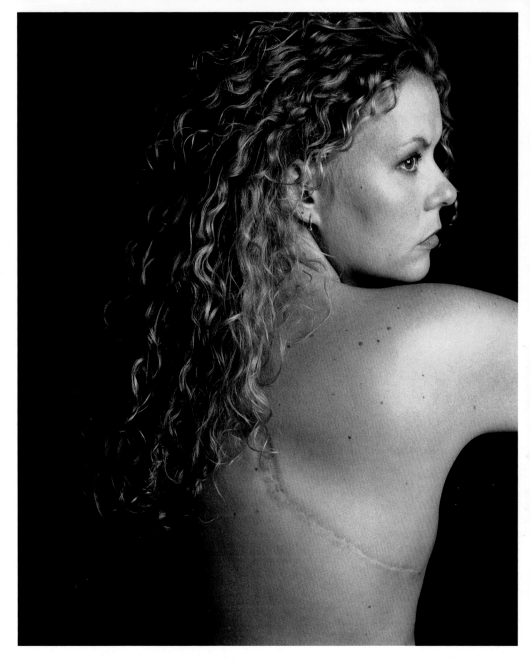

Second major operation. 'Adventurous surgery' 1996

Both photographs by her brother Robert

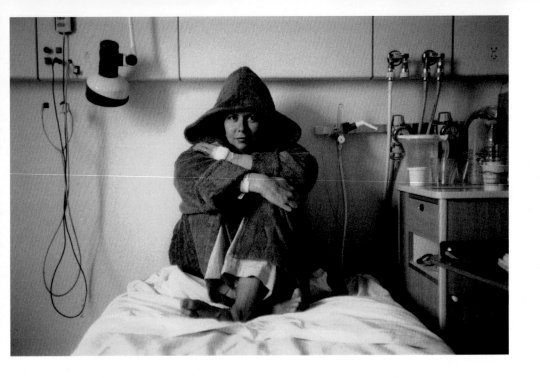

Elizabeth Ward,
Brompton Hospital, the place where Anna felt safe

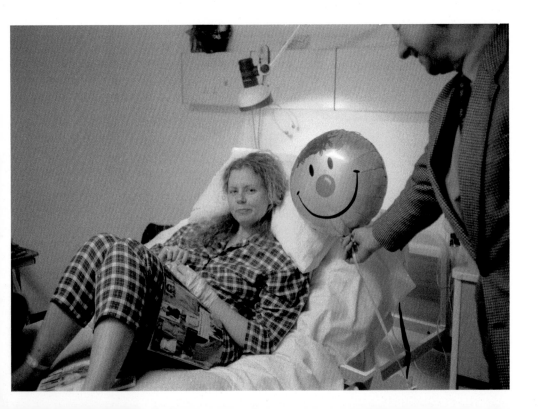

Two boiled eggs, after Anna cuts off
Mitchell's hair to match her own

Holding back the tears on *This Is Your Life* programme, 2 November 1998

Surrounded by family at the *This Is Your Life* after party. Her Auntie Liz and cousin Helena.
Last photograph taken of Anna

Daddy My Daddy

30 October – 10 November 1998

'What do you think to this colour Dad?'

Bob was unsure about the blue nail varnish that adorned Anna's toes but since his taste was not exactly high fashion he decided to accept an education in modern beautification.

'Are you sure you haven't got frost bite?' he teased.

Manicures and pedicures had become a very special part of Anna's routine and made her look a little more feminine than she felt. It was therapeutic, helped time pass quickly and gave those around her an excuse to pamper her in an acceptable way. Today it was my turn to apply the polish, though more often than not Sarah took charge of manicures.

'All I need now is a party!' She flashed me an impish look and I returned a smile of affirmation. Today we were celebrating Bob's birthday but in three days time we would be in the television studios for *This Is Your Life*. We were delighted that everything seemed to be going well. Arrangements were all in place and secret coded phone calls had been passed back and forth from Threepwood to the BBC, back out to friends and onward to family.

A coach would bring all Bob's nearest relatives down from Lincolnshire to Teddington Studios whilst another would pick up our closest friends from Brookmans Park. The Derbyshire contingent had a minibus whilst others coming from Spain, America, Sheffield and other far-flung corners would make their own way by car and taxi.

Anna had been out of hospital a week, during which time the Macmillan nurses had begun to make visits to help Mitchell and me to cope with the emergencies that might arise whilst she was at home. The tumour on her spine was trapping the sciatic nerve and she had been in excruciating pain, requiring pethidine injections to ease her plight. We were worried that too much pressure was being put on Anna to be well.

'Just don't worry about it. It doesn't matter *how* bad I am, I will *be* there.'

It was whilst I was painting the blue nails that my mobile rang. It was our friend Jill Dando who had been one of the main presenters on *Breakfast Time* whilst Bob had worked on the programme. We knew that once Bob had been 'caught' by presenter Michael Aspel and the red book, he would decline the tribute on the grounds that his daughter was not well enough for the programme to go ahead. It was necessary for someone to be there to assure him that it was going ahead with Anna's blessing and with her involvement.

'Oh hi Sarah!' I said hoping to deceive Bob as to the caller. 'You'll have to hold on a moment, I can't hear you. I'll take the phone out to the garden where I've got better reception.' My days as an actress had paid dividends over the past few weeks and Bob had absolutely no idea of all the subterfuge that had taken place in order to surprise him.

Jill was checking on Anna and the final details of what she should be saying to calm Bob and persuade him that all was well enough to go ahead. She too was excited since the plan was to catch him at the training ground as he coached the goalkeepers. Jill was to join the rest of the Arsenal team for some pre-filming at Sopwell House Hotel and then travel with them and join in their warm-up lap as they ran past Bob's goalkeepers, who were already training.

'Thank you for doing this Jill, it's the only way we can think to guarantee his participation.'

'I can't wait to see his face,' she said in return. 'See you Monday.'

Robert and Sarah had surprised Anna and bought her an Amanda Wakeley dress to wear. She'd never owned anything that had a designer label inside and she couldn't remember the last time she had worn a dress. More recently she had opted for the comfort and safety of black trousers and T-shirts. I'd found a strappy pair of sandals that would complement the ensemble perfectly so she needed her toes to be looking their best.

Anna and Mitchell had decided that the weekend was going to be ultra-quiet. No visitors, no getting up early − just rest until Monday morning when the car would arrive to collect them.

'Have a nice day!'

In all our thirty-four years of marriage I had never said such a thing as Bob went off to work. He confessed afterwards that he had found it odd and wondered for a few seconds what I had meant by it. As soon as the door was closed I raced to his wardrobe to get ready for the day ahead. Would he want to wear the blue jacket with the red tie or the brown jacket with the spotted tie, or even the checked jacket and the dark shirt? Variety was the best policy so the clothes were stacked into hanging bags ready for packing into the car with shoes, socks, pants and belts. If I only took a choice of one it was bound to be wrong so I played safe.

It was 2 November, the planned day to record *This is Your Life* and right on time a lean stretch limo glided into the drive and whisked me off to Knebworth where yet another load was waiting to be packed – wheelchair, nebuliser, portable suction unit, pillows, kitchen paper, water, and clothes for later.

'You know I feel really good today,' said Anna as we sped round the M25. I had been amazed at how well she looked when I arrived and was delighted that so far everything seemed to be just perfect.

The plan was to catch Bob just as he was starting his training session with the goalkeepers. He'd spotted a cameraman lying in a ditch pointing a lens in his direction but was assured by David Seaman that it was the BBC filming a documentary on him. It wasn't until the whole of the Arsenal squad came jogging in an unusual direction that he became suspicious but was equally baffled to see Jill Dando, dressed in training gear, come running towards him.

The ruse worked and Bob was totally shocked as he was presented with the famous red book, the Arsenal squad cheering the occasion. But, as predicted, he expressed his deep concerns about continuing and, as hoped, he was soon persuaded otherwise by Jill.

'He'll have been caught by now Mum. Phone him!' Anna was beside herself with excitement, wanting to know how he had taken it.

'I can't phone him, I'm not allowed to speak to him.'

Anna grabbed my phone and dialled Bob's number. On his mobile the words 'Megs Mob' appeared and he presumed it was me.

'You ★★★★★!' He said teasingly. He was surprised at the answer.

'Hi Dad! It's me and I'm ready to party!'

– and she did just that. She and Mitchell were first to be invited to take up their places on the stage followed closely by the rest of the family and friends taking part. She felt as though she was at her wedding again, everyone in turn giving them a hug as they made their way to designated places.

We were nervous of Bob's reaction on being led out on to the stage to be faced with all the people that he held dear. But today was about celebration and we had been assured that not one word of Anna's illness would be mentioned during the programme.

The familiar musical fanfare that opened the show caught our breath and we saw, for the first time, the film showing how Bob had been taken by surprise. The doors at the back of the stage opened and Bob and Michael Aspel walked tentatively into the spotlights to the cheers of the audience.

He'd had time, between being caught, driven to the studios and waiting in a dressing room to imagine who would be there from his past to tell their stories. He'd prepared himself for seeing his friends, his family and those with whom he'd shared so much.

But nothing could quite prepare him for seeing Anna, flanked by Robert, Mitchell and John, proudly applauding his entrance. Anna was not dressed in the Amanda Wakeley and the strappy sandals, but in black trousers and a black shirt. The dress had kept riding up over her knees and if she'd had to stand in the shoes she would only manage it at an angle of forty-five degrees, so they'd been abandoned in favour of comfort!

For an hour Bob was greeted, hugged, surprised and moved. A parade of embarrassing photos, forgotten stories, and gilded memories peppered the stage as he was reunited with team-mates, college friends, colleagues and heroes. And at the end of the programme, Bob was led to the front where he faced an audience packed full of friends, all waving white handkerchiefs that had become such a tradition after his 'father of the bride' speech at Anna's wedding.

For the next few hours we experienced shared joy that we wouldn't have thought possible. It was a party where Anna was one of the guests, where she could join in the gossip, catch up with cousins and chat to her grandpa. She was wheeled from group to group laughing at stories, conversing with friends and just being her normal self.

She spent some time with Jill Dando and with Helen Rollason; both had worked in TV with Bob and become such good friends of ours. Little did we realise that eight months from this day, all three women, each in their thirties, would be dead.

Jill would meet her death on her own doorstep the following April at the hands of a gunman, a shocking end that would appal the nation and start a manhunt of massive proportions.

Helen, the first woman sports presenter for the BBC, who had been fighting her own battle with cancer would die the following August. She and Anna always had so much in common comparing treatments, hair loss, symptoms and food. Helen had done much to educate the public articulating her own positive attitude to cancer through a television programme that followed her day-to-day life with her daughter.

But at the party, the future still hid its tragic revelations and no one would have guessed the final outcome for each of the beautiful women who laughed and chatted that night with so much vitality and life.

We were worried what we would find the next day as we made our way to Knebworth expecting Anna to be exhausted and frail. But instead she was flying!

'Tell me about the catch. Did you ever suspect? What did you think when you saw … '

We had never heard her talk so much for months. Adrenalin was pumping through her veins ignoring the lack of platelets and red blood cells, charging her batteries to the full and creating a surge of energy unseen for weeks.

It lasted for ten days during which time Anna's quality of life was quite remarkable. She was still having problems with clots of blood forming around her windpipe and we perfected the technique of tipping her over the edge of a chair then patting, rubbing and applying physio to her back forcing the offending matter up and out of her body. But generally her mood was good and she was almost free from pain.

The programme was due to be transmitted just one week after being recorded and we watched it with Anna and Mitchell, Dennis and Jan and their sons Nick and Matthew who had driven all the way from Christchurch to be with us at our home. It was difficult to believe it ever happened, but there it was on the television screen. We laughed, we cried and we were delighted at the result. As the credits rolled we took ourselves off to a nearby restaurant where stories and confessions had us all rocking with laughter. Since Anna had become seriously ill she enjoyed shocking us with revelations of shameful acts and deeds of daring.

She asked if we could all remember a time when she and Mitchell had arrived at Christchurch with a plate of fairy cakes. She'd offered them round and we had all eaten one, impressed at the fact that Anna had suddenly become very domesticated. Dennis and Jan had been with us and we had all eaten at least one, enjoying them as an accompaniment to a cup of tea.

She confessed across the table that evening that they were hash cakes containing a small amount of cannabis from her painkilling supply and delighted in telling us the hilarious effects it appeared to have had on us all. Nick and Matthew were flabbergasted as were Dennis and Jan but it caused so much hilarity between us that the rest of the customers must have wished they were at our table. Tears of laughter rolled down our faces as Dennis threw his arms in the air and declared with great astonishment and delight, 'I've done drugs!'

Always Came Too Soon

The euphoria of *This Is Your Life* lifted Anna's spirits and allowed her to be mostly symptom-free for ten days afterwards. The adrenalin that accompanied the planning and the excitement of the occasion helped her cope more easily and the pain seemed to be much more bearable than before.

She had enjoyed celebrating Mitchell's thirty-second birthday and had bought him a large stone with a hole in the middle, six bags of pebbles and a pump – much to Mitchell's amusement. His DIY skills were not always known as the best. The two of them had often sat by and admired the water feature in the foyer of the Brompton Hospital. It was calming and peaceful, the water tumbling over the large round stone on to the smaller pebbles that formed a stream. It would be replicated, on a smaller scale, in the garden of Gun Lane, but professional gardeners might have to be called in to install it otherwise it might sit as a pile of dry stones for ever.

On 16 November Anna was admitted to the Brompton so that Mr Goldstraw could check the stent and clear away any debris under anaesthetic. She had become very poorly the previous two days, running a temperature from an infection and in excruciating pain from her hips. Her antibiotics were doubled and she was given four bags of platelets in preparation.

The period of time she'd experienced without symptoms was a welcome respite but her return to hospital brought her frustrations flying to the fore. She began to cry so I tried to console her. But the crying set in and wouldn't stop. Stroking her had no effect, talking likewise. She just wanted to cry. Then she began to talk.

'I want Mitchell. I just want him here to be near me'

Mitchell was her soulmate and healthy counterpart. But he needed space. The reason I was the one who did the hospital runs was to give him a break. He looked after her every need, day and night and he deserved time by himself. She had periods of calm, but they were soon followed by inevitable tears. The relentlesness of the interminable treatments were beginning to drag her down to a place she rarely visited.

A phone call and a couple of hours later Mitchell arrived and Anna's delight at seeing him was all-consuming particularly since he was going to stay the night, sleeping in the reclining chair next to the bed. It would put her in a better frame of mind for her visit to theatre.

We had nearly lost count of the times she had gone through the routine of preparations that preceded operations. It had become a way of life and the staff on the ward and in theatre had become Anna's friends. They were the people whom she trusted and turned to in times of real need who would always have a solution to the gravest situation. They were the ones who could turn Anna's fear into optimism and were always willing to 'give it a go'.

This time was no different. Anna had gone down to theatre wheezing and rattling through her throat and she came back with a smile on her face and the ability to breathe easily. Mr Goldstraw was pleased with his work and had managed to clean out quite a lot of clots that were clinging to the sides of the stent. Away from Anna's room Bob asked about the tumour and what we could expect in the near future. Mr Goldstraw told him that he had been able to see the tumour at the bottom of the stent and had simply pushed it away so as to keep her airway as clear as possible.

The next stage would be guided by Anna. If she wanted him to have a go at changing the stent then he would try. He would burn off as much of the tumour as he could see and replace the stent but he stressed that with her problems such an operation would be very dangerous. If she didn't want him to do that then he would do his best to get her through Christmas and into the New Year.

With each sentence we were being given the warnings that Anna's fight for life was nearing its end, but it was difficult for me to accept that one day Anna might not come back smiling and joking as she had done so many times before. She was my daughter and she was invincible. But Anna had no fear of facing the operations as she felt that if she were to die under anaesthetic, at least she would know very little about it.

By the following week Anna had spent an uncomfortable few days at home and she was aware of a swelling over her chest area which gradually spread to her neck and finally her face. Adrian, Mr Goldstraw's junior doctor suggested Anna return to the Brompton.

'How much more do I have to take, Mum? I must have done something terrible in my life. What else can happen to me?'

The questions bubbled out of Anna's mouth between sobs. She lay on her tummy in the familiar surroundings of Room 3 on Elizabeth Ward trying to ease the pain in her hips. She was exhausted, holding my hand tightly, rubbing my thumb with hers.

'This is going to destroy you Mum.'

'No darling, I won't let it. All I want is for you to be out of pain; out of all of this. I want whatever you want.'

Adrian took one look at her face, at the raised veins on her nose, temples and neck and recognised the problem.

'I need you to have an X-ray but what I am sure has happened is that the tumour is now pressing on the superior vena cava, the main vein going into the heart. It runs alongside the trachea and is being squashed by the tumour.

'I don't know how much more I can take Adrian.'

'I'm sorry Anna. It must be awful for you. There's nothing we can do surgically but I want you to start taking steroids to help relieve the pressure. I've rung the Middlesex who want you to go to radiotherapy before nine o'clock on Friday morning so they can give you more treatment to your chest.'

Anna then began the questioning. 'Will it give me a heart attack? Will it cause an aneurysm? How long will it take to finish me off if I go on diamorphine? If I need hospitalisation can I come to the Brompton instead of a hospice?'

Her mind was in overdrive considering all the options that might lead to her death. How Anna would die was not a subject that had ever been raised, but it was certainly in the forefront of her mind now.

The steroids took very little time to do their work and by the following day she sat at home with a big smile on her face, the swelling reduced considerably from the day before. Her appetite had returned and she was able to take simple pleasure in her once favourite pastime of eating.

Bob was in Barcelona and, as usual, it was difficult to convey all the details without worrying him unduly before he went on air. He hadn't wanted to make the trip in the first place, aware of how critical Anna's situation was. The stresses were telling on all of us but Bob had to put on a public face and appear to the world as though there was nothing wrong. His body told a different tale as it was covered in a rash from top to bottom.

On his arrival back he made a decision to stop work for the foreseeable future and told ITV that he would be taking time off. He was frustrated at not being available all the time, at being unable to be of help when urgent situations presented themselves, and suffering the pain in hearing upsetting news from such a distance. He decided that he could act as Anna's chauffeur and spend as much time with her as possible.

The very next day he was able to transport us up to the Middlesex where Anna underwent more X-rays and consultations regarding her radiotherapy. We returned home to find that Mitchell had cleaned the house from top to bottom and had been out to get in all the shopping.

Not only did the weekend bring a period of calm when Anna felt so much better in herself, able to eat and to enjoy her time at home, it gave the two of them time to sort out their heads, trying to put their crumbling world into some sort of perspective. Robert and Sarah had joined them and were able to help in voicing the realities that were now emerging.

'You know,' said Anna, 'this thing isn't going to let me go quietly. It's going to drag me kicking and screaming.'

She told them she was very happy with where she was and that she now found it hard to comprehend the feeling of finality that had enveloped her during the last week. She was feeling so much better that she phoned me and suggested we should do her Christmas shopping the following day.

It was 30 November and, as we turned into the car park Anna's delight was obvious at the sight of all the shops looking their festive best. She was excited that once more we were able to enjoy our annual magical day. We entered Habitat and the sound of Christmas music brought a smile to her face, prompting memories of Selfridges, stretch limos and Lakeside shopping centre. As Anna wheeled herself round the shop I followed dutifully with a trolley, which gradually filled to the brim as Anna chose a present for everyone on her list. She stopped at the top of a long steep ramp; at the bottom was an area of glass picture frames, piled high and stacked together. She flashed me a mischievous grin and I could imagine what was going through her mind.

'I think I might have to take control down here,' I said, picturing Anna sprawled amongst broken glass, and I grabbed hold of the wheelchair handles to guide her down at an acceptable speed.

We went back to the car to load the presents when she suggested we pop in to Tesco to pick up one or two things that she needed. Anna hadn't been shopping for six months and the idea of her wanting to go round a supermarket seemed unbelievable. By the time we came through the checkout she had filled four carrier bags.

Mitchell was totally shocked when he helped us empty the car and couldn't believe that Anna had been able do all her Christmas shopping in one go, let alone push herself round Tesco.

There was no doubt about it, the steroids were giving her a break from intense pain and discomfort and we were all immensely grateful. She was so excited that at last she could believe Christmas was on its way and, in turn, her thirty-second birthday. I had booked tickets for the family to see one of her favourite musicals, *West Side Story,* at one of the London theatres in the hopes that she might be well enough to enjoy it.

The following day Bob and I called to take her up to London for her radiotherapy sessions and the bubble had somewhat burst. The sciatic nerve pain had returned and the situation had been compounded by her coughing up fresh blood. I rang the Middlesex hospital and they advised me to bring her in since they felt that radiotherapy would help to stop the tumour from bleeding.

So reluctantly Anna said goodbye to Mitchell and, armed with the usual supplies of water and kitchen paper, we set off in Bob's car to London. The whole day became a nightmare as Anna went from radiotherapy planning down to radiotherapy treatment. We looked on the board and noticed that the machine which was scheduled to be used had broken down and there would be a two hour delay.

'I don't know how much longer I can sit here Mum,' she said despairingly after an hour had passed. She was sweating profusely and her cough was still producing fresh blood.

We didn't reach home until 3.00pm and all Anna wanted to do was be lowered into a hot bath, where her body could be suspended in water giving her relief from weight-bearing pain. We laid her on top of the duvet and put a towel over her to help her cool down.

'I'm all right now Mum; I'll be able to go to sleep.'

We left for home at 4.00pm and Mitchell took himself upstairs and lay on the bed with Anna. But by 4.45pm she was having difficulty with her breathing.

'It doesn't sound good. Don't you think you should ring your mum and dad and think about getting to the Brompton?'

'No, I'll be all right. Just give me some time.'

'I'm not happy Anna, I'm going to phone your mum.'

She had been in the process of filling herself with chocolate bourbon biscuits, a particular favourite at that time, and took the phone from Mitchell's grasp, spitting out half the contents of her mouth as she said, 'Oh all right, I'll do it!'

I was making a stack of shepherd's pies, knowing that Anna was now on a steroid-induced eating binge.

'Mum, I think I might have to go to the Brompton. My breathing's changing. Will you phone Adrian and ask him what we should do? I need to be quick though.' she sounded concerned.

'Why doesn't Mitchell bring you over?'

'No we don't all need to go. Come over here while I pack a bag and Dad can take us in.'

I flew round, throwing my pies into the fridge, packed some clothes for an overnight stay and arrived at Knebworth with Bob at the wheel. Mitchell opened the door and there was Anna sitting on the bottom stair, looking fairly frail.

'We're not going to the Brompton. Anna thinks we should get to the Lister, have them stabilise her by putting a line in and blue-light her into London,' said Mitchell.

So Bob took Anna and the wheelchair and drove the ten minutes to the Lister Hospital's accident and emergency entrance, taking directions from Anna's gestures. Mitchell and I followed behind planning our method of attack in preparation for our arrival. I would be in charge of Anna's Filofax whilst he would go to register her name at Casualty. So organised was Anna that she had put all the history of her illness on to one page for just such an emergency so that if she couldn't describe her medical problems, one of us would be able to.

Bob got out of the car and began to struggle with the wheelchair.

'Dad, over there!' Anna shouted. He looked round and saw that Anna was pointing to a stack of wheelchairs. He rushed over and at that moment bumped into two paramedics who were coming out.

'In need of help mate?' they asked.

They soon had her out of the car and on oxygen and by the time Mitchell and I arrived on the scene they were wheeling her across the road towards Casualty.

I only had to look at her face to know that she was in a serious condition. She had gone white and breathing was extremely difficult.

She was wheeled straight into the resuscitation room where she eased herself on to the bed, declining help in order to protect her painful bones. Her breathing consisted of loud bubbling sounds. Bob and Mitchell went to either side of her whilst the doctor arrived to ask questions.

'How long has she been breathing like this?'

'About forty-five minutes.'

I then went quickly through her condition. 'She has a tumour perforating her trachea. It's haemorrhaging. She has a stent in the trachea and she has a platelet problem. Her count is only about twenty-two. She normally has platelet transfusions. We were on the way to the Brompton where she is being treated.'

I gave them the page from her Filofax which summarised her whole medical history. The staff were quite calm and it struck me that it was never like this on hospital television dramas where stretchers come rushing through doors and orders are barked out to the duty staff.

She was attached to the monitor behind the bed so that the rhythm of her pulse could be heard and vital signs seen. Her breathing was getting worse and we were all aware that this time the battle had reached a critical point.

'Please do something!' pleaded Mitchell to the bemused staff.

It was fairly obvious that Anna's case was presenting them with a few difficulties. Other doctors were brought in and again we had to explain the problems in detail, but her condition was alien to them and they couldn't quite grasp the reason she was struggling for breath. I asked for a phone to get in touch with Adrian at the Brompton.

'Adrian, it's Megs. We're not going to make the Brompton. We're at the Lister in Casualty and Anna is very ill. Please can you speak to them because they don't know what the ✱✱✱✱ they're doing!'

It was the quickest way I knew of communicating the very dire situation that we found ourselves in. We had always been comfortable with crises before because Anna was always surrounded by those who knew exactly what action to take. Here we were with strangers who had to assess a situation that had only just presented itself to them. And all the time, Anna's breathing had worsened.

The anaesthetist, who had been on the phone to Adrian, asked if he could speak to me. He explained that they didn't have any room in intensive care at the Brompton until tomorrow, so the Lister would probably ventilate Anna and find an ICU bed at another hospital. In the meantime, if the situation changed then he would let us know.

'We're going to have to take Anna to the operating theatre and give her an anaesthetic. We will then try to get an airway into her lungs to help her breathing and we may have to put her on a respirator. What you must realise is that this procedure in itself is very dangerous with

Anna in this condition.'

'Please, just get her out of this distress. I don't want her to be in this distress! I understand what you're saying but you have also got to realise that Anna wants no more of this,' I pleaded.

They prepared to inject Anna with a mild sedative whilst Mitchell talked to her constantly.

'Come on, Willow, you can do it. We've been here before and we know you can do it. Just breathe in and out slowly. They're going to give you some sedation and you'll be OK soon. Just hang on. Not long now and you'll be asleep.'

She was conscious and hearing every word Mitchell was saying. The room was filling with people and the medical staff were starting to show concern.

'As long as you want to be here that's all right with us,' said a lady doctor, reassuringly.

Bob moved round to be next to Mitchell who had been given a chair and I stood on her right. We were all holding her hands. She began to fight for breath and threw her arm across her chest thumping herself twice as she often did to relieve a clot that had stuck there. As she did so the rhythmic sound of her pulse stopped and was replaced by a single high-pitched tone. The nurse standing by the machine flashed a look at the doctor and tactfully switched it off. Anna's right hand had dropped by her side and I looked at it lying open; the very hand that I had been holding only a few seconds ago and through which I had been willing her continued hold on life.

'Has she gone Bob, has she gone?' Mitchell's despairing cry rent the air, raging at the injustice of it all.

'Yes she's gone Mitchell.'

For forty-five minutes we had watched as Anna fought the final throes of her battle against a virulent enemy. Surrendering her ground had never been an option and her determination to stare defeat squarely in the eyes had filled us with optimism and pride. She had been quite right to foresee a less-than-peaceful end, and the only crumb of comfort to be gained was that we were all three with her when she drew her final breath.

We were led to a private room where we could stay with Anna for as long as we wished. We stood round her, numbed by events. I stroked her forehead and bent over to smell her, knowing that the memory would have to last me for ever. I kissed her face and held my cheek to hers feeling the warmth and softness of her skin for the last time.

Bob asked the male nurse in attendance if he would help him wash her and tidy her up whilst Mitchell removed her rings, including the one he had placed on her finger the day they were married six years earlier. We stood there hugging each other as we had done so many times before, often wondering what the future held, but this time knowing how and where and when.

We had travelled a long way since the day she entered the Lister Hospital as a trainee nurse full of enthusiasm for her chosen profession. This was where she first encountered the face of her foe and where that enemy finally seized her life.

We were numb on the short journey back to Gun Lane. For the past few weeks we had never left Anna alone in hospital overnight without one of us being with her. Now we were leaving behind the most precious part of our lives.

I Can See Clearly Now

Robert and Sarah spent the night with Mitchell but none of them had slept until the early hours. The suddenness of yesterday had shocked us all and questions flew in and out of our minds. The expectation had been overtaken by the unexpected. We all knew that the inevitable would one day happen. We kidded ourselves that it wouldn't be this week or even next week. It would be sometime in the future when we were more prepared - or not.

Perhaps this was the right time. The first day of Advent, seven days before her birthday, twenty-four days before Christmas and only thirty-one days before New Year. December was the most exciting month in Anna's year, when she and Mitchell first went out together and the month in which they became engaged.

Anna had faced up to the cancer eyeball to eyeball right up until the end. She challenged it all the way, never shrinking from its meandering journey, its devastating effects, never giving into the easier option of diamorphine or overdose. And always she thought of us. She worried how we would react after her death, what we would have to endure beforehand and what we would see at the end. She always tried to protect us and wanted only to enjoy the time that she had left. Her death marked the end of her final challenge.

Jane had worried how she should tell Louis and how he, in turn would interpret the information. At breakfast the day after Anna died she broached the subject.

'Louis, you know Anna has been poorly?'

'Yes Mummy,' Louis said with nonchalance.

'You know she's been very poorly?'

'Yeah, yeah!'

'Well Anna was so poorly that she's died.'

'You mean Anna's dead?'

'Yes and she's now in a really lovely place called Heaven.'

Louis jumped down and went over to his toys and began playing. After ten minutes he said, 'So Anna's dead Mummy?'

'Yes darling.' He continued to play for another few minutes.

'So is Anna an angel?'

With much relief that Louis seemed to be getting the right idea Jane confirmed the fact. It was another fifteen minutes before Louis said, 'So has Anna got wings?'

'Yes, she has.'

'And is she still in her wheelchair?'

The picture was perfect.

On opening up Anna's Filofax we had found her funeral planned in every detail, a wish to replicate her wedding day, the happiest day of her life, a desire to reflect her taste in music and the instruction to 'PARTY'.

How ironic it was that her funeral should take place a year to the day that Anna lost her hair. She was cremated at a private family service wearing her wedding gown, her feet bare and her head covered by a circle of anemones. It was strange to have a family gathering without Anna and it was difficult for Mitchell not to have her by his side. Colin and Paulene were devastated at losing a very-much-loved daughter-in-law but were there to help and guide Mitchell through his ordeal. An hour later we gathered at the tiny church in Knebworth Park where a lone piper reflected Anna's Scottish ancestry and her love of the bagpipes.

We were amazed to see just how many people had come to pay their respects to Anna and we were grateful for their comforting presence as they spilled out into the churchyard. Nurses in uniform from the Lister, staff from the Brompton, top personnel from ITV Sport, half of the Arsenal team plus the manager and coaching staff, ex Arsenal players, close friends, distant friends, the whole of the staff from the surgery where Anna worked, patients, headmasters and many whose lives Anna had touched in some way. We belted out 'Praise My Soul' as loudly as we could for the second time in six years, just as we had here at the wedding. The service finished with a recording of 'I Can See Clearly Now' by Hothouse Flowers, the words of which would confirm to everyone that Anna was at last free. It turned out to be the most magical celebration of her life.

But the most moving tribute of the whole day was Bob's address. His voice was powerful enough to stop his tears but his words left no one in doubt as to the true influence she'd had on the family. He was driven by the memory of Anna telling him that there must be no white handkerchief waving on this occasion, but it was hard when it came to expressing gratitude to Mitchell:

> *Anna's greatest worry was not in dying. That's never been her fear. Her worry was and is, how Mitchell will cope. Well my darling daughter, have no fear. Of course, it will be with difficulty, but Mitchell will cope. Mitchell, we marvel and thank you for*

completing and truly fulfilling Anna's life and happiness. Six years as man and wife is not enough, but eternity would not have been enough for you two.

And so little Willow, continue to show us all the way. Smile as you've always smiled and fill our lives daily, until we meet again.

As we left the church I suddenly realised two things. That I didn't feel at all cold in the pink suit and that we were almost in the same order as the wedding day. I looked round and saw Mitchell being hugged by both Robert and John, as in her vision.

'I keep seeing my funeral, Mum. I see Colin in pieces, I see Robert and John holding Mitchell on the path of the church and I keep thinking of all the people that will be there. Do you think we could have my funeral before I die so that I can party with them?'

Part 2

from Death to Life ...

Fresh Roots, Green Shoots

The grounds of Knebworth House had become a major venue for open-air rock and pop concerts since 1974 when The Allman Brothers Band attracted 60,000 at the first large concert held in the park. Since that time it had been the scene of outdoor extravaganzas featuring Pink Floyd, The Rolling Stones, Genesis, Frank Zappa, Led Zeppelin, Mike Oldfield, The Beach Boys, Cliff Richard, Deep Purple, Queen, Paul McCartney, Eric Clapton, Elton John & Dire Straits and in 1996, Oasis, when Anna and Mitchell had danced and partied their cares to the wind as Liam and Noel had seemingly visited them in their back yard.

But now it was Robbie's turn. On the first three days of August 2003, Robbie Williams performed at Knebworth, drawing crowds of over 375,000, and a further 3.5 million who watched live on television and online. This was reputedly the biggest UK pop concert ever and caused a huge traffic jam on the A1(M) as an estimated 130,000 cars tried to reach the venue.

The stage where Robbie performed was alongside the plot that we had chosen four years earlier as Anna's resting place. She had wanted to be buried in Knebworth Park and a suitable site was chosen with the help of Lord Cobbold – close to water with a clear view of the house and church that had meant so much to her and Mitchell. Anna's ashes were buried under a willow tree close to the river. We had planted it in November 1999, eleven months after her death, when close members of the family and Lord Cobbold stood round a small sapling as its roots were dug in over the casket.

It would be a place to come and talk, to have picnics and feel close. It would for ever be Anna. It would see fireworks, streamers and flowers at celebratory times and particularly at Christmas. And as we grew old, the tree would get stronger and stronger. The deer would pass and rabbits would make their homes, whilst shrubs and brambles created their own secret garden. But we never thought that one day Robbie would be there to sing 'Angels' for her. She had a front row view and she could dance and shake her hair as much as anyone else.

We had chosen a willow tree to reflect the names that Mitchell called her –'Wills', 'Willow' – its branches and soft cascading leaves would always remind us of Anna's long curly hair framing her smiling face.

The diary I had started at the beginning of her illness ended the day after her funeral. I couldn't bear to write about life without her as it would somehow magnify the emptiness of our days. For the five years previous our every waking thought had been of her, of her treatment, of what emergency might occur and how we could make her life living with cancer more comfortable.

But it took Tim, the minister who conducted her funeral service, to put into words what we hadn't realised. He had asked if he could listen to our stories of Anna, to discuss what we would want in the service, the music and the memories. For three hours we talked, laughed, sang and finally prayed. Tim thanked God saying 'that in the five years in which Anna was dying, she taught us all how to live.' We were astonished at his perception, his understanding and his use of words. He had listened, digested and understood, in the space of three hours, something that we had only just begun to comprehend. Anna's philosophy was simple. She needed quality of life and quality of time, the two things she had asked for when diagnosed, but most of all she needed fun. She wanted those around to be smiling and was determined to banish thoughts of the future and to live in the present, to make the most of what she could do with those she loved most and not contemplate what might be ahead.

Bob's mum – Nan Wilson – was famed for the laughter and cheerfulness she brought into people's lives. She could only ever see positives, even when she lost her two eldest sons in the Second World War, both shot down in the planes in which they were flying. Hers was a life to be admired for the way she had dealt with the inevitability of war, never blaming, never asking for sympathy but turning again to life and living it to the full for her sons' sakes. 'Everything is sent for a reason,' she believed. She was her father's daughter, he a Scottish Presbyterian minister, the Reverend Robert Primrose, whose sermons were renowned throughout his parish for their perceptiveness and warmth.

I knew that Anna's story should never be lost to the family. Her example in living with cancer was extraordinary and I decided to edit the diaries down into a book, there being too much emotional detail in the original text for others to digest. So the hole that I now lived beside started to be filled with hours in my office writing up a book that I would call *Anna's Legacy*. I had no idea what I could do 'related to all of this' but at least I could try and make some sense of it for others to read.

It was on 20 January 1999, the month after Anna had died, that we received a letter from the editor of the *Welwyn and Hatfield Times*, the local newspaper.

> *I hope you will forgive me writing to you in this manner, but I have an idea I would very much like to talk over with you. All of us at the Welwyn and Hatfield Times were extremely saddened to hear of the tragic death of your daughter Anna. Her bravery, especially, moved us all.*
>
> *So many young people seem to be stricken by this disease these days. We would like to do something to help and thought about launching a fundraising campaign, via the Welwyn and Hatfield Times and our sister papers in Hertfordshire, to raise much needed money for research and those who care for sufferers.*
>
> *With the permission and backing of her husband, yourself and her family we would like to set up this appeal in Anna's memory.*
>
> *I hope this project would meet with your approval and look forward to discussing it with you.*
>
> *Yours sincerely*
>
> *TS Mitchinson, Editor*

Life had begun to turn to 'normal' for most of us. A new norm had replaced the old norm. Bob had to return to presenting ITV football, John to the BBC, Robert to his photography and Mitchell had to start searching for a job. He had good friends who helped with the harrowing days and nights that had to be filled without Anna, but he was creative, uniquely talented and highly employable.

I contacted Terry Mitchinson and thanked him for his kind thoughts and suggested we meet. I told him that I had thought of doing something in Anna's memory but was not clear what that would be. I didn't want to replicate anything that was already being done and it had to be appropriate to Anna's age group. I suggested we meet with representatives from the local hospitals and hospices from the North-East Hertfordshire area where Anna had worked as a nurse. It would be wonderful to be able to give back to the community she served.

In four weekly meetings Terry and I were joined by the CEO's from the QEII and Lister Hospitals, Allison Cooke and Heather Lawrence, the Chair of Trustees from Isabel Hospice, Barbara Doherty and the Matron from Garden House Hospice, Trudy Bunday. We talked through ideas and they listened to my stories of Anna and how she managed to educate us in the needs of someone with a terminal illness. In recounting Anna's last five years I told them how she had seemed so much better when she or we had planned an outing of some sort. The day we went shopping in a stretch limo with her closest friends; concerts of Take That, Oasis, Barbra Streisand; Arsenal matches, a trip to Paris and her father's *This Is Your Life* programme. She had always seemed energised after each occasion when adrenalin had taken over and symptoms of her illness had seemingly disappeared. Laughter, enjoyment, sharing with friends and family had all helped cancel out the greater picture.

I also pointed out that when we had looked at what help was available for Anna's age group, there seemed to be nothing. There were wonderful charities for children up to the age of sixteen, Teenage Cancer Trust for those needing help in hospital, and the amazing hospice movement that catered mainly for older patients. But for young adults struggling with serious illness and a home life, there was nothing. But what constituted a young adult? Anna was twenty-seven when diagnosed and thirty-one when she died, a time when her personal and professional life had been blossoming and thoughts of starting a family were uppermost. It would be the same for most at this age.

The gathered professionals were in agreement saying that the National Health Service could provide diagnosis and treatment; what it couldn't do was give quality of life. Wouldn't it be wonderful if there was a charity that could provide a patient, struggling with treatment, a meal out with their partner, or a trip to the hairdressers to lighten the burden – a special day? It would be unfair to give this only to those with cancer so I suggested that all serious illnesses should be included.

So in a room at the QEII Hospital, Welwyn Garden City, it was agreed that I set up a charity that could give Special Days for Seriously Ill Young Adults between sixteen and forty. All it needed was a name.

Willow

But that *wasn't* all that was needed! My enthusiasm had carried me away and I had to speak to the family, in particular Bob and Mitchell. I knew nothing of how to set up a charity and of what pitfalls there might be along the way, but I felt the necessity to spread the word. 'If Anna's special days worked for her, why shouldn't they work for others?' I said to Bob. 'And by the way, will you help me?'

Grief takes its own course in many different ways. Some people will be privately distraught, some will remain obviously bereft for years, some will become angry. Others, seemingly controlled, find outlets in creativity or group activity. It leaves a mental scarring not easily healed, damaged goods unable to be returned. Its shadow will be permanently discernible, sometimes faint, sometimes harsh, not always obvious.

Everyone is different. Bob would go to training at the Arsenal, be the first to change, run out to the goalkeeping area, sit on a ball before the players arrived and bawl his eyes out. Once joined by others, he'd be controlled but ready to smash as many balls at the goalkeepers as his artificial hip could manage.

He was as enthusiastic about setting up the charity as I was and was very happy to be of use in whatever way he could, understanding my new resolve. We talked with Mitchell, who was thrilled and we asked what he thought it should be called. The Anna Carey Fund? It was too personal and too closely linked to Anna. It needed a name that was not too subjective, but was simple, memorable and recognisable.

'What about her nickname, – 'Willow'?' suggested Mitchell, and thus Willow Foundation was born.

It wasn't until 25 August 1999 that we launched Willow at Brocket Hall alongside the Laura Davies golf tournament. Piggybacking on to a marquee erected for the event, the whole family gathered to give the charity a good start. Mitchell, being a graphic designer, had come up with a logo that not only symbolised a willow tree but to us, had echoes of Anna's high cheekbones and Raphaelesque hair. Meanwhile Robert agreed that the photo he had taken of Anna just before she lost her hair, and which he had given to me as a Christmas present, should be used as a reminder of Willow's raison d'etre.

Whilst walking back from the marquee to the golf club I was

joined by a tall distinguished-looking gentleman who had been present at the launch. He introduced himself as Peter Wilkerson, a local printer and owner of Herts Offset. He had been moved by what he had heard and offered help in any way he could. Over the next few years he and his wife Rosey became huge supporters, printing our quarterly newsletters free of charge, our stationery, and leaflets, and sponsoring fundraising events that we held at Brocket Hall.

Terry Mitchinson of the *Welwyn and Hatfield Times* had been a great help in publicising the launch and in making Willow their charity of the year. But I knew we would need a little more assistance, so I asked him to announce that if his readers raised money in various ways, much like Red Nose Day, Bob and I would go along and receive the cheque to say a personal thank you. I also asked that he print a story about Willow every week for a year – and he did. He accepted my request that he become Willow's first trustee, a post that he served for the next thirteen years.

We were fortunate to have a spare room that acted as an office. It had been used frequently during our Bob Wilson Goalkeeping School days and I was accustomed to working on a computer. So we set about promoting Willow and visiting the many local groups that raised money for us. There were pubs, clubs, motorbike groups, schools, companies and individuals who had taken on board our cause and helped us raise the money we needed to bring the service to North and East Hertfordshire. They enabled us to create our very first Special Day. Bob had said to me as we approached Christmas – 'All these people have been enthused by the cause – you really have to give a Special Day for someone.'

We approached Isabel Hospice, one of the organisations who had helped me formulate the idea, and asked if they had anyone within our criteria – seriously ill, aged sixteen to forty. Yes, they had and she would love to go to London with her husband to see *Mamma Mia*.

We contacted the manager of the theatre and he donated a box for the couple. A good friend's secretary's husband was a black-cab driver who offered to pick them up, wait and drive them back. Remembering Anna's discomfort in cars towards the end, we sent pillows and a hamper of food and drink and instructed the driver to take them to a restaurant, should they want, after the performance.

They were elated, but had been too tired to go onward for a meal. They so appreciated their night out that they sent a lovely letter and a cheque for thirty pounds to enable someone else to have a Special

Day. Our second recipient was a young man who wanted to see Sting at the Royal Albert Hall and once again the wheels went into motion to organise the evening.

We were very grateful for the publicity surrounding the setting-up of Willow which included television appearances, radio and newspaper interviews. This in turn inspired others wanting to help and very soon I had a group of volunteers who were willing to file, phone, enquire, organise and work to lay the foundations of the charity.

I took a call from Jerry Golland who was one of the founders of the Sylvia Adams Trust, a local Hatfield charity giving grants to deserving causes. They had taken over a disused doctors' surgery and turned it into office space and decorated it in art deco style in memory of the late Sylvia Adams whose antiques legacy facilitated the work of the charity.

'Would you like office space?' Had he seen my office at home he would have realised that this would make my life ultimately more structured. Try as I might, the files of correspondence were beginning to overflow and I spent days locked away, seldom leaving our home. Through meetings with Jerry and his co-founder Alan Morris, the Sylvia Adams Trust offered office space for the next 6 years and they also gave Willow a grant to pay for a PA to work alongside me.

So it was that Willow began a life of its own away from our home 'Threepwood', out into the world of planning, meetings and organisation. Working as Director and Chair of Trustees, I had managed to persuade several good friends and family to come on the board alongside those who were familiar with the workings of charity and its unique laws. These would be the founder trustees who would steer Willow on an upward course over the next few years making it a very successful local charity.

I also had my own PA, Pam Meiklejohn, our first employee, who fortunately had a great work ethic and an even better sense of humour; and we had a group of volunteers who were enthusiastic and dedicated to providing quality Special Days.

But like Anna, I also craved fun in my life. I needed a group of people around me who didn't take life too seriously but who looked at life in a constructive and upbeat way. And I was lucky that those who at first got in touch to say they would like to volunteer their time, were just that. Willow was like a magnet, drawing in the most positive, enthusiastic, engaging, creative and supportive people who were attracted by the cause and who wanted to be part of the process. They were a remarkable group of ladies, who all eventually became paid members of staff, once the charity could afford such. It is they who were responsible for the care, the thought, the look, the feel, the ethos and all the detail that created the backbone of Willow.

The work they did was not a chore, it was a joy. The enthusiasm they showed shone through every phone call made, and every conversation had. The embryo that was Willow began to grow, slowly at first, but strengthened daily by the nurture and care that was plied. Like any growing child, it responded to the environment in which it was being reared. Consequently my own life was also enriched by working alongside Pam Meiklejohn, Sue Parslew and Suzanne Brennan, by the fun, laughter and tremendous hard work that took place. There are too many good people to mention, who volunteered their time, but it was these three who gave the charity the best start in life that it could possibly have had.

The massive publicity that the *Welwyn and Hatfield Times* generated became the lifeblood of the charity. One of the receptionists at the newspaper put me in touch with her brother who would be able to supply me with second-hand reconditioned computers – free of charge! What a godsend! I was also approached by a very kindly gentleman who suggested a website. Rikki Bellamy soon created our first online presence and it was a truly proud day to see www.willowfoundation.org.uk adorning the internet. Like many who gave their time for free, Rikki never sought any recognition. He was happy knowing that he was contributing and helping those whose lives had taken a very disruptive and unfortunate turn.

Similarly, Jerry Lovejoy of Inver Systems was happy to supply all our technical support and he was called on many times over the years to work on our software, hardware and problems that only a specialist could. These people were truly philanthropic – not with finance, but by giving their time and expertise in abundance.

Usually, help was offered because the cause resonated. Over and over again we heard stories of others' relatives or friends who were going or had gone through tough times with serious illness. They could understand the strain that such situations entailed, not just for the patient but also those surrounding them.

Because our recipients were going through treatment for a serious illness, we had to make sure that their Special Day was just that, one that would allow them to think exclusively of the enjoyment of the day. They only had to get themselves ready for whatever they had requested and Willow would do the rest — the transport, the tickets, the refreshments, the overnight accommodation, the entertainment. So an itinerary had to be detailed and specific, everything checked and double checked for possible mistakes so that nothing could go wrong.

Once we were operating smoothly, we received the letters emphasising just how much the Special Day had provided for recipients friends and families alike. How it had given them back a normality that had disappeared from their lives, and had allowed them to talk and had helped them forget the negativity surrounding treatment. How it had empowered them to do something for themselves and how it had made them smile.

We will be eternally grateful to all those who gave us support during those early years when we were feeling our way, and forging ahead through uncharted territory. We weren't surprised that Special Days had been so enthusiastically welcomed by medical professionals and recipients alike, but we had not expected the number of enquiries we had from people outside Hertfordshire asking if they could take advantage of our service. Very soon Willow spread to the eastern region and adjoining areas to the north and west whilst gradually our volunteers and staff grew accordingly.

Looking back I now realise that writing the book and setting up the charity was my own process of grieving, although it must also have been a subconscious way of staying close to Anna, a problematic situation when other members of the family are there and in need of close attention. It was two years into the life of Willow that my daughter-in-law had to say to me, 'Don't forget you have two other children.' John had called many times asking if I could babysit Louis, but often I had a meeting to go to or an event to attend. Robert, so strong through Anna's illness and death, had been finding life so hard without his sister. So determined had I been to make sure Willow was a success I had channelled all my energies into work and ignored those whose hearts had been broken as much as my own.

Infancy

I was determined that Willow should be built on a solid foundation, one that would withstand the inevitable tremors, shakes and earthquakes that might come its way. Most charities are created following a tragedy, whether it's famine, flood, destitution, family illness or desperate need. All are worthy and maybe there are too many that replicate what is already there. In founding Willow we were sure, through our meetings and consultations, that we would be providing a unique service particularly for an age group that had so far been virtually ignored. Sixteen to forty is a time when life is about furthering education, forging a career, creating a family, enjoying a social life with old and new friendships, and enjoying being an adult, capable of appreciating life as it unfolds.

A diagnosis of a life-threatening illness shocks the system, alters perception and changes life as planned. The pressures of diagnosis, treatment and recovery can have a devastating effect on work and family so Willow would try to redress the balance, providing unique and unforgettable Special Days tailored to specific needs.

I knew little of how a charity worked, of its laws, its regulations and its governance procedures so I had to do some research. We would need a board of trustees who would have overall control and be responsible for making sure Willow was fulfilling its charitable purpose. I would need to find people who would accept responsibility for the work of the charity to further and support its function. I didn't want to involve the boys as I realised this was my way of coping and it would be unfair to force it on them. They needed to move on forging their own lives with their young families but I knew they would always give their support.

I had already asked Terry Mitchinson to be a trustee, whilst Bob and I made three, but it would need better minds than ours to steer a straight and lawful course. The Sylvia Adams Foundation in Hatfield not only provided us with an office and my very own PA, they also offered the services of their director, Kate Baldwin, who was expert in all things charity. They allowed me to lean on Kate and grill her as to whether we were going in the right direction, as I was so anxious that the charity should not move too quickly without the proper structure in place.

It happened that Kate too had experienced loss, that of a sibling, and therefore she had huge empathy with what we were trying to achieve. I found her advocacy so crucial that I asked her to be a founder trustee therefore giving substance to any decisions that were taken. Willow owes a lot to her guidance as she had an academic mind aligned with common sense and much of her wisdom helped build Willow from the basement upward.

I invited Louise Hickson, Anna's best friend and bridesmaid who had also studied to be a nurse, onto the board. Louise had gone on to specialise in cancer treatment and was familiar with the difference a diagnosis meant to someone's life. Whenever she'd been to see Anna during her illness she stayed so positive and happy, not changing her attitude as a friend or being over-sympathetic. She was delighted to be involved and it was Louise who eventually guided Special Days so professionally along the appropriate path. Her mum Sue also accepted my invitation to be a trustee and it was she who worked so hard alongside me in the very early days, traipsing round doctors' surgeries, hospices and the like in order to get the word out. It was Sue who organised the first Special Days and who rigorously maintained the required standards.

My father had been a newsagent in Chesterfield and I often delivered papers or served behind the counter in the shop. He taught me how to wrap rolled newspapers in string then cut it against its own tension round my hand and how to count change into people's palms. I found this pretty easy as he was a good teacher and made it so simple. However, I didn't fare as well in the formality of school maths and I failed my 'O' level three times, proudly achieving forty percent on my final attempt. I had at last begun to understand geometry thanks to a change in teacher and was quite excited when the penny began to drop. Sadly the pass mark was forty-five so my education in numbers finished there.

But it had given me a good basic understanding of maths and I was therefore quite capable of running the domestic and business side of the Wilson household. However, being responsible for the money that people gave in good faith to Willow would be a huge task and would require a proper accountability and a transparency which followed accepted fundraising practices.

I was introduced to Sarah Price by the CEO of the QEII hospital as a potential trustee. She was an accountant by profession and a willing volunteer in many areas of the county. She listened to the proposal for Willow and the invitation to become a founder trustee and to my delight accepted. My relief at there being someone to oversee the finances was huge and I felt lucky that a jigsaw was beginning to come together. Sarah was a joy to work with, having a wonderful sense of humour and an astute mind.

When Anna was eight she had been bridesmaid to our niece Heather, with whom we had always been close, ever since Heather and her husband Rino lived with us briefly during their early married years working at the Middlesex Hospital in their roles of doctor and nurse. Rino had been in the CT scanner department at the Lister Hospital the day Anna's tumour had been found and he was a wonderful sounding board throughout Anna's illness. Heather in the meantime had become a talented florist with great organisational skills and she had arranged the flowers both for Anna's wedding and funeral. We asked Heather if she would represent the wider family members on the board to which she agreed.

But a business brain was needed, one that would think about sustainability and growth with honesty and professionalism. Chris Measures was a very dear friend, someone on whom we could always rely, who would do anything asked of him and had a sharp brain in business. He was the epitome of calm and reasoned thought and someone who would feel as fervent about giving back as we did. Chris and his wife Jayne had been in South Africa at the time of Anna's death attending their son's wedding. As soon as they heard the news they cut their extended visit short in order to be there at Anna's funeral. He accepted our invitation without hesitation.

But although the idea of appealing to local people to raise money for Willow was succeeding, it would only be a short-term measure as there would be a finite period for enthusiasm. Returning again and again to the same audience for funding was not an option.

In 1991 the England 1966 World Cup team had been invited to a dinner at Wembley to celebrate twenty-five years after winning that illustrious trophy. It was arranged by the charity SOS who asked Bob to be the chair of the organising committee. During this time we made very good friends with a lady called Pippa Forster, a charity fundraising and public relations consultant. Of course I wrote to her in the hopes that she might advise. In my letter to her on 31 August 1999 I said:

> *The response to the charity tells us that we seem to have struck a chord with people. It's only right that we make sure the foundation is administered properly.'*

She replied:

> *I would be greatly honoured to give you some help with setting up the charity. One of the few talents I have is steering newly founded charities onto a secure financial path so that they are enabled to fulfil their mission. So many scrabble about trying to keep things ticking over, when with some sound advice and practical help in things like setting up a proper administration and developing a longer-term fundraising strategy they could achieve so much more. I always advise new charities to think of the longer term.*

Pippa became a trustee and wrote our very first five-year business plan and strategic framework. I called Pippa and Kate Baldwin my two pillars as between them they could guide us on fundraising, strategy, charity governance and charity law. In between those two pillars we had to make it up as we went along!

During the charity's infancy I relied heavily on the prudence of the board of trustees, all of whom felt passionately about creating a service that could benefit seriously ill young adults aged from sixteen to forty. They were all enthused, creative, determined and committed. It was this group of people that allowed Willow to grow organically into a service that became much appreciated by medical professionals and recipients alike. It was these people who made sure Willow's own roots ran deep for stability and support and allowed Willow to discover its own unique place in the world, being the only charity offering Special Days for this particular age group.

Special Days

Serious illness brings with it a new normality, one that involves doctors' appointments, medication, hospital visits, and very often, an abundance of daytime television. The treatment can sometimes be worse than the illness itself when dignity and hope can regularly be stripped bare. What we had learned from Anna was that every time she had her own Special Day, whether it be shopping, concerts or a simple meal out, it generated smiles and a chance to experience normality and crafted memories that still help us connect with Anna, even today.

It was important that those applying could understand who would be eligible and so the criteria were set for those living with and under treatment for life-threatening and life limiting-illness. It was imperative that a Special Day needed to be of good quality, reliable, fulfilling and satisfactory. It necessitated careful planning, dedicated, skilled and sensitive staff, an understanding of serious illness, a huge variety of contacts and sufficient funding.

We were fortunate enough to have the most amazing volunteers who later in the life of Willow became employees. There had to be a consistency to all the work that they did. Nothing could go wrong with a Special Day and they had to provide the recipient, friends and family a once-in-a-lifetime opportunity to choose something uniquely tailored to their needs. They could choose whatever they wished and we would do our best to create that experience for them. There would be no means testing, no discrimination. It opened the door to the most varied choices of Special Days and some of the biggest challenges for the staff. The majority of applications preferred a weekend away, an overnight visit to London's attractions, a sporting occasion or a meet and greet with a celebrity. These were the moments that replicated the lost normality that had suddenly become out of reach. Not because it wasn't possible for them to organise one for themselves, but the fact that the time and thought required in planning an outing had become burdensome. All energies were sapped and engulfed by the-day-to-day management of a serious illness, accounting for the consequential disinclination to increase the load.

A letter from the wife of a recipient, illustrated this fact after an overnight stay in London with a visit to *The Lion King:*

To this day I don't know how Graham managed to take such a full part in the trip as sadly he died only ten days later. The fantastic organisation, kindness and consideration of all those involved in arranging and providing services to the trip has to be a major factor. My daughter and I are eternally grateful for that as you provided us with positive memories, laughter and excitement at a time that only seemed negative and hopeless. I know for a fact that we would not have felt confident or energetic enough to have packed our bags and arranged the trip ourselves and I am forever indebted to the Foundation for these special memories that we shall treasure forever.

Serious illness steals the spirit and sense of being and a day spent totally away from the new normality of it is a day that would often modify future thinking. A young gentleman living on the Isle of Wight requested a day at Highbury to watch his beloved Arsenal play at their home ground. Stephen was in treatment for a brain tumour and it would make his day if his mates could go with him. A mini bus was ordered, return tickets for the ferry, tickets for the match and a meet with Bob before kick-off to say hello.

The group arrived at the arranged time and we all met on the steps of Highbury exchanging greetings and chatting about their journey. They were a cheery bunch, excited to be attending with no worries about transport, parking or queuing and hugely grateful for the chance to just be lads together. It raised our own spirits to see how much it meant to them all and a win by the Gunners would eventually make the day perfect.

It was only a month later, as we were climbing the steps to the marble halls ready for another home match; we heard a shout from nearby. There was Stephen with the same group of lads ready to cheer on their team once more. We stopped and asked how this had come about. One of the friends said, 'We were scared to do it, scared that we could somehow cause damage. But you showed us not to be afraid and to just get on, do it and live for the moment.'

It was only then that we realised how Special Days could be quite so empowering. Over the years, this example of empowerment would be replicated again and again in many different forms by those who thought that serious illness restricted freedom. Only when they had experienced their Special Day would they write to us and say that Willow had shown them 'how to live'.

When we started Willow, it was intended as a way of giving something back to North and East Hertfordshire where Anna had trained and worked as a Community Nursing Sister. As the effects of a Special Day became apparent to more people, the word in the medical world had spread and we received requests from those outside of Hertfordshire and much further beyond. The medical professionals told us that they saw it as another tool in their bag, something they could offer amidst the seemingly negative and debilitating effects of essential treatment. We received these words from a Macmillan nurse:

> *Today I had a call from a truly amazing 16-year-old – Lisa. She absolutely sparkled as she told me of her stay at Alton Towers and all the antics she and her family enjoyed. Chemotherapy and symptoms all forgotten – magic! I just wanted you all to know that whilst you make/help those struggling with disease enjoy special times, you also help those professionals privileged to know them. Many thanks for lighting the darkness, theirs and mine.*

Mitchell was particularly pleased with the way the charity had been welcomed and always came round home to chat about life and unload baggage that was stored in his head. The five years of illness had thrown us together in the most unforgiving of circumstances but it was a passage of time where our relationships had intertwined so massively that he was very much more than a son-in-law. His closeness to Robert, Sarah and John was particularly important to us all and we would always be thankful to have Mitchell there to make us laugh uncontrollably, even during the most tearful of times.

On one particular visit he seemed edgier than usual and we realised he needed to get something off his chest.

'I've got something to run by you which I really need to speak to you about.'

He was hesitant, even uncharacteristically restrained. Was it his job? Money troubles? Problems with his health? Over the substantial period of time that had passed since Anna's death he had coped brilliantly in work and in keeping the house looking smart. Our curiosity was sparked and he had our full attention.

'You remember Debbie Smith? Well she's been really good to me, coming round and chatting about everything. You remember that when she was burgled Anna suggested to all our friends that they club together to buy her a new music system? Debbie and I have become very close friends and she's asked me if I'll go on holiday with her. She thinks it would be good for me.'

It wasn't the fact that Mitchell had formed a friendship with another female that surprised us, but that he felt he should seek to gain approval from us. Anna had always anticipated that it would happen one day and had indeed given Mitchell her blessing – with some comical provisos! But we were very humbled that we should be asked for some sort of blessing.

We were relieved that his dilemma wasn't of a negative nature and anything that lightened his solitary life could only be good. We were happy that Debbie had given him time to talk and was offering him a chance to get away from the loneliness at home.

It would be a chance for him to step out of the enveloping darkness that sometimes travelled with him and which could often cloud his day. It would be a time for him to be given a chance to look to the future rather than always being reminded of the past, and to experience his own special day in a totally different environment.

Nursery/Childhood

The first year in the life of Willow was sustained and funded by the people of Welwyn and Hatfield who rose to the challenge to raise money for our cause. We will be for ever grateful for the support they afforded us at a time when we had no notion of where this all might lead. When I was asked what sort of sum I had as a target for raising in the first year, I plucked an amount out of thin air saying 'one hundred thousand', never really knowing if it was even a possibility.

None of those who worked for Willow had any previous experience of charity employment so it was a matter of making it up as we went along and learning by our mistakes. Our fundraising was mainly event-based which was hard work but we had fun devising ways to raise money week in and week out. There were many people who were moved by the cause and had the means to help and over the years some have stayed with us and others moved on.

The inaugural golf day at Brocket Hall in June 2000 was to be our first proper formal Willow fundraising event. It was attended by many of our 'celebrity' friends from the fields of football and entertainment. The atmosphere of that day would never really be replicated again, everyone attending willing it to be a success. It raised over £60,000, a sum way beyond our expectations. So as we passed the first anniversary of our charity we couldn't believe that with monies donated by third parties plus the golf day we had raised a total of £195,000.

Our first Willow Ball was the next event and this was again at Brocket, in a marquee erected at the back of the main Hall so that we were able to use both the house itself for the reception and the marquee for the ball. It was a magical evening, the house looked magnificent and once again all the guests believed that what we had created was unique and worthy of their support.

Rick Wakeman had agreed to travel all the way from his home in the Isle of Man to provide our main entertainment for the evening and we were thrilled that he declined any payment except for his expenses. He sat next to me at the dinner and I thanked him for his time, assuring him that we would pay all his travel costs, requesting him to let me know when he was back in the Isle of Man.

'Oh don't worry about the return ticket. I'm not going back.'

'Oh, so you have another gig whilst here on the mainland?' I asked.

'No, my car is packed with all my things that I need. I've left home.'

'What do you mean?' I asked, not quite sure if I had missed something.

'I left my wife and home and came straight here and I'm never going back.'

Rick gave an amazing performance that night at his piano, never showing any glimpse of the stress that he must have been going through. It was the start of a new life for him and for Willow, neither party knowing what was ahead, but both stepping into the unknown with fingers crossed.

If year one was successful in that we provided seventeen Special Days, a fact that we continued to marvel at, then year two saw the team getting into their stride, learning to add value to the days, receiving feedback as to how we could improve. More and more requests were coming from outside the county of Hertfordshire and increasingly we were able to respond accordingly. That year we delivered thirty-two Special Days and in the third year another fifty-one.

Brocket Hall was not only our base for golf days and the ball, but it was where we held our 'Evenings With' providing us with the most prestigious facilities we could hope for. Michael Parkinson agreed to be the subject for our first-ever 'Evening With' and the tables were turned with Bob asking the questions and Michael telling the stories. Over the following years such stars as Rick Wakeman, Jasper Carrott, Alistair McGowan, Aled Jones and Rory Bremner came to entertain and help us raise money.

Arranging the Brocket events was always stressful – selling the tickets, obtaining auction prizes, dressing the room, balancing the entertainment. But one particular 'Evening With' brought its own challenge. We had asked Paul Gascoigne, the ex-England and Tottenham footballer, if he would be willing to be the main subject of the night and he accepted immediately. He was keen to help us and we sold out the evening very quickly once the event was advertised.

Hertfordshire was, at that time, the home to many Arsenal and Tottenham fans so it was easy to see why Paul would be a popular choice. However, he had also courted the attention of the press through his problems with substance abuse and alcohol and it would be interesting to be able to hear Paul's own thoughts on his colourful life.

We had been in touch with him in the weeks leading up to the event and on the evening before his appearance on the Saturday, Bob decided to give him a call to make sure he was ok for transport etc. Paul answered his phone.

'Hello?'

'Hi Paul, it's Bob here. Just checking that everything is OK for tomorrow and that you're quite happy for the car to pick you up at six o'clock?'

Paul didn't seem to hear the question and replied, 'Hi Bob, you've just caught me at Gatwick Airport where I'm about to get on a plane to America.'

'Why are you going there?'

'I need to get to the clinic out there to dry out. I've been in a bad way.'

Bob didn't even mention the event the next day but wished him well and put the phone down before he began to panic. We had sold 120 tickets, paid Brocket for food and drink, decorated the magnificent dining room, laid on a PA system, video footage and stage, recruited an auctioneer and brought in volunteers to help manage the guests. And now we had no subject for our 'Evening With'.

Bob's mind began to race and quickly went to our stack of videos where he had footage of footballers he was close to. 'How about I do a Goalkeepers evening? I've got footage of David and Pat which we could show and I'm sure they'd help out if they are free.'

David Seaman and Pat Jennings had been two of the goalkeepers that Bob had coached at Arsenal. They were all very close, not just because they had all been custodians of the Arsenal goal, but because they shared so much over the years.

Pat and his wife Eleanor had been so caring during Anna's illness, always asking after her and, as devout Catholics, had given us holy water and sent up prayers in hopes of a recovery. David was there on the training field through the whole time that Anna was ill and knew full well what Bob had been going through. He became very fond of Anna and Mitchell and could see the strain that Anna's battle for survival was putting on Bob.

During the first year of Willow, Bob had been invited to be a guest on an ITV programme not dissimilar to *This Is Your Life*, where David was the subject. Bob was invited to speak about their times together as coach and player and towards the end of his tribute Bob mentioned that we had set up a new charity called Willow. He then asked David if he would agree to be the very first ambassador for the charity – rather difficult to say no on live TV!

Consequently, in the aftermath of Gazza's revelation, Bob rang both David and Pat to see if they might be free the following evening and would step in at short notice as main guests for a question and answer session. Fortunately they were both free and agreed, but of course we still had to placate those who had bought tickets on the premise of seeing Paul Gascoigne! Just one table out of the twelve were angry that Gazza was not appearing, but by the end of the evening everyone expressed their delight at hearing the wonderful stories told by the three goalies who put their keeping skills into saving the day.

A lady called Sharon Dyer had been watching the TV programme on David Seaman when Bob asked him to be an ambassador. Before he moved to Arsenal, David had played for QPR - Sharon was a huge fan. So much so that when she was working for Chase Bank in the USA, she would fly to the UK and back every weekend to see her beloved team play, home or away.

Sharon was also a David Seaman fan and the programme sparked an idea which made her get in touch with us. She was currently working for RBS and was aware that the committee responsible for Swapsball, an annual event organised by the financial markets of the City of London, was meeting soon to decide which charity should be the recipient of their September 2001 donation. She suggested she would like to put Willow forward to the ball committee but warned us not to get too excited as there would be many other charities applying.

We were astonished to find we had been chosen and were alarmed to learn that it would mean giving a five minute presentation about Willow. We had been warned that in the past the charity representatives had found it very difficult to get the attention of those attending as the traders were hellbent on enjoying the night to the full.

Traditionally, it is a night of revelry and charitable donation. The centrepiece of the evening are the post-dinner auctions that see traders bidding absurd amounts of money for an eclectic selection of luxury items – Mediterranean cruises, celebrity lunches and VIP tickets to rock concerts. Over the years, the testosterone and alcohol-fuelled bidding had helped raise huge amounts for various charities, but this year the atmosphere was totally different. The traders would be using the evening to help assuage their own sorrow at losing so many good colleagues during the week past in the tragedy of 9/11.

As we stepped on to the stage to give our presentation we realised just what a difficult task it was going to be. Bob spoke into the microphone asking for quiet, but the clamour continued, undiminished. He asked once again for just five minutes of their time, to no effect. And then he stopped speaking. He stood there, and stood there, until gradually table by table the noise abated.

When finally we told our Willow story the response was amazing. The whole room stood up and applauded and we were relieved that we had managed to get their attention. Being a young audience, Willow's focus on youth had resonated with them hugely and they totally understood the cause.

The largest single donation of the charity's life at that time came from the evening at the Grosvenor House. In excess of £215,000 was raised on that one occasion. This ball and its organisers will always have a special place in the heart of the Willow Foundation for it was this single donation that allowed the charity's work to spread beyond the core area. It gave us the opportunity to invest in new computers that would allow us to run a much-needed database, so vital to the coordination of our work. The balance of the money was invested in the charity's Development Fund.

The lady who had made all of this happen, Sharon Dyer, was then driven with a passion to help Willow further. Her job at RBS was as a technical fixer, not of the IT sort, but a solver of the unsolvable, a troubleshooter working in a mainly male environment that was driven and competitive. On meeting Bob her boss once said, 'We do not know what she does or how she does it, but she gets us to change and do the right thing!'

Over the next few years Sharon persuaded RBS to support us in a UK-wide road show where local RBS management invited their clients to hear Bob's after-dinner speech about football and TV. I would pop up between the main course and the dessert to tell them all about Willow. It was an amazing opportunity to bring the charity to a different section of the population, corporations and businesses who might want to adopt Willow as their charity of choice. And it was good to travel places like the Isle of Man, Jersey and Ireland which enabled us to bring Willow to people it could otherwise never have easily reached.

Sharon's loyalty to Willow was extraordinary as she would always see an opportunity where we couldn't. Over the next few years she was the enabler and networker who raised more money for Willow than any other individual person.

Willow continued to take over our lives although we changed tack and made sure that we were mindful of our growing family and had some quality holiday time. 'Anna would be mad as hell with you if you didn't,' was the reminder from the boys. It was true that whilst we were trying to improve the lives of others, it was important that we too lived by Anna's mantra.

When Mitchell once again arrived on our doorstep we were not unduly surprised when he asked our opinion about Debbie moving in with him. They had become incredibly close and were happy together but Mitchell's sensitivity to the whole situation meant that he sought our approval before going ahead with the move. We had no hesitation in giving them both our blessing, relieved that there was sunshine in a life that had been clouded by grief.

It was that sunshine which began to spread its rays even more widely for them the following year when they announced that they were expecting a baby. No one could have been more delighted for them than Bob and I, but Mitchell knew that this was the one blessing that Anna had always longed for, but was so cruelly denied. Once again he was sensitive to our feelings and came round to tell us personally. He had always been afraid of parenthood, denying that he would be a good father, despite the obvious natural compassionate traits that others saw in him. Now he was so much more experienced in life, wiser, unselfish and ready to share his amazing imaginative charismatic personality with his offspring. And no son or daughter would ever be the poorer for that.

The Willow Years

This is Robert's photo of Anna given to Megs as a Christmas present, and subsequently adopted by Willow as the image which was to represent their work and ethos.

The 'Willow' logo was designed by Anna's husband, Mitchell.

Terry Mitchinson, editor
Welwyn and Hatfield Times

Pam Meiklejohn and
Suzanne Brennan,
Willow's first staff

Rosey and Peter Wilkerson, our generous first printers

David Seaman, Willow's first Ambassador with his coach

Swapsball, Back row: George Graham, Natasha Kaplinsky, Bob, Megs, Simon McCoy, Linda Lusardi, Frank McLintock, Mary Nightingale. Front row: Jim Rosenthal, Richard Keys, Richard Dunwoody, September 2002

Ladies Lunch at Brocket Hall. Megs and Rosey Wilkerson with Julia Hawthorne (left) who gave a talk entitled *Knickers through the Ages*

Bob·Wilson

MARATHON MEN BACKING BOB'S CHARITY

Three of the Arsenal staff - and one former staff member - will be running in this year's London Marathon for Arsenal's 'Double' winning goalkeeping coach Bob Wilson. No, Bob hasn't hit hard times, he and his wife Megs have launched a charity in memory of their daughter Anna, who died of cancer a year ago, aged 31.

Anna was a great Arsenal fan and loved her days out at Highbury but the more sick she became the more precious such outings were. The family soon began to realise that special days out helped relieve a lot of the symptoms she had and also lifted the spirits of those around her. The adrenaline that came with the excitement of doing 'normal' things often helped more than the drugs with which she was being treated.

Last August Bob and Megs launched the Willow Foundation, a charity giving special days to seriously ill young adults between the ages 16-40, an area so far untouched. The four Arsenal men, Don Givens (former U19s coach); Neil Banfield (U17s Coach); Lawrence Huthwaite (youth team kit manager) and Kam Bhabra (youth team physio) have chosen to raise money to help the charity by

(L-R) Lawrence, Neil, Don, Bob, Megs and Kam.

running the London Marathon on April 16.

The name of the charity stems from Anna's nickname of Willow, given to her by her husband Mitchell - and the one Bob was known by in his playing days.

Initially the charity is concentrating on the Hertfordshire area, where Anna trained and worked as a Community Nursing Sister. Within three years the aim is to go national, but that will only be possible with the help and generosity of people like Don, Neil, Lawrence and Kam and donations from football fans.

Imagine if everyone here today contributed £1, the Willow Foundation would benefit to the tune £38,000!

If you would like information about the charity and how to apply for special days, please contact the address below and should you wish to help the cause, please send your donation to:

Willow Foundation, c/o Bob Wilson, Goalkeeping Coach, Arsenal Football Club, Avenell Road, Highbury, London N5.

GunnersLine Live Commentary & Ticket News 0906 474 4444 (calls cost 60p per minute at all times)

Arsenal Football Club 1

Encouragement from Robbie Williams after meeting Bob in the Directors Box, Highbury

Harry Redknapp helping Willow raise money in the City

Pat Jennings and David Seaman. Perfect cover for the absent Gazza

Renowned sculptor Frances Segleman creates a likeness of Bob 2005

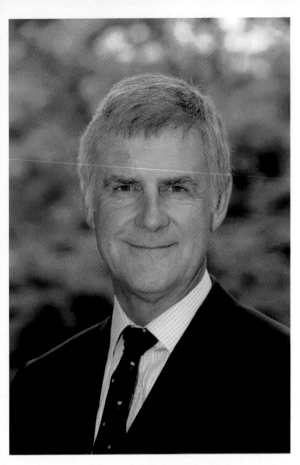

CEO David Williams OBE, who took the charity to national status

David Williams amongst the rubble, as the building was changed from a bank to Willow House

Willow House, and below, Willow staff celebrating 2,506 Special Days

National Launch of Willow: l-r Jim Rosenthal, David Seaman, Natasha Kaplinsky, Megs, Bob, Richard Keys, Gary Mabbutt 2008

National tour, spreading the word, Glasgow. Photo *The Scotsman*

Growth Surge

I remember Anna saying to her dad, when he called round stressed with work at ITV, 'Dad, it's not important.' Well we could see her point, lying there, her hair gone, without the energy to get herself off the sofa. Nothing in life could be more important than time with family and friends. She looked at existence from a new perspective and taught us that quality of life and quality of time were the things that we should hold the dearest.

In 2003 Bob had the opportunity to step out of the world of television that he had worked in for over thirty years. He had reached the top of the tree in two professions and managed to continue his love of all things football by coaching the goalkeepers at Arsenal until his legs finally told him that they too might need to be considered, particularly following two hip replacements.

But the charity had taken over our lives, and the energy and enthusiasm that Bob had always applied to whatever he was doing had been seamlessly transferred to the needs of Willow. We were passionate about getting the message out, to be able to offer the service to as many seriously ill patients as was possible, and making sure we had sustainable funds to be able to provide for the many applications that were now landing on our desks.

To maintain the business model viable over a long period of time, meant we needed to be more professional, more challenging and more imaginative in diversification of fundraising and the delivery of Special Days. Being so close to the product often meant failing to see beyond the obvious, not thinking 'out of the box' and so therefore not moving forward. So by year four it was decided to appoint a CEO who could look at Willow from a different perspective, and refresh the brand and inject some new energy.

Air Commodore David Williams OBE was in the process of retiring after thirty-five years in the RAF when his PA spotted an advert for the CEO position. She encouraged him to apply, knowing that his particular abilities might well fit him for the role. David described his introduction to Willow thus: 'After two rounds of interviews I received a request for a third interview. It was explained to me that the trustees liked me but were worried that I knew nothing about charities. As this was totally true I went on a weekend course – 'How to be a Chief Executive of a charity'. Returning for a further interview I don't think the panel thought this was the same person they had interviewed a few weeks before.'

Although not an obvious choice, as lack of experience weighed heavily against him, he was an easy candidate to appoint as his style was inclusive and respectful, he showed effortless communication skills and self-evident leadership quality. His love of sport was a big plus coming into an environment that relied on our sporting connections, but the one aspect of his life that would provoke much rivalry was his love of Tottenham Hotspur.

David began in June 2003. It must have been a huge shock to his system − coming from commanding thousands of mostly male disciplined service personnel, to a small office inhabited by nine females of diverse backgrounds, all working mainly part time. His dedicated team were as follows:

Pam Meiklejohn – Office Administrator and PA
Suzanne Brennan – Director of Operations
Sue Parslew – Special Days Co-Ordinator
Louise Hickson – Medical Advisor
Annie Lambert – Events Co-ordinator
Lauren Caisley – Event Admin Assistant
Wendy Upton – Press and PR
Debbie Birtwistle – Bookkeeper
Sue Oughton – Admin Assistant

Before his arrival we made sure that everything was clean, tidy and looking quite organised as we imagined his own office to have been. He was welcomed in as the sole male, the only full-time member of staff, who would need to be educated quickly in the current workings of Willow. However, the fact that David had no previous experience of charity brought freshness to Willow and being so well trained in RAF discipline, David was prepared to aim high and be adventurous. He was a quick learner, was keen to succeed and brought renewed energy and determination to make Special Days available to a greater geographical spread.

His arrival enabled me to step back from the everyday running of the charity and it was the beginning of a great working relationship between David, Bob and me. At the time of his arrival Willow was providing 123 days per year; in 2004 it provided 249 and in 2005 it was 407 making a total of 1,021 days completed since the start of Willow.

Over the first six years of Willow's life, Special Days grew organically as we responded to requests that landed on the doorstep. We were used to those coming from all the counties adjacent to Hertfordshire but word of mouth meant that we were receiving applications from as far away as Manchester and Newcastle. We surprised ourselves with our ability to respond with ease and it gave us confidence that we were now ready to step away from the constraints of being regional charity.

In October 2005 Willow was launched as a national charity with much fanfare and publicity at the County Hall Hotel, Westminster Bridge. Natasha Kaplinsky, who had worked alongside Bob on *Breakfast Television*, agreed to be there to give greater credence to the work we were publicising.

It was followed by a countrywide road show promoting our service delivery and reach, educating the medical profession in the benefits of the Special Days that Willow offered. Before the launch we had needed to draw up contingency plans for the surge in applications and be prepared to cope with the increased work that this would involve. But the thought that we would be able to give even more seriously ill young adults a chance of a Special Day drove us on. We began to tour the country, speaking in big city hospitals, meeting with nurses and medical professionals to bring the story of Willow and what it had to offer them in the way of Special Days.

We were in Glasgow at the end of the day and just about to go for a meal when our PA back in the Willow office telephoned. She was beside herself with excitement – we had received an email from Robbie Williams asking Bob to get in touch.

They'd had a chance meeting four years earlier before an Arsenal home game. Before the match Bob had wandered into the Directors' Box to take a look at the ground before it began to fill with fans. Sitting reading the programme was Robbie Williams who looked up at Bob and said 'Oh wow!' to which Bob replied 'Oh wow!'

Robbie had been reading an article in the programme about four of the backroom staff at Arsenal who had chosen to run the London Marathon for Willow, and indicating the aims of the charity. The two began to chat, Bob telling Robbie how much of a fan Anna had been and how she would have loved this moment. They talked about the name Willow and how it was used as a nickname for them both.

'Is your real name Robert?' asked Robbie.

'Yes it is, and presumably it's yours?' said Bob.

'Of course. So you're Robert Wilson and I'm Robert Peter Williams. I don't suppose you're middle initial is P, is it? RPW?'

Bob's heart sank at the thought of revealing his middle name so merely said, 'Yes it is! What a coincidence.'

With that Robbie took hold of the programme and across the article wrote: *To Willow from Willow, With love, Robert P Williams – Robbie.*

To this day, that programme is a precious reminder of that meeting and is framed and hangs in a special place at home.

Four years on and Bob was somewhat surprised to get a message from Robbie asking him to get in touch. He was in Mexico and had been looking through the BBC news website and had come across an article about our tour of the country in publicising the charity and the story of Anna. They had exchanged emails and pleasantries when Robbie wrote: 'When we last met, we talked about having the same initials RPW. But you never told me what your P stood for.'

Bob's heart once again sank and he took a deep breath before replying.

'Well, the P of my middle name stands for er … um … er … um … er … er … Primrose! Quick explanation – Scottish tradition dictates middle name to reflect mother's maiden name! My mother was Catherine Wingate Primrose.'

The reply was immediate. 'Well, er … um … er … um … er – that word just happens to be the one used by our family for a fart!'

Robbie kindly invited us to his next concert at Milton Keynes, where we partied and danced like the teenagers we weren't. Conspicuous as we were, being at least thirty years older than those around us, we had a great time, enjoying the atmosphere that our daughter would have delighted in. As the last song was announced, we decided to leave and the words that Anna had adored followed us all the way to our car.

> *And through it all she offers me protection*
> *A lot of love and affection*
> *Whether I'm right or wrong*
> *And down the waterfall*
> *Wherever it may take me*
> *I know that life won't break me*
> *When I come to call, she won't forsake me*
> *I'm loving angels instead.*

Without Whom ...

You can lead a horse to water but you can't make it drink. Similarly you can set up a charity but you can't provide the service without a level of support. Unless you are a person of means, founding a charity relies on the ability to attract those who can relate to the cause and are enthused by the service provided. Willow had the added advantage of having a founder whose face was familiar, whose reputation was sound and whose character was warm, inviting and well-regarded. 'Your husband is a legend and a gent,' are words repeated to me time and again. I have no doubt that others had opinions of an opposite persuasion, but generally speaking he was respected and brought the right kind of credibility to the charity.

Willow's sustainability was very dependent on the success or otherwise of the fundraising and this in turn was very reliant on the gravitas that Bob brought through his credibility as a footballer and TV presenter. Bob has always been a very good communicator and enjoys interacting with people so it was natural for him to be able to tell the Willow story in a personal way. He was tireless in attending events, giving talks, meeting people who were interested in helping Willow reach its targets. He was the face of Willow and that opened up doors which would otherwise have been closed to us. His network was extensive and such was the respect people had for him, very few requests were turned down and many more were offered up unasked. He was unselfish in his desire to thank those who offered support and would go out of his way to talk to people about the charity, its aims and its objectives. He cried a lot.

In 2003 he published his autobiography charting his career in football and television and told of the deaths of two brothers during the war and the more recent loss of Anna. As a result the story of Willow reached a wider audience and the book was a trigger for several significant meetings that would help shape our future financial security.

Doug Fisher of Leisure Link, a company specialising in golfing holidays was an Arsenal supporter whose wife had undergone treatment for breast cancer and so was linked to Willow on two counts. He could empathise enormously with what we had been through and understood why Willow was such an invaluable charity. He offered to put on a golf competition where supporters and friends could enjoy a few days away playing golf, raising essential funds at the same time. It proved to be so popular that the event has been organised every year since in France, Belgium or the UK and I'm pleased to say that the Bob Wilson Golf Classic continues to this day.

Since our children were young we have taken the majority of our annual holidays on the Algarve in Portugal and this tradition continued with grandchildren. On one particular visit, Bob had taken grandson Louis to the nearest shop to buy a beach ball, when he was stopped by a gentleman who apologised for disturbing his holiday and introduced himself as Roger Riggs.

'I've just read your book and the last chapter about losing your daughter made me cry. I want to support the charity you've set up and when I get home I'll be in touch.'

Bob thanked him for his interest and provided his email address. Having got used to people promising such things Bob never expected to hear from Roger again, so it came as a pleasant surprise that he kept his word. He wanted to put on a dinner in Bristol and a golf day and was intent on spreading the word to the good people of the south-west.

We hadn't taken into account the character of the man, that when Roger had made a promise he would move more than himself to fulfil it. He believed that what we were doing was significant and was even more supportive after meeting those beneficiaries who spoke at each of the events he organised and who voiced the profound effects that their own Special Day had had on them and their family. Over the next fourteen years, Roger continued to repeat his dinners and golf days which not only raised considerable sums but also spread the awareness to many who would never have heard of Willow.

Golf was always going to be included as one of our annual events after the first one had been such a success at Brocket Hall. We were always lucky enough to find a sponsor and those have included Ron, Iris and Steve Unwin, Tony Berry, John Livock, Kevin Keegan and more lately, Duncan Sinclair. Bob played in one of the many other charity matches that he was invited to and was partnered with Duncan who was CEO of a property trading company called Mountview. They got on well despite the fact that Duncan was a huge Tottenham supporter, a minor detail that would always be a source of banter between them.

Duncan was attracted to Willow and expressed an interest in our golf day which he began to attend and eventually sponsor each year. Sadly his lovely wife Pam, a champion swimmer and golfer in her time, suffered a very severe stroke soon after they had built themselves their dream home which contained a huge swimming pool.

Pam and Duncan looked forward to the Willow social calendar and began sponsoring not only the golf, but also the annual Willow Ball. Duncan would sponsor the events but also spent a huge amount of money buying auction prizes, bidding up the lots and helping the totals rise beyond our expectations.

Pam's progress was slow, but she was a determined lady who worked hard at her mobility and speech, which had been seriously impaired by the stroke. They both felt that Willow taught them much about living with her illness: making the most of every day, looking forward to occasions when Pam could dress up, put on a face and join in with the fun.

She always had a smile, and loved being taken on the dance floor in her wheelchair to move around to the music and forget about her disabilities. These were her own Special Days when she could mingle with people she knew and loved and over a period of ten years her progress was remarkable. Her speech improved massively and she would insist on getting up and down stairs on her own, even if it was on her bottom.

It was a very sad day for everyone in 2013 when news came in of Pam's sudden death, just at a time when her quality of life seemed to be improving. Duncan said to Bob, that Willow meant so much to them both and that they had learned how Special Days could impact on Pam with her condition.

In 2015 Duncan took the Willow golf to new heights arranging for the charity to be the main beneficiary of the senior tour when the competition was hosted at Hanbury Manor. The Willow Senior Golf Classic took place on three consecutive years when the Willow logo was beamed through the marvel of TV as a background to much of the play.

Of all the people that have readily supported Willow, Duncan Sinclair showed himself to be a true philanthropist with a generosity of spirit that had few bounds. His willingness to fund golf days and the Willow Ball enabled the charity to open its arms to others who might never have otherwise come into contact with our cause, thus allowing us to spread the word to a wider audience. His contribution over the years helped us provide thousands more Special Days than would otherwise have been possible and we at the charity are deeply grateful for such long-term funding.

Golf has brought on board many people who learned about Willow through attending and playing the game they love. One such is Bob Weston of Weston Homes, a man who believes in our own mantra of enjoying the moment. Bob has a huge heart and loves nothing better than improving other people's lives and his method is quite simple. When attending any event and there is a fundraising mechanism – bid! Bid for memorabilia, for holidays, for dinners, for sailing across the Solent – even if you hate water – and win as many as possible.

Bob Weston's place of work also acts as a gallery where items, which he's purchased at the variety of charity functions he has attended over the years, are displayed; framed boxing gloves, shirts, cricket bats, football boots, golf clubs, all signed by heroes of that particular sport. And if he decides he can do without an item he's purchased, he recycles it and presents it to another charity for them to be able to reap the benefit of a gifted auction item.

The advantage of having an active bidder like Bob Weston in your audience is that an item will very seldom be sold for less than its perceived value. He doesn't always win, but he makes sure that the hard work a charity has put in to sourcing such valuable treasures is not wasted.

Back in 2005 the much-revered sculptor Frances Segelman invited my husband to have his head sculpted in front of an invited audience of like-minded local artists. She wanted Bob to speak about the charity and once the head was finished, would gift the final bronze piece to Willow.

It was an amazing experience to see a skilled artist create a likeness out of lumps of grey clay. Her hands and eyes worked in harmony, the one creating the features that the other could observe. Bob sat close to Frances for two hours and in that time she was able to build, mould and tease her material until it became the recognisable face that was with me every single day.

Another sculptor, Anna White, was there watching with her husband Paul, who was an avid Arsenal supporter. He listened intently as Bob told the story of Anna and how Willow was created, its charitable purpose and the resulting Special Days that were giving such relief to those who were eligible.

Paul approached Bob, telling him that he too would like to support the work that we were doing, and once again, he turned out to be a man of his word. Paul not only put on large fundraising events for Willow, where those in the property world that he inhabited would be in attendance, he also led by example by signing up for an incredible challenge – a triathlon! Never having done anything like this in his life, he set about training and then persuading his colleagues at his company Frogmore to join him.

Since that time, Paul's contribution to Willow's stability has been incalculable. He became the first chair of our development board, introducing the charity to some very influential contacts; he also took part in an extraordinary golf challenge.

On 21 June 2009, the longest day of the year, four men whose ages were 28, 38, 48 and 58 planned to do something never done before. To play 108 holes of golf in one day – not on one golf course, but on six courses, three of which were in the south-east and three in the north-west! The courses had to be those on which The Open was played and there would be only eighteen hours of daylight in which to complete the challenge. Everyone, except those taking part – Paul White, Mike Balfour, Justin Jeffrey and Alistair Hunter – felt that it was an impossible task as the distance between Kent and Lancashire was impossible to cover – unless by helicopter.

The only person we knew who might have the size of helicopter needed for four players, one reserve and all the golf bags, was Michael Owen, the ex-England and Liverpool footballer. He agreed to our request for his pilot to fly the players at a given time from the last of the Kent courses to those in Lancashire, where Bob and I would be waiting to greet them.

The rules were stringent: every hole had to be played and all scores kept and verified. They met in Sandwich as dawn broke and at 4.12am began their marathon rounds of golf playing Prince's Golf Club, followed by Royal St George's at 6.30am and then on to Deal and the Royal Cinque Ports at 9.00am On completion of their round at 12.34pm the helicopter was waiting for the journey to Liverpool and Hoylake Golf Club.

Bob and I had travelled up to Liverpool by car and were awaiting their landing at Hoylake where we greeted them and quickly caught up with the morning's adventurous rounds. The Willow golfers were feeling tired but fired up to complete the challenge they had set themselves. The flight had given them some respite but it was already

1.20pm and the next three courses had to be finished in daylight which would only last until about 9.40pm

From Hoylake they flew to Royal Birkdale near Blackpool where Bob and I were waiting between the eighteenth green and the first tee, where a safe landing space had been designated. What we hadn't taken into account was the very serious match between the Birkdale captain and the captain of another local club who were finishing their round on the eighteenth green. The helicopter landed and the rotor gradually came to a halt allowing the passengers to disembark safely. We all greeted each other with enthusiastic hugs and were in the middle of comparing travel notes, when the Birkdale captain came striding over to berate us all for the terrible distraction it had caused during his putting on the final hole of his match, which he'd subsequently lost!

Finally at 7.15pm, the four competitors hit their balls from the first tee at Royal Lytham & St Anne's, their closing golf course and managed to hit their final shots up the eighteenth fairway in the rapidly fading light.

At 9.50pm we were all drinking champagne on the final green to celebrate an achievement that had never previously been completed. They were exhausted but the thrill of reaching the culmination of weeks of planning kept them happy and buoyed at the thought of all the sponsorship money that they could now claim.

Everyone stayed the night at Dormy House but it wasn't until the next morning that we learned that Paul had spent the night in Blackpool hospital having collapsed in the bath and frightening everyone with thoughts of a heart attack. Fortunately the problem was a result of exhaustion and dehydration and could be quickly righted by hospital infusions. Challenges can be fun, but they can also be extremely physically demanding of the body's resources.

On the 24 February 2016 Bob and I were thrilled to be invited by Paul and Anna to Buckingham Palace to witness Paul receiving an MBE for services to charity from Her Majesty the Queen. His support for many causes is widespread and it was truly wonderful to see this recognised by the awarding of a national honour.

Willow owes Paul White, Duncan Sinclair and Bob Weston a huge debt of gratitude for their unstinting support over many years and for enabling thousands of seriously ill young adults to have a Special Day of their choosing and in doing so experiencing fun and laughter with friends and family. Those without whom Willow would find it difficult to exist come in all disguises and are mainly revealed gradually over a period of time.

Richard Davis was queuing in a bookshop in Bournemouth to get his copy of Bob's autobiography signed. He spoke gently and sincerely and told Bob that he would try to raise some money for the charity that he'd read about in the book. He turned out to have his own building firm and spent his time on such places as tall scaffolding, or surrounded by demolished structures ready to be cleared and rebuilt. He promised nothing, but over the next ten years we witnessed the extraordinary determination of the man and his sincerity in being able to provide for those whose lives serious illness had blighted.

Every few months money would arrive in the office with a brief explanation of where Richard had been and what challenge event he had completed. His energy and athleticism were admirable and the distances he travelled to compete were extraordinary.

In 2018 we presented the 'Willow at Heart Award' to him in recognition of his outstanding support over a ten-year period; he had completed ninety-five extreme events and raised in excess of £80,000. Since his first fundraising exploit in 2008, the Tokyo Marathon, he cycled, climbed, swam and ran his way not just in the UK but on the seven continents and in twenty countries. Every time he competed he paid his own expenses and insisted on getting sponsorship for Willow from friends and business associates. He scaled such heights as Kilimanjaro, cycled the Pyrenees and pounded marathons in New York, Cape Town, Las Vegas, the Arctic Circle and places too numerous to mention. In the twentieth anniversary year of Willow, his aim is to kayak solo around the Isle of Wight and as I write, his training has begun in the hopes of perfecting another sporting skill.

All of the supporters mentioned are among those who look on Willow from the outside, recognise the value of Willow's activities and who have been moved by the work of the charity. But support also comes from the inside, from those who have experienced a Special Day and wish to give something back in thankfulness.

Lee Dunford was seventeen years old and diagnosed with lymphoma. His request came through for a Special Day which Willow quickly organised. His great passion was music and he especially wanted to share his day with his closest friends Adam Tozer and Andrew Heller. The consequence is best described by Adam who continues to embrace the experience:

At 17 you're invincible, or so you would think. Being diagnosed with Hodgkin's Lymphoma at such a pivotal age is incomprehensible.

I remember being physically stunned when Lee told me of his illness. I didn't know how to feel, and it wasn't me that this was all happening to. I sometimes try to imagine what it must have been like for him, but I don't think I could even come close to how he must have felt.

During the four and a half years of his illness Lee underwent several bone-marrow transplants and countless rounds of chemotherapy. Through it all he retained his impeccable sense of humour: always greeting people with a smile and never wanting to be a hassle to anyone. In spite of his illness he lived life to the fullest that he could: playing in gigs with his band, the mighty Postillionage; returning to Sixth-form College at Sudbury Upper; even enrolling in an Open University natural sciences course.

The two days I was lucky enough to spend with him and Andrew in London were amazing. Everything was thoughtfully organised and prepared by the charity. They listened to Lee's requests and ideas and formulated a great trip to the City for us.

It was the summer of 2005 and The Willow Foundation had arranged for us to spend a couple of days in London, with one of them being at Slap Studios, Brixton. They put us up in a five star hotel, the Grosvenor, Marble Arch, and gave us £100 spending money. We travelled down early on the first day in glorious sunshine, and spent it mooching round the music shops off Tottenham Court Road. In the evening we grabbed a bite to eat and went to the Comedy Store.

The next day was the day of the recording session in Brixton. The studio was in an old building, like a converted Victorian warehouse, it was also in the same building that Basement Jaxx has a studio. The engineer, Rory, was a smashing chap that did a great job of producing the track 'Did You Ever?' a band favourite, penned by Liam Steer, and adapted for this such recording by Lee and Andrew. The day flew by, with only occasional stoppages for cups of tea and pizza. In the end we produced a masterpiece of a song with a solid poignancy that hits me every time I listen to it.

I will cherish the memories of those two days forever, as I'm sure will anyone else who has benefitted from the work of the Willow Foundation.

LeeStock [Festival] is a great and positive thing to come out of such a tragedy as losing Lee. It's such a fitting testament to the guy, as he loved music and socialising, and a fantastic way to give back to charity and help others in need.

Lee was, is, and will always be, an inspiration.

Adam Tozer

That inspiration moved Lee's friends, Edd, Matt and Pete Keogh to create music for public viewing in a village hall attended by 300 people in order to raise money for Willow and naming it LeeStock. It was so successful that they repeated it a second year but this time as a two day event. But they had no idea just how popular they would become or how LeeStock would evolve on the back of their enthusiasm and organisational skills. Each year saw more demand for the event and each year the friends stretched themselves to put on a bigger and even better festival, first at the local White Hart pub, where they turfed the whole car park, and eventually to the grounds of the National Trust property of Melford Hall, Suffolk.

Thirteen years later the LeeStock Music Festival features well-known bands that perform to more than 3000 individuals and families over the weekend, camping and enjoying the amazing facilities offered. And because of the hard work and dedication of Lee's friends, over £170,000 has been raised so that other seriously ill young adults can have a Special Day of their own choosing. It is the most wonderful tribute friends could ever pay to someone who inspired them and taught them so much about how to react to adversity with positivity and enjoyment. Lee's parents Rob and Rosie Dunford lost a beloved son, but they are so proud of the festival of music which brings fun and laughter to many thousands and which his friends have lovingly created in his memory.

There are so many more people who have supported us through the years, too many to mention individually, but our gratitude to them is no less real for their dedication and loyalty in raising funds and awareness of Special Days.

Teenage Angst

I had been regularly advised by trustee Kate Baldwin to beware of 'Founder's Syndrome'; where the person or persons who originally founded the charity hold too much power and influence following the initial establishment of the organisation. She had become aware of how toxic this could be.

Despite the personality and passion that founders may display initially, division and discord may arise and ultimately have the effect of limiting further growth or bringing failure. The trustees at the start are usually friends and colleagues who wish to support the original cause but this too can eventually restrict the capability of the organisation in growing in an organic way.

During Willow's infancy the team, consisting of trustees and volunteers, literally made it up as they went along. They sought advice and listened but we were in new territory creating an outlet for a need which had not previously been recognised. No one before us had proposed a concept for providing Special Days for this particular age group. We had to devise a vision, a mission, structure, strategies, governing documents, application forms, a logo, accounts, a website, an Advisory Board, a Development Board and a thousand other necessary practicalities. The workable vision had to be understood and communicated to everyone who joined the organisation.

With David Williams at the helm and my position as Chair of Trustees still on-going we seemed to have the charity really well established with a team that fitted together like the perfect jigsaw. We had moved from our original office in Sylvia Adams House and, with an amazing donation of £500,000 through Michael Spencer's 2003 ICAP charity day, we were eventually able to purchase a stand-alone building in Old Hatfield which we called Willow House. It was a converted bank, and offered us so much more space to grow following the national launch.

We now had areas for staff to take breaks and eat lunch in a dedicated kitchen space, for trustees to meet within the charity's own walls, and for Special Days and fundraising teams to have their own designated office areas – we were beginning to look more professional and with that came a new confidence that we could make Willow a substantial enterprise.

But no matter what else happened, the biggest boost to us all were the letters we were receiving from those who had experienced a Special Day. They constantly echoed our own experiences with Anna and emphasised that the Special Day had given them the excitement of expectation, some wonderful memories, and helped bring normality back into their lives at a time when it was most needed.

The majority of requests were very simple: a chance for friends and family to enjoy time together during weekends away, sporting occasions, concerts and family parties, though occasionally there was something quirky or it took so much more effort to put together.

A request came through for a night in a haunted castle, something the recipient had always wanted, and eventually the venue was found in Northumberland. We arranged a Ghost Tour and an overnight stay at Chillingham Castle, which is widely regarded as one of the most haunted places in the country with hundreds of paranormal events being recorded.

But the one that caused everyone at Willow to put on their thinking caps was the request from a lady in Portsmouth. It was nearing Christmas and, being very ill, she was confined to the local hospice. But what she wanted more than anything else was to see her young children playing in the garden at home in snow, on Christmas morning. There wasn't much time as this was the week before, so the staff started making enquiries as to who could transport real snow to the south coast ready for Christmas morning.

They tried snow-makers, snow domes, snow slopes from the north of Scotland to the south of England. All presented difficulties with the snow, transportation and the date, with the added problem that it was unusually mild. But the emotional appeal of the request and the thought of what it would mean to the mother spurred the staff on ensuring they researched every possibility. The whole office came together in an attempt to find a solution to fulfilling the request.

It came in the guise of Coca-Cola. They were running a competition to 'have your garden filled with snow' as the first prize and it was spotted by one of the Willow staff who asked the company if they would consider doing a second garden. Sadly it couldn't be done on Christmas Day as no one would be working, but they suggested Christmas Eve. The relief all round was huge and the team set about making sure all other details were organised. An ambulance was arranged to collect the lady from the hospice and take her back later that day. Harrods agreed to send a Christmas hamper and Woolworths, who were still in business, sent warm clothes for the children to wear as they played snow-balls and ran around enjoying their own special winter – on what was a fairly mild day!

Lorryloads of snow arrived early morning and one by one the trucks deposited their cargo across the back garden – which was not small by any means. A Christmas tree was placed in the middle of the lawn and once it was all ready the ambulance arrived bringing the mother home.

The office received a call from her trying to express just how much it meant to her. 'Thank you, thank you all of you for making this amazing day – I now believe in Father Christmas!' Everyone was relieved that it had gone well and that the various elements to the day came together. Many phone calls had been made, before and after, thanking those who pulled out all the stops to achieve what had seemed impossible. We were all very saddened when we were informed of her death soon after but happy that we had raised a smile and made some memories.

Often the simplest of days has the most lasting effect and nothing illustrates this better than the instance of a lady, again nearing the end of her life, who asked if we could arrange a casting of her hand so that when she was no longer there to be with her children, they could put their hands in hers for comfort.

The gentleman who agreed to do the casting arrived with a bucket and mixed the contents to a paste as the lady reached her arm down into the soft warm mixture to create the mould. The cast would eventually stand in an upright position so that as the children walked past it, they could hold on to their mother's hand and remember her touch. It was the first time we had been requested such a day but, for the Day Maker who arranged everything, it was one of the most moving. She later received the following letter:

Dear Rachel

My beautiful wife Val, died aged 37yrs at The Hospice of St Francis in Berkhamsted in Aug 2009. She fought a brave battle against breast cancer but died after many opportunities to make so many special memories for me and our two young boys Matt and Alex who are now aged 9 and 11yrs. Val never was able to see Matt start secondary school in his new uniform this year, but with the memories that charities such as Willow Foundation created for us and other families like us we had so many special times in the months leading to her death.

Willow Foundation created the opportunity for a specialist company to come to our house to take some hand castings. It was quite a funny afternoon as we were all covered in goo whilst the people made the casts in our kitchen. It has been a special memory for us to hold now, the boys often talk about how messy it was and how fun it was.

The finished product was a beautiful bronze style casting of all 4 of our hands entwined together. It remains at the boys request on the hearth in our front room. Val also wished to have 2 individual hand casts made so that the boys could always hold her hand if they wished during sad times. Only last night, before I knew of any of this, Matt was holding her hand whilst he played on the computer. It is a great source of comfort and positive memories for such young boys who miss their mum terribly. I like to hold her hand too!!

The charity put this request together very quickly for us through the Hospice and the whole procedure took place in a couple of weeks. It was truly amazing and is obviously a great source of comfort to me too, knowing that Val had successfully managed to fulfil another of her many ambitions for us.

With many kind wishes to you all.

Yours sincerely

Paul Kingdon, Matt and Alex

It is words like these that mean so much not only to those who work to create these days, but to those who support us by helping to provide the funds to underpin the infrastructure of such an organisation. The letters are a huge source of strength and an endorsement of the positive effect a Special Day can have not only on the recipient, but on the whole family. If the one who is ill can smile, it infects those around and helps them cope with all the trivial hindrances they face.

One day in November 2007 a very formal confidential letter arrived home addressed to Bob. It came from the Secretary for Appointments at number 10 Downing Street and said:

The Prime Minister has asked me to inform you, in strict confidence, that, having accepted the advice of the Cabinet Secretary and the expert Honours Committees, he proposes, on the occasion of the forthcoming list of New Year Honours, to submit your name to The Queen with a recommendation that Her Majesty may be graciously pleased to approve that you be appointed an Officer of the Order of the British Empire.

Before doing so the Prime Minister would be glad to know that this would be agreeable to you.

Bob was stunned and a little concerned. He realised that this award was for his tirelessly devoted work in helping to found Willow and was very appreciative of the nomination, but he said that there was no way he could accept it. He felt that it should be me that had the recognition saying, 'I am only the face of Willow, you are the one that did all the work'. He was upset that we hadn't both been included in the award and said he would turn it down. It took quite a lot of persuading before he agreed to accept it on behalf of all those who had helped to create Willow; those who would be proud to receive acknowledgement of our efforts and pleased that our 'figurehead' would be the one to shine a light on the charity itself.

We were able to surprise the family around the Christmas dinner table with the news before it was announced in the New Year Honours list. And all we could then do was wait and see when Bob would be receiving his award. It was rather unfortunate that the date set for the investiture at Buckingham Palace was the 25 June 2008, only ten days after I had an operation for a replacement ankle. But after communications with the Palace we were able to reassure our sons Robert and John, who would be accompanying us, that because I would be in a wheelchair, we would get preferential treatment over everyone else!

The special car park ticket arrived and instructions to go the Choirmaster's Door where we would be met by a Palace official, which we duly did. All other guests were using the main entrance and the red staircase but we would be treated as special! Arriving on crutches and in a large surgical boot was not ideal and my outfit for the occasion had to be based on wide-legged trousers and a large hat to distract attention from the encased leg. I sat myself into the wheelchair the Palace had kindly provided and kept reiterating to the boys, 'Stick with me and you'll be treated as special'.

We entered the Choirmaster's Door to be faced by six steps; at the bottom was the largest stairlift I have ever encountered. I was wheeled on to it and waited for the action. Slowly, very slowly, the stairlift took me to the top of the flight. I hardly dare look at my family knowing what might be going through their heads – this was not quite the entrance I had in mind! At the top we turned to face the doors of a small lift which opened to allow us in. It was very tight, my large hat being squashed against the sides, as the official said proudly, 'You are now in the lift in which the Queen's lunch is delivered every day.' I was wheeled out to join the other guests on their way to the ballroom, I said, 'See, I told you it'd be special.'

Even if the entrance wasn't what I had imagined, the rest of the day lived up to expectations. Tradition is often the glue that binds a nation and that day was a huge insight into the workings of an investiture. Military precision and pageantry was noticeable in every moment from the time we were invited to be seated until the end of the event.

The National Anthem was played and the Queen entered the room attended by two Gurkha orderly officers, a tradition begun by Queen Victoria in 1876. The Queen's Body Guard of the Yeomen of the Guard were in attendance and the military band played a variety of music while the recipients were called forward one by one by the Lord Chamberlain.

Because I was in a wheelchair, we had a prime view − front row for me and the seats immediately behind me for the boys. 'There, you see, I told you the wheelchair would make it special!' However, the boys became very concerned about me in the middle of the ceremony when they saw my shoulders shaking. 'You all right, Mum?' they asked, assuming the emotion had got to me and I was crying. But I was trying to control a fit of the giggles that overpowered me at the sight of some of the recipients' unbalanced bows and over-rehearsed curtseys.

Each person was made to feel that their moment was singular and when Bob approached the Queen, she told him that she understood that it was he who had founded Willow. He explained that we had done it together and she offered her hearty congratulations and pinned to his lapel his much-deserved OBE. On our way out the boys declined the offer of the lift and said they would rather use the grand staircase and take in the royal ambience. They would meet us in the courtyard. Bob kindly stayed with me until we had negotiated the backstairs exit.

Family pride was on full show that day; sons for their father and wife for her husband captured beautifully on camera. I abandoned the crutches and the wheelchair, determined not to spoil the photographs that would be a reminder of our very own special day.

It was about this time that I felt my own position at Willow needed reviewing. After steering the charity as Chair of Trustees for nine years, I was very anxious to avoid Founder Syndrome setting in, so decided it was time to step down and allow someone else to take hold of the wheel. It would be good to have a new pair of eyes to appraise the organisation and bring greater experience to the table and expand the service further.

We set up a recruitment drive to find a suitable candidate and soon appointed Tina Tietjen, someone with both corporate and charity experience, whilst Bob and I settled into our new roles as Founder Presidents. The original founding trustees had gradually stepped down and new ones had been appointed in their place. Willow was beginning to change in many ways and I had to learn to accept that it wouldn't always be my baby. Decisions would be made that I didn't always agree with and I began to realise that some were for the good. But there were some that I really couldn't stand by and let happen, particularly if they would damage the very sound vision and values upon which Willow had been built.

This also coincided with the financial crash of 2007/8 which affected not only banks, businesses, personal wealth, mortgages and the stock market, but the income of all charities. Supporters could no longer give their spare change to great causes, or spend their corporate budgets on entertaining, so the income that we relied on so heavily began to decrease, which ultimately was reflected in the number of Special Days we were able to grant. Over the next four years our totals dropped from 1,395 to just 777 but we were determined to work hard to maintain both value and quality.

At the very onset we were lucky enough to have a fundraising team led by Suzanne Brennan, who was brilliant and probably could have managed Willow single handed. Over the early years she helped forge the Special Days department into an efficient machine. Creativity was her forte and her imaginative thinking saw her fashion each department in turn from Fundraising to Communications.

She started a Willow newsletter, creating a modern and more professional look for all our letter-heads and logos and infected the rest of the staff with her enthusiastic innovative ideas. Each year she came up with concepts which we hoped would attract a range of different audiences who might also spread the word, as well as offering opportunities for supporters to find diverse ways of giving to Willow.

Brocket Hall was the main venue for Evenings With, but we also hosted Ladies Lunches where talks were given by the hilarious Rosemary Hawthorne on *Knickers Through the Ages*, Hilary Alexander of the *Daily Telegraph* on *Fashion* and the wonderful Gloria Hunniford, who had similarly experienced the loss of her daughter Caron to cancer.

But Suzanne saw the art world as an avenue to explore. She created Impact Art where famous sports-people directed their ball, glove, golf club through paint in order to create a unique canvas. Sportography was a huge collection of iconic sporting photographs all signed by the sportsperson and displayed and auctioned at an exhibition at Bonhams. Stars on Canvas invited artists, celebrities, architects and children's illustrators to decorate in their own way a canvas 9"x9", to be exhibited and auctioned on ebay. Just One Word was an initiative where well known photographers were invited to photograph Special Day recipients and illustrate the one word that they used to describe their day. Keepsakes exhibited photographs whereby the subject was pictured with a particular item that meant much to them. Ozzy Osbourne, Professor Robert Winston, Sir Alex Ferguson, John Cleese and many more celebrities as well as Special Day recipients, were all willing to sit and have their portrait taken holding or wearing their keepsake. I was asked to participate and delighted at the chance of donning Anna's original denim waistcoat, onto which she had sewn and pinned her collection of Arsenal badges. A photo-shoot with son Robert saw me sitting inside the giant concrete A of Arsenal against the background of the Emirates Stadium.

That particular period became a difficult balancing act between the push for expanding our fundraising, which always had to be reinvented and refreshed, and keeping up the quality of Special Days. We would never let standards decline as recipients only ever had the chance of one Special Day, and that day had to be for ever sealed in their memories as unforgettable.

It was the letters from those who had also experienced all Anna had taught us, which continued to be the energy behind Willow – letters like this:

> We first became aware of the Willow Foundation when my Husband had been admitted into hospital having being taken seriously ill. I genuinely didn't think that there would have been anything that would have put a smile on his (or my) face at that time. However, planning our special day with our young family made us think beyond chemotherapy, consultants and hospitals which was such a relief at that time. It gave us something as a family to aim for, for this we are immensely grateful.
>
> The break away to Center Parcs was the BEST holiday ever! We genuinely had to keep pinching ourselves that a charity had organised the whole thing, even our dog Webster came with us.

The time spent as a 'normal' family was precious and Alan and I along with our 2 children had an amazing time.

When someone has cancer the world revolves around that person getting better and everyone else gets pushed to one side, children included. You brought my family together and for that a simple thank you seems worthless. I know it sounds soft but the Willow Foundation restored my faith in people again as you begin to question everything when someone you love gets diagnosed with something that may kill him. You made us feel special and helped us enjoy quality time together to make us realise what is truly important.

I know this is yet another cancer survival story and I have gone on a bit, however, I wanted you to realise how much your charity helped us deal with what was happening to us. Without giving Alan something to focus on in hospital it would have made it a great deal harder for him to keep strong. For that I give you the most heartfelt thank you I think I have ever given someone.

Reading such words was emotional for everyone and testament to why we worked so hard. It gave us the impetus to create more and more Special Days for those in need. Willow was experiencing some difficult times, which we managed to resolve and overcome, but I didn't see the dark clouds that were gathering on the horizon, and were to bring more personal anguish to the Wilson family.

Celebrating Robert's 40th birthday. l-r John, Debbie, Megs, Tessa, Sarah, Robert, Mitchell, Bob

Mitchell and Debbie Carey

Early golf sponsors, Steven and mother Iris Unwin

Sharon Dyer, one of Willow's earliest and most loyal supporters with Bob and Megs

Nervous time; waiting in the
wings of the annual ball to
update the Willow story

Pam Sinclair, wife of Duncan,
who always felt that Willow
taught her much about
living with illness

Paul White and team in the midst of the Open Golf Courses Challenge. June 2009

Mission accomplished, as daylight fades. 18th green Royal Lytham & St Anne's

Paul White together with his wife Anna at Buckingham Palace, after receiving his MBE in 2016

Pat Jennings with Duncan Sinclair, whose support and sponsorship took Willow to new heights

Bob Weston of Weston Homes, a supporter whose generosity to Willow knows no bounds

Staff, trustees and volunteers celebrating 10 years of Willow, 2009

Willow volunteers cheering on our runners at the London Marathon

Thierry Henry taking part in the *Impact Art* project

Dennis Bergkamp creating his own canvas for *Impact Art*

Display of contributions to our *Stars on Canvas* exhibition

Robert with his contribution to
Just One Word

Megs, photographed by son Robert at the Emirates Stadium. Anna's denim waistcoat with Arsenal badges, for *Keepsakes* project

OBE for Bob at Buckingham Palace, 25 June 2008

Bob Wilson's Soccer Cycle begins at Craven Cottage, home of Fulham FC. l-r David Tweddell, Bob, Steve Cliffen, 18 April 2011

Grandsons Tom and Max wish Papa luck for his 530 mile ride

The cast of Val Kingdon's hand for her sons to hold, the most poignant of Special Day requests

A Special Day at Cranwell for Beth Ritson looping the loop, which brought unexpected delight 2013

Willow *Herts100* bike ride attracts all modes of cycles!

Fun and enthusiastic cheers for finishers of the Willow *Herts100* bike ride

Amazing Willow supporter Richard Davis on the summit of yet another mountain

Richard Davis with well deserved *Willow at Heart Award* November 2018

Bob outside our first Willow shop
in Welwyn Garden City

Ian Wright winning *Outstanding
Contribution to London Football* 2018,
photo Robert Wilson

Spurs Manager Mauricio Pochettino
winning *Manager of the Year* 2019, photo
Action Images

– both awards presented at the
Willow *London Football Awards*

Jackie Scully and Duncan getting married on the Cutty Sark before running the London Marathon

Jackie and Father of the Bride finishing the London Marathon. Photo *Virgin Money*

The happenstance moment on Lions Head, Cape Town. Bob leans on the fence then realises the word Willow is carved into the wood

The Wilson family gather at Megs' birthday May 2017. Back row l-r: Megs, Tessa (holding Jock), Louis, Ali (Louis' girlfriend) John, Bob. Front row l-r: Robert, Max (holding Charlie), Georgie, Tom, Sarah

Bob and his Mum, whose positive philosophy has always guided the family

Live a Life you Love

The past year had brought challenges to the whole of the charity sector and it was no surprise that in January 2010 Tina Tietjen decided to step down as Chair of Trustees. She had successfully steered the charity over a two year period that needed careful governance and a tight hold on the financial reins. I was relieved that Willow had been in steady hands during a very rocky period with someone who could stay calm and collected during testing times.

In the event, Richard King took over as Chair, an accountant by profession, working as a Managing Partner at Ernst and Young, bringing commercial and operational expertise to the board, and it was only by witnessing other people's skill at chairing the committee that I realised that my decision to step down was the right one. I had been the correct choice at the beginning and for most of Willow's infancy, but it was becoming a larger beast baring its teeth and at times needed a more experienced hand than mine to deal with it.

There was much discussion to be had as to the roles that Bob and I now had to play and just how much time we could spend away from our fundraising and promotional duties. We would never step away from what we had created, but we had to gradually let others take over the running of the charity for us to be able to spend more time with family.

Our grandchildren had arrived thick and fast. John's son Louis was the only one born when Anna was alive and the only one that had her attention at a time when she herself was denied the possibility of ever having children of her own. But now the family had grown into a very different dynamic. Robert and Sarah had married the year after Anna had died and Mitchell, being Robert's best man, made sure that plenty of humour was brought to the proceedings. Rob and Sarah gave us two more grandsons to love and adore – Tom and Max - whilst Mitchell and Debbie were blessed with two sons of their own, Dylan and Euan. After John and Jane parted they both moved on. John married Tessa who gave birth to Georgie giving Louis a much loved half-sister and since Tessa already had two children, Max and Maya, our family had grown delightfully beyond all our expectations. There were now so many lives to share, so many young people to watch grow and develop in their own unique ways that we were able to appreciate the closeness of a loving family.

Robert and Sarah had booked a villa holiday in Portugal during the August holidays but Robert, being a freelance commercial photographer, was always at the beck and call of any large jobs that came his way. Thus it was that he landed a particularly important and well-paid assignment which would take him to South America for three weeks but which sadly cut right across the Portugal holiday. The boys Tom and Max were still quite young, energetic and loved activity no matter where they were. It was decided that in order to help Sarah, her mum would stay with her the first week and we would fly over for the second week.

It was a lovely chance to be with them in the sunshine and be able to join in with fun and games both at the villa and the beach. Robert was able to keep in touch although much of the time he was beyond contact as he travelled through the mountain terrain of Peru towards Brazil.

Our holidays had always included a visit to the Algarve, ever since our own children were young, so we were familiar with the area both inland and by the coast. And it was to the sea that we went at the end of the week, taking the boys on to the beach where we made sandcastles and swam in the cool Atlantic.

We went to one of our favourite restaurants for lunch, Julia's, where we could find shade and have a rest from the exertions of beach games. We had just ordered our meal when my phone began to ring and I was surprised by the caller's name: Paulene Carey, Mitchell's mum.

'Hi Paulene, this is a surprise, we're in Portugal.'

I still find the words she spoke quite the most distressing I had heard. They changed our mood, they changed our world, and they changed the very symmetry of our lives.

'Megs, Mitchell's died.'

I always thought that seeing people in films collapse as a reaction to bad news was a complete exaggeration, but the words ripped away a part of me that had always been my link to Anna. Mitchell had continuously been there at every step of Anna's journey, her consultations, her operations, her setbacks and her roller-coaster ride. He was the one who made us all laugh, who had the most unique way of putting life into a different focus, of changing the dials from off to on. Following Anna's death, he had continued to be in touch, sometimes phoning me just to talk at moments of doubt or despair or even in times of joy. We had a special bond that would never be broken and his own joy at finding Debbie and in becoming a father of two sons seemed to be recompense for all that had gone before.

The ache in my chest was real, the thoughts racing through my mind were spinning with despair and my physical reaction shocked those around me. It was hard to take in the whys and hows as Paulene explained to me what had happened. She had been such a wonderful mother-in-law for Anna and now here she was, telling me of her own son's death. She'd had no warning; no time to understand that death might be an option, no preparation for what 'might' could ultimately bring. Hers was the greater loss, but she was the one who was calm in delivering the news.

Food became superfluous and we left Julia's, all devastated by the news. At the time, the shock was all encompassing but it never occurred to me to soften my reaction to the news for the sake of Tom and Max. I have often thought since that this must have been as shocking for them, just witnessing our reactions.

Our first thoughts were of how we could relay the news to Robert, out in South America travelling from country to country on his shoot. What sort of effect would it have on him? He of all people had such a bond, such an understanding and a love of the madness that was Mitchell.

We had travelled no more than half a mile in the car on the way back to the villa when my phone rang. It was Robert sounding very distant and quizzical. He had noticed a missed call from us but more strangely two from Justin, Mitchell's brother. This was going to be a difficult conversation and it was everything we feared. The effect of distress was obvious, even from half a world away. Robert's instant reaction was, 'I'm coming home.' He couldn't bear to be anywhere else other than close to Mitchell.

Sarah is a lucid and sensible person, one who will think through a situation and be able to rationalise logically and soundly. We were thankful that she was able to persuade Robert that there was absolutely no value in his coming home, abandoning probably the best job he had ever had, as there would be some time before more was known about Mitchell's death.

Debbie, the boys and Mitchell had returned from a wonderful sailing holiday around the Greek Islands. Just before they came home, Mitchell had trodden on a sea urchin, a pretty painful experience and rumour had it that this was the cause.

From what we could gather he had collapsed at work twenty-five minutes after eating a corned beef sandwich and was rushed to the Lister Hospital in Stevenage with suspected food poisoning, but discharged the same day after being given painkillers to treat stomach cramps and diarrhoea.

The following day he received an injection from his GP to treat the sickness that had continued all night, but had to be rushed back to hospital after collapsing at home. Doctors resuscitated him after he suffered a heart attack in A and E but he never recovered and was pronounced dead thirty-six hours later on 18 August.

We couldn't believe what we were hearing, not only about Mitchell's death, but the irony that he had been treated at the very same Accident and Emergency where he had witnessed the trauma of Anna's death. How cruel, how tragic and how heart-breaking that Debbie and the boys should lose him so early in their life together in such a dramatic way.

But if we were surprised by the events that were unfolding, we should not have been surprised by the reaction of the press. It was only the day after it had happened when Debbie, in deep shock and distress, went to answer a knock on her front door. She was in her dressing gown and was greeted by a young reporter wanting to know more about her husband's death – and could she confirm that he had been married to Anna and was Bob Wilson's ex-son-in-law!

We had immediately returned from Portugal and once home I had a call from Justin warning us that the press were wanting to speak to Bob and were trying to find him. He was cleaning the car so I warned him but at that very moment, a young woman approached him and asked if he would like to say a few words about Mitchell's death.

There is no tact in seeking out a story and no sentiment in reporting it, as long as the headline can grab the attention. This was Mitchell's family's tragedy and the last thing they needed was mindless press banging on the door asking inconsiderate questions.

But there were many questions that Debbie needed to ask. She resolved to seek out the truth of what happened over that distressing period of time. She was the one who had been with Mitchell, had seen his intense pain, his vomiting, his heart attack in the ambulance, his fight for life over those long tortuous hours and his last breaths in hospital. She would seek out the truth and find out that if anything different had been done, could his life have been saved.

We all gathered at Knebworth village church to say our farewells on the 27 September, five weeks after he had died. His family did him proud with the most amazing remembrance service, reflecting his personality, his charisma and his sense of humour. And Robert was able to stand up and give his particular tribute to the person he loved and admired most next to his own family:

> *To meet Mitchell was to know Mitchell. One meeting was usually all it would take to fall in love with him. The outpouring of emotion, grief, disbelief at his passing is testament to the person he was. He was a one off, he was unique. He would change the dynamic of any room just by walking into it.*
>
> *That wicked sense of humour and incredible charisma went hand in hand, and everyone that knew him has a story to tell. For instance, only Mitchell would think of, and get away with, gift wrapping a telephone box. Not in a slaphappy vandal way, but with care, attention, pride and leaving it so that you could still insert your 10 pence piece and use the phone. He once wallpapered the outside of a school sixth form block. If the pattern on the paper didn't match up, the piece would have to come down and he would start again.*
>
> *As for charisma, he could hold any crowd captive for hours. If Mitchell was on a roll, it would be a night you would never forget. I remember not too long ago we were at the 02 Arena to watch the Foo Fighters, having been invited by the guitar technician. Whilst we sat at the bar before the gig, Mitchell had convinced a group of, what had started out as rather loud aggressive blokes, that he was in fact Dave Grohl's long lost English half brother. The charade was only enhanced when we sauntered off through the back stage door and on to the side of the stage. In fact, the only time that group of blokes might have had their suspicions was when he convinced himself and me, that we should follow the band out to centre stage half way though the gig. The sight of us being dragged back stage by a group of burly security guards was probably enough for those guys to realise that they were in fact in the presence of one of the great storytellers.*
>
> *Stories about Mitchell will either have you in tears of sadness or tears of joy. He covered the whole spectrum; there were no half measures.*
>
> *He was the smartest, most empathetic, compassionate guy most of us will ever meet. He had a knack of filtering out the good from the bad, the important from the banal. With him by your side it felt like that no problem was too big and no challenge too difficult.*

And what now?

Now we grieve. Don't be afraid to shed many tears for Mitchell. If ever there was a person who deserved a lifetime of happiness with their beautiful family, it was he. People like him don't come around too often. We have all been blessed by his presence. He was one of the true greats and his loss is one that deserves to be mourned with all our hearts.

If you knew Mitchell, then a piece of you will always be Mitchell and with that piece there lies a responsibility. His loss leaves a void so large it can never be filled, so use the love we have for him to help those most affected by his absence, for he was a son, a brother, a husband and a dad.

The only way to try and make sense of his passing is to ask the question, 'What is more important, is it the years you spend on this planet or the way you choose to use them?' Forty-three years feels cruel and premature, but my god how he shone during that time!

He once told me that if I ever missed him, I should reload and try again. He always had a quote for you and usually from his favourite songs.

Live a life you love, use a god you trust, and don't take it all too seriously.

Love and Rockets Mitchell

We miss you.

It wasn't until 1 February 2011 that Mitchell's family had to sit through the findings of an inquest at Hatfield Coroner's Court. It initially found that Mitchell had died from an extremely rare form of food poisoning after eating a corned beef sandwich.

He had suffered multiple organ failure after contracting clostridium perfringens type A, a condition that had only been recorded seven times across the world. The court heard that Mitchell had collapsed only twenty-five minutes after eating the sandwich and was rushed to hospital but discharged after being given painkillers to treat stomach cramps and diarrhoea. By the time he was taken to hospital a second time his liver, heart and lungs were in such a bad state nothing could have kept him alive.

Gastroenterology specialist Dr Martin Carter, who worked at the Lister Hospital, told the inquest: 'I've never seen a case of clostridium perfringens in the blood in my entire medical career.'

Coroner Edward Thomas recorded a narrative verdict, and said:

'Rarity creates sadness and unexpectedness.'

However, it later transpired, after more microbiological tests, that the poisoning had not come from the corned beef, but from meat he had eaten the day before he left Greece forty-two hours before his collapse.

The traumatic time that Debbie had spent with Mitchell, watching him in such pain and being so ill over two days, has to be one of the very worst experiences anyone could go through. But she had to return to her boys, Dylan, nine and Euan, seven, and make sure they would all cope with the loss of a larger-than-life father and husband. Mitchell would be proud of the way she managed and of how she continues to live her life with smiles and laughter.

As I look at the photograph taken on Anna's and Mitchell's wedding day, it is hard to comprehend that two young people who had so much going for them could both have their lives ended by some rare form of illness. But the mark they made on this earth during their relatively short lives will endure through generations. 'I want quality of life and quality of time, but most of all I want to have fun,' were Anna's first words after being diagnosed. It was her and Mitchell's mantra and we will always do our best to keep that at the forefront of our minds.

Adolescence

During the seven years of David Williams' tenure as CEO the number of Special Days rose to an amazing 1,350 with a staff of forty and an income of £2.5 million per year. He didn't sit behind a desk and issue orders. He rolled up his sleeves and dived into the work of making Willow a vibrant charity available to all who were eligible. He made sure that, as the charity charged towards its adolescence it was secure in its foundations and basic values. And thank goodness it was, as the financial problems of the world were having a toxic effect on donations and fundraising in general. His CEO report for December 2009 shouted louder about the financial turmoil that charities were facing more than anything I can write.

> *Twelve months ago the Willow Foundation faced its most demanding year – a proposed deficit budget to cover an expected increased number of special days in an extremely difficult fundraising climate. There is no question that 2009 has been the most difficult twelve months in the Charity's ten-year history but I think we can look back with a degree of satisfaction that we came through relatively unscathed.*
>
> *The Charity is judged on its special days and in 2009 we funded and organised more special days than ever before; 1325 days were provided and, although the quantity is short of the target that we set at the beginning of the year, the quality did not drop. However, we have been able to lower the average cost of the days by compiling the days with extra efficiency and by aggressive purchasing whenever appropriate.*
>
> *The primary reason for the drop in numbers was because the income in the first quarter was so disappointing; a decision was taken to drastically reduce the profile-raising work of the Medical Advisors. As we moved into the second half of the year the Medical Advisors picked up the pace and are now promoting the Charity again.*
>
> *In January we faced a deficit of £435,000. Internal cost-cutting measures followed and we have been able to reduce the anticipated deficit month on month. We end the year with a deficit of £139,349, but even a born optimist would not have predicted such a change in fortune. Income was down but expenditure was down by a far greater margin. The adverse financial climate has had a significant detrimental effect on events and, in particular,*

sponsorship. This problem will not go away in the near future and so we are reducing the heavy reliance that we have always placed on our historic big earner of major events and realigning more effort towards trusts and individuals.

David and the team worked incredibly hard that year to stabilise the downturn in income and were successful in making sure that Special Days would not suffer any loss of quality despite the decrease in funding. At the end of 2010 he stepped down as CEO but continued to work for Willow for another seven years in a capacity that made use of his amazing ability to organise the important sporting events that the charity relied on for income. His life in the RAF had seen him serve in many places including Berlin, Moscow, the Gulf war commanding 55 Squadron, Akrotiri and Belgium. His experiences were scary, dangerous and exciting. It was David who, with his adventurous spirit, led Willow into its adolescence with values and purpose intact and for that will be for ever grateful.

Gill Edelman was appointed in his place and one of the very first tasks she had to deal with was Bob's determination to set a good example to the rest of our supporters by raising a large amount of money via a challenge. Bob himself wrote:

> *It started with thoughts about how I could celebrate my seventieth birthday, how would I mark the year, the day? A family lunch and a weekend away sounded perfect but I was restless to do more. I'm not overtly sentimental, but it was basically the numbers – my 70th/71st year was so synonymous with my football career – winning the "Double" in 1970/71.*
>
> *Football, television and my family have been my life but I wanted to celebrate by raising money for Willow. We've always enjoyed cycling but it was very much a pastime, a pleasant way to spend a Sunday afternoon – never a serious interest. How could I combine cycling with football in order that Willow might benefit? The answer – I'd visit every Premier League club, meet old rivals, relive memories, raise the profile of the charity and its work and, through sponsorships, raise £25,000 for Willow.*

Two great friends Steve Cliffen, fifty-seven and David Tweddell, seventy-eight signed on as co-riders and what started as a relaxed discussion became an eleven-day, 530-mile pedal-powered road trip from Fulham to Newcastle and all the Premier League clubs along the way, culminating in a visit to Hampden Park, where Bob first played for Scotland. We had known David for over forty years and his skill and love of cycling had seen him as reserve for England in the 1956 Olympics. Even at seventy-eight he would pound the roads every day defying the years and putting much younger athletes to shame. Steve on the other hand just loved the thrill of the challenge, any challenge, so was willing to put his heart and soul into the project.

Gill Edelman, the new CEO, was totally enthusiastic about the assignment and we put together the logistics of how this could be achieved. Gareth Parker, an events and marketing consultant was appointed project manager to work alongside the Willow team in organising the details. It helped that he was a football enthusiast and Arsenal nut! The route, transport, sponsorship, health and safety, cycling kit and equipment, press and PR, social media, training runs, accommodation, insurance, risk analysis and a hundred and one things had to be considered. It took many hours of planning and discussion but was finally agreed that 18 April 2011 would be the starting day at Fulham finishing in Glasgow on 29 April.

Basically the team consisted of four couples – Bob and myself, Steve and Maureen Cliffen, David and June Tweddell, Mick and Becky Lee plus Gareth Parker and Tom Bunning, the latter being the photographer who would capture the official record. Becky and Mick, a seasoned cyclist, would be in charge of the technical support vehicle and all equipment that would be needed during the road stages. My own role was route direction, media, PR and football clubs whilst Maureen and June travelled ahead to make sure that all the essentials were taken care of: food, hotels, kit, laundry, meeting and physio room arrangements.

On Monday 18 April we gathered at Fulham Football Club and were joined for the first day by additional riders. Les Ferdinand, who had completed the Dallaglio cycle challenge the year before, Lee Dixon looking like a professional Tour de France veteran and Yanto Barker, a real professional cyclist looking sharp, fit and very young compared to the seniors. We were also joined by Jim White of the Daily Telegraph, who showed he had the energy to cover a story in practice and The Goalie, David Seaman who, as our first Willow ambassador had accepted our invite to give Bob the encouragement needed.

On the first day we started at Fulham and travelled the two miles to Chelsea then another twelve and a half miles to West Ham, a further nine miles to Arsenal and The Emirates followed by five miles to Tottenham. The London cabbies were amazing hooting and cheering the group as they travelled the capital and as each of the stadiums came into view the support outside was heartening. Each of the clubs welcomed them into the ground, had photos pitch-side, offered refreshment and presented them with commemorative shirts.

From Spurs we left London and headed north to Hertfordshire and the overnight stop but it was only then, when the adrenalin began to cease flowing, that the task the group had taken on began to sink in, and a massage became the most welcome activity.

The next morning they called at the Arsenal training ground where Arsene Wenger and all the team wished them well. Jens Lehmann, the current custodian of the number one shirt said, as he waved the cyclists on their way, he now had further proof that all goalkeepers were crazy.

The next two days were spent riding north towards the Midlands where there were four more clubs to visit: Birmingham, Aston Villa, West Bromwich Albion and Wolves. So many familiar faces arrived to greet us and at West Brom, there in his black cycling gear was Brendon Batson, Bob's former Arsenal team mate, ready to ride alongside for the rest of the day. Sadly he had lost his own wife Cec only eighteen months previous and the memories were obviously still painful for him.

Bob's diary from that time reads:

> *Royal treatment from the Wolves. Stan Cullis would be so proud. A cheque for £1000.00 from the Wolves Community fund and sandwiches to boot! What a class act. Billy Wright's imposing statue guards the gold stadium where he was a heroic captain. He was also the manager who first signed me as an Arsenal player. To complete the day we were able to stretch our legs for 30 miles in order to rest our heads at Stoke. I'm finding the whole experience exhausting but invigorating and surprised how well we are holding up. We got through the last 5 miles by singing every Elvis and Everly Brothers numbers we could think of.*

Stoke City's legendary goalkeeping World Cup winner Gordon Banks was there to greet us at the Britannia Stadium before the cyclists tackled the undulating terrain through Stoke. The steady rise past Jodrell Bank and Alderley Edge took them down to the city of Manchester and the imposing Etihad Stadium.

Family and friends were there to greet us as well as a warm welcome from Mike Summerbee before setting off to visit the other Manchester club at Old Trafford the next morning – a Saturday.

For both Manchester United and Liverpool this was a match day so visiting both clubs meant arriving early morning at the first, where Sir Bobby Charlton and Sir Alex Ferguson wished us well, and at 1.15 at Anfield, well before kickoff. With the recent anniversary of the Hillsborough disaster the Shankly gates and memorial were covered with wreaths. However, the Scouse humour and wit was in full throttle and it was amusing to witness the repartee between the crowd and the cyclists.

From there we visited the Everton and Wigan grounds, eventually arriving for an overnight stop in Bolton where ice baths and massages were on offer. It was here that we coincided with the Bolton v Arsenal match, one that we had to attend, but which put a damper on the proceedings for Bob by an Arsenal loss. After the match we met up with a Willow beneficiary, Jan O'Brien and her family who had raised more than £10,000 for Willow since her own Special Day. She told us, 'It was the turning point in my battle against cancer and it showed me that there was still living to be done.'

The cycle team needed no further inspiration than hearing that.

The seventy-four mile ride to Blackburn over the Lancashire moors was challenging but inspiring as the amazing vistas provided views of green fields, pink blossoms, yellow buttercups and new-born lambs. From Ewood Park, where the Blackburn team had waited to wish us luck before catching their team bus for their game, to Blackpool where there was a great welcome by Arsenal and Blackpool fans alike.

Throughout the journey we had met many people who had experienced a Willow Special Day. It was always so heart-warming hearing their stories and their gratitude for time spent with loved ones at a difficult moment in their lives. But one particular moment stood out for Bob as written in his diary:

> *We made our way to Poulton Le Fylde and on to Cockermouth when I spotted a lady waving me down at the side of the road. She said her name was Karen and had just come from her farm up the road. As she walked towards me she was crying. She knew about the ride and wanted to tell me how much her son's Special Day had meant to him. He was 23 and had been treated in the Christie hospital but sadly died a year ago. She wanted to say thank you and we had a hug before we went on our way. It was a difficult journey for me from then on, moved by her story and thoughts of her loss.*

Day nine of our challenge saw us begin the west to east coast jorney across the Pennines. So far the ride had been broken up and made more bearable by stopping at the grounds, meeting the staff and players and accepting great hospitality. We knew now that the next part of the ride would test the fitness of all the cyclists and the gradients would get steeper and steeper. It took three full days before we reached Sunderland and in that time no matter how high we travelled we never seemed to come the same distance down to sea level. We had expected the steepest of descents but for the amount of climbing we did the decline appeared to be deceptively short. On day eleven we finally arrived at St James's Park, Newcastle, our final Premier League club and a huge surge of adrenalin masked the fatigue that each and every one of us harboured aligned with the emotion of finishing.

This was where we said goodbye to the rest of the team. Tom, Gareth, Bob and I then set off for Glasgow and Hampden Park where Bob made his first full international appearance for Scotland in 1971. It is the stadium that, in its original form, was opened in 1902 by Bob's great-uncle, Sir John Ure Primrose, who was the Lord Provost of Glasgow and Chairman of Glasgow Rangers. There to greet us was a welcoming committee in the shape of the Arsenal Scotland Supporters Club singing a rendition of 'Good Old Arsenal'. We all went down to the hallowed turf and Bob was able to ride round the pitch on the cycle that had travelled the length of England and to the twenty Premier League clubs, bringing the challenge to a fitting conclusion.

Bob was totally bowled over by the reaction of so many friends and strangers who chose to encourage him by sponsorship and he couldn't believe it when the final total came to £375,000. But the real heroes were those behind the scenes who enabled it through the donation of equipment, overnight stays, recovery massages and logistics, not to mention 'the team'.

Coming of Age

Over the next seven years Willow's ride was pretty rocky. There was a deep need for continuity as the role of Chief Executive Officer changed hands four times between 2010 and 2017. Fortunately the charity was steered by Richard King, a Chair who was capable of dealing with the most difficult of situations and a board of trustees who were devoted to keeping Willow on course. They were an essential voice through all the difficulties that presented themselves to ensure the charity carried out its purpose for which it was set up and complied with its governing document and charity law. It always took informed decisions acting prudently when necessary and using sound judgement when needed. Every member of the board cared deeply about Willow and worked tirelessly to ensure its stability.

Bob and I were made Life Presidents and it was clear to us that our opinions would always be sought and listened to. It was highly important that the governance of the charity be in tune with the management and that the vision and values laid down in Willow's infancy be adhered to. Quality of work, of ideas, of events and of Special Days should be at the forefront of anything Willow was aligned to and the raison d'être always be acknowledged. Anna's mantra of 'quality of time and quality of life' would flow through the charity like letters in a stick of rock and her philosophy of making the most of each and every day, influence the thinking of all who continue to work there.

In 2015 the CEO at the time, David White, recognised the need for diversifying our income as we were so heavily dependent on events. As a way of creating guaranteed income each year the trustees therefore agreed to the opening of Willow shops. So in early 2015 four shops opened locally which would give Willow a presence on the high street and a stream of continuous income through retail. One at a time we attended the opening of first the Welwyn Garden City, then Barnet, Hatfield, Hemel Hempstead and Stevenage shops. We were proud to see Willow amongst what is a very competitive market. And once again, the quality mantra was applied and it continues to give us a great thrill to walk into a Willow shop and see the effort our staff put into making the stock and surroundings look inviting.

David White also recognised the inefficiencies of working in Willow House. When the building was first purchased in 2005, we all thought that the charity would be there for ever. It had enough space for the various departments, a large meeting room, a kitchen and plenty of areas for the stock that always lived with us — buckets, T-shirts, auction items, raffle prizes, banners etc. We could never have envisaged that Willow would grow to such a size that more office space would be needed. But needed it was. The building was old, it couldn't be extended or altered any more than it had been, it was too hot in summer and too cold in winter and maintenance was becoming costly.

At first the problem was solved by renting a large room for the Special Days department to work in a building located a few yards from Willow House. But clearly this was not satisfactory as it was important for all the departments to be able to interact with one another. The motivation for those who worked in Fundraising was hearing the current stories of Special Days, of the unusual, the emotional, the funny and the uplifting. And the Special Days team needed to appreciate the work that the fundraising team had to organise in order to pay for those days. Being a split office therefore was far from ideal.

It would also make financial sense to sell Willow House, and better use the income from the sale to rent more modern office space where the staff could work as one. David White found just the right premises in Welwyn Garden City, close to the station where the whole charity could work on one floor within sight of each other.

At the end of May 2015 the sale went through and the move to Gate House was completed. All departments were now able to work closely, interacting with each other, understanding each other's roles and feeling more like a team than ever before.

Team Willow continues to fill us with great pride and love and we can never thank them enough for their loyalty and hard work. Over the years we have been very fortunate to have the most amazing people work for Willow. It is heartening to hear them talk about the 'Willow family', even when they have left to move to new pastures. It is hard to say goodbye when they inevitably move on in their careers but it is also a great joy for us to see how much they care about the work they do and particularly the people they do it for. Whether they have worked in Special Days, Finance, Challenge Events, Community, Marketing, Philanthropy, Corporate, Major Events or Retail, they are all an important part of being able to provide for those who will benefit.

In August 2017 the charity was rocked by the news of David Williams' death, our very first CEO. He had been battling illness for over a year but had been working for Willow in his changed role until the very end and the measure of his standing came in the flow of letters and emails from those with whom he had come into contact over the previous decade and a half. His funeral was full to brimming with those who had shared his years in the RAF and latterly Willow and the celebration of his life was a truly fitting one. To everyone's amusement, it transpired that David had written his own eulogy, a task which had obviously filled his immobile hours. It was very moving to hear his own words spoken by family friend Rev Paddy Cable but particularly humbling to hear about his time at Willow.

'I would like to think that I have achieved much in my life but nothing compares with providing special days/memorable events for seriously ill young adults.'

I was able to tell David in the weeks before he died that he would be the very first recipient of the 'Willow at Heart Award' which would be presented at the Ball in November. He was speechless but very moved and promised he would do his best to be there. In his place that night to receive the award were his wife Sue and sons Jamie and Simon. A fitting and heartfelt ovation was given.

But in saying goodbye to David Williams we had also welcomed in our newest CEO Jonathan Aves who, coincidentally, was recruited from Hertfordshire Community Foundation, a charity that worked alongside Willow in the Sylvia Adams Offices, Hatfield, in the very early days. The HCF collaborates with private philanthropists, family trusts, businesses and the public sector to provide local charitable funding. Willow welcomed Jonathan's specialist fundraising knowledge and a chance to bring some much needed continuity at the helm. It therefore would be a very different charity for Jonathan to steer, one that was national, had a service delivery and relied on the many events that had become established over the years.

The event that has been consistently successful is the Willow Ball and it remains the one occasion when the charity is celebrated by long-term and new supporters alike, showcasing the work carried out all year round and recognising some of the amazing people who go that extra mile in order to help Willow continue its work. It is one of the events when we particularly rely on the support of our dedicated and loyal volunteers. Without those people who are willing to give their time for nothing, at all hours of the day and night, the charity could not survive. At our golf days they stand out in the rain, stewarding the course; at our challenge events they marshal the fields; at our Willow Ball and London Football Awards they greet guests, sell raffle tickets, monitor the auctions, and run around as necessary; at our Carol Concert and Folk Concert they rattle the tins and man the stalls; in our shops they deal with all things retail and in the office they are given a variety of tasks from folding, printing, researching to packing.

From year one it was important for us to be able to gather the Willow family together and give thanks for those who had helped in whatever way. A carol concert was planned and we were lucky that one of our volunteers, Ed Giberti, was attached to the delightful St Francis of Assisi church in Welwyn Garden City. For the next ten years the Willow Carol Concert was a place where volunteers, staff, special day recipients, their families, friends and stakeholders of any hue, gathered to celebrate with a different choir to lead us each year, appearing in all sorts of guises. Some were big, bold and brash, some rather tender and shy. But I remember one particular year a group arrived looking rather like a hippie gathering with long flowing dresses, men in head bands and all with children in their wake or arms. Their singing was fairly free but with an understated restraint, the tambourines and bamboo flutes slightly jarring with the church organ.

It is usual for either Bob or myself to stand at the end of the service to thank each and everyone for their participation, but that year my thanks to the choir came out in a bit of a muddle between what I was supposed to say and what was really in my head. 'Thank you so much that was …interesting.'

For the past ten years, thanks to the generous sponsorship of Rae and Carol Borras of Borras Construction, we have been privileged to hold our service in St Albans Cathedral, the size of the Abbey allowing far more people to join us at what has become one of our favourite events of the year. The amazing Hertfordshire Chorus, with their conductor David Temple, lead us in the singing and are a pure joy to listen to, whilst the readings and other individual performances reflect both Christmas and the work of Willow.

Because of Bob's background in football, it was inevitable that Willow became aligned to that particular sport. Throughout the years footballers and clubs have given great support to the charity and indeed it was predictable that a fundraising dinner with a sporting theme should emerge. The London Football Awards is a night that has grown on a grand scale over the past few years. It started out as a London Legends evening, recognising those players who played for London clubs, but has become an evening that now recognises excellence at all levels and areas, be it on the field or in the community. It showcases all aspects of the game in London and gives opportunity for football clubs at each professional level to come together and celebrate the beautiful game.

It is because of football that we have been fortunate enough to attract some high-profile names who help promote Willow – and not only Arsenal ones! Since day one when David Seaman agreed to be the very first ambassador we have been very lucky to have some truly amazing celebrities, who are all committed to helping us raise awareness of the work we do. They represent not only football, but show business, television, rugby, golf, tennis and news. They have rallied to the cause and are always there to help endorse the effects of Special Days. Being a public figure can be a powerful tool in mobilising support and they have all, at some time, donated to our auctions, helped with a Special Day or drummed up support from their own networks.

They even join in our challenge events, including The London Marathon, the Willow 10k where Lord and Lady Salisbury allow us to use the delights of Hatfield Park, the Herts 100 bike ride and our annual clay pigeon shoot day, courtesy of the Royal Berkshire Shooting School.

Being event-based means that the charity is not entirely in control of how much income it can raise in a year. It can budget and estimate, but unless tickets are sold, weather permitting and sponsorship secured, it is never certain of delivering the necessary income. Hence the importance of individual donations, corporate partnerships and trust support all of which are the backbone of funding.

The sole purpose of all of this is to ensure that we can continue to provide Special Days for seriously ill young adults! A lot of work takes place; crucial decisions, time-consuming meetings, constant reinvention of fundraising, juggling of budgets, networking, phoning, researching, speaking, all done with huge love for the end product. At every level of the charity the joy of a Special Day is never forgotten. The letters that come in to the office from recipients thanking us for taking them back to 'normality' and giving them a chance to forget about illness and treatment are always read and continue to inspire.

They give a very small insight into the turmoil that serious illness has brought to their everyday lives and the effects that it has had on every member of their families. After a trip to Center Parcs with her two daughters, a young mother wrote to us and said: 'Since our trip to Center Parcs I have decided life really is about enjoying the good times, and if you look hard, they are everywhere.'

She also enclosed a letter from her 9 year-old daughter:

> *Dear Bob and Megs and all the people at Willow Foundation. Thank you for helping me, mummy, nanny and Lily to go to Center Parcs, it was very fun. At Christmas mummy was not feeling very well and I was a bit upset and I cryed a bit but she told me about it and I wasn't that scared after a while.*
>
> *And then she kept on going to the hospital and sometimes Lily and me went to the hospital with her and it smelt like old women and baby food. And I thank you very, very, very, very, very, very much for helping my mum and cheering her up. And when we went to Center Parcs the first thing that popied in my head was 'CAN WE GO SWIMMING!' And we went to a shop and I got a snorkel for £10 pounds and when we went swimming I used my snorkel and I drinked some water which I was not supposed to happen. After that I went down the rapids and when my mum went down it a man was all over the place and made mummy laugh.*
>
> *Then I went rock climbing and the coach was called Simon and my nick name is Graciebean so I told Simon and he called me bean. My sister Lily wanted to go horse riding but it was raining. So we ordered bikes and by myself I went a little way round and I fell in a ditch and a woman came past and sore me fall in the ditch and I went all red.*
>
> *And mummy had a massage and fell asleep! See you one day*

In 2013 we had arranged for twelve young people and their responsible companion to visit RAF Cranwell where they would experience a whole day visiting the hangars, trying their hand in a simulator and being taken up in various light aircraft by pilots who had volunteered their services for the day. Afterwards we received a letter from Tim Ritson who had been accompanying his daughter Beth and who expressed so eloquently his deep feelings:

> *The pleasure on the day for the beneficiaries was obvious and a welcome escape from the grinding drudgery of the treatment many were enduring or had just completed. However, in our*

case, equally important was the anticipation and build up to the event, which provided a diversion to look forward to whilst lying down being burned by radiotherapy or made increasingly ill by intra-venous drug regimes – apparently the possibility of vomiting from looping the loop is a positive experience, whilst vomiting as a result of chemotherapy is definitely not.

Once again, thank you for a great day and for helping me see my daughter at the happiest she has been for a long time.

Or the 19 year-old who just wanted to have fun with his friends at Alton Towers:

During this time I forgot that I was only 19 years old and that my life was potentially being threatened by an illness over which I had no control. I have lots of really close friends and I have always been a party animal. I almost forgot to enjoy my time with my friends and that is where you made me the happiest bloke on the planet.

I could never have afforded to say thank you to my friends for all their support and comfort through my illness. They have visited me in hospital, cooked for me, cleaned my house, taken me shopping etc.

The fact that I could do something for them, treat them to a weekend break at Alton Towers was such a fabulous thing. The Willow Foundation made it possible for me to say thank you to all the people who really matter to me, you made me feel in control again and you made me feel positive about me.

Perhaps the most rewarding news comes through those who have experienced a Special Day and who then feel empowered to go out, shout from the rooftops, and raise money for Willow. Jackie discovered she had breast cancer just as she'd become engaged to be married. She celebrated her engagement with Duncan her fiancé on a Willow Special Day aboard the Orient Express during treatment. She said she wanted to escape being a patient and Duncan could play partner not carer:

It was a turning point for us as I realised that cancer can take a lot of things, but it doesn't have to take your smile.

Once treatment was over Jackie dedicated her non-working life to challenge events and volunteering. She and Duncan began to run and built up their distance over a period of time. Then she planned her wedding.

It's fair to say, the last few years have been one big adventure as we've volunteered, travelled, run and laughed our way through each day. And, it has been a real privilege to go on that adventure with Duncan by my side. So it seems only fitting that our wedding should follow a similar theme. That's why at 7.30 a.m. on 23 April 2017 we will be pulling off a world first and getting married on the Cutty Sark before running the London Marathon. Then we'll be heading off on a trek of the Great Wall of China for our honeymoon. It's the big charity fundraiser wedding.

Jackie and Duncan were as good as their word and were married aboard the Cutty Sark dressed in lycra. Willow ambassador and *Dancing on Ice* professional skater Frankie Seaman designed and made Jackie's dress so that it was both bridal yet easy in which to run. And off they set – along with the father of the bride and some of the wedding party! All completed the London Marathon and the most unique wedding day ever with huge smiles and donations in place of wedding presents! In raising money for both Willow and Breast Cancer Care, Jackie said:

We are proud to be able to make our happy day one that will help many many more people find happiness and support in the future. It's not what happens to you in life that defines you, it's how you choose to respond.

Just as important are the family and friends that bear witness to all the baggage that serious illness drags with it. Often they feel helpless to soothe or comfort when symptoms or reaction to treatment take a hold. Atmospheres can be created, tensions built and thoughts of the future are clouded in grey mists of the unknown. Special Days are not necessarily the answer, but they are sometimes the spark that shines a light on what can bring happiness back. Jess Hill wrote:

My Special Day reminded me how good life can be amidst experiencing the hardships life can offer. It is so easy to let negative thoughts manifest and circle around in your head when you're experiencing something so challenging, but having the Special Day to ponder over and anticipate provided our lives with so much light.

To quote Dumbledore 'Happiness can be found even in the darkest of times, if one only remembers to turn on the light.' Thank you to Willow for showing me and my family where the light switch was.

'It will all turn out for the best'

As I write in 2019, Willow remains the only national charity working with seriously ill young adults aged 16 to 40 providing uplifting and unforgettable Special Days. Experiences that enable them and their families to reconnect and refocus on each other whilst enjoying time together, creating memories that will last for ever.

Currently the average period of time for a Special Day is three days but if the request is for accommodation nights in a hotel, holiday park or lodges then they are mostly between one and four days depending on the distance travelled. Each day is specifically tailored to the recipient's needs and requirements and it is important that the Day Maker who is arranging all the details, listens, tries to make it personal, and leaves nothing to chance.

We are approaching Willow's twentieth birthday and are on course to provide 1300 Special Days this year. In Willow's lifetime over 16,500 Special Days have been provided and on average four family or friends have shared the day. Therefore over 66,000 people have experienced the effect it can have – enough to overfill the Arsenal's Emirates stadium! And in total over £45 million has been raised from the most generous of donors, whether individuals, groups, companies or trusts, in order to provide those days.

In writing this book I realise I have only mentioned a minuscule number of people who have had such faith in our vision and given us the support that has allowed us to help so many seriously ill young adults; forgive me for not mentioning you all. We are eternally grateful to everyone who has touched Willow in whatever way and hope that they feel the connection to its growth. Willow is in a good place, its roots have spread and deepened and we are so grateful for the blessings that abound.

It's almost unbelievable for Bob and me that twenty years have elapsed since Willow was created, two decades of keeping Anna's philosophy alive and in so doing providing a higher degree of quality of life and quality of time for people in a similar situation to herself. But it is mainly about the smiles, the normality and the memories generated that counteract the current challenges and heartaches. It is about creating an excitement in looking forward to and taking part in something so pleasing; an adrenalin rush which, for the moment, takes away the symptoms and routines that have become the norm and about sharing fun and laughter that can bind family and friends.

Since we lost Anna, the memories of her life both as a joyous child and a wise young woman never leave us. She may have only lived for thirty-one years but the mark she made on those who met her, befriended her, were nursed by her or who in turn nursed her, was deep and lasting. Even though her death left a void in our world, we feel she is still with us and would be incredibly proud of how many people have benefitted from her legacy.

During Anna's long illness, daytime television became a friend, taking her mind away from the routine of treatment. But one morning Mitchell came down from upstairs to find her crying and asked why.

'I'm watching such an emotional story. This lady's young daughter was very ill but every so often the little girl had a smile on her face. When her mum asked why she was smiling she said that a lovely lady had come to see her. Every so often, and after these incidents the mum would find a white feather, and following her daughter's death, she found more in strange places.'

'You mean a bit like this?' Mitchell opened up his hand in which he was holding a white feather. It slightly freaked Anna. 'Don't worry; I've picked it up in the bedroom. It's obviously come out of one of the pillows,' said Mitchell dismissively.

Anna took great delight in recounting the story and we all laughed at the chance he should have a feather in his hand. But it was to resonate with us, more than we expected.

It was the week after the funeral and I was walking our dog Remi through the woods, talking to my daughter, unable to come to terms with the loss. 'How can you possibly be happy anywhere other than here, with us, with Mitchell, with your brothers? I need to know that you're ok. I need to know that you're happy.' Over and over I repeated the words through my tears, desperate for an impossible answer.

As I approached a large pond, deep in the dell, a large white feather came floating down, gently swaying from side to side landing softly on the water beneath. I smiled at the coincidence and looked fondly at the feather as it lay gently on its new resting place. I walked on and between there and arriving at my car a mile away, I picked up twelve more white feathers. I finally said to the sky, 'Alright Anna, you can stop. I believe you now.'

Bob returned to work and the very first interview he did just so happened to be back at the Arsenal training ground, London Colney. He had gone through preparation as to his line of questioning, picked up the microphone and told the cameraman he was ready. But just as he was about to start he was aware of something above his head, a white feather coming down towards him. He put out his hand, and it landed right into his palm. He was stunned. He had been interrupted once before at a first interview, but that was by Anna personally giving him the news that she was free of cancer.

The morning after Anna had died, I suddenly remembered that the fountain she had bought for Mitchell's birthday was due to be built that day, but fortunately I was able to catch the gardener before he set off from home. The large stone sphere water feature with pond and pebbles would replicate the one they had come to love at the Brompton Hospital. It was intended to provide a place of peace and tranquillity for them in their garden but would now take on greater significance.

Much to Mitchell's disappointment, the eventual building of the water feature and fountain was a bit of a disaster. It was neither symmetrical nor was the pond the shape he had wanted. He knew it wouldn't be what Anna intended so rather than upsetting the gardener, he set about demolishing and rebuilding it himself. It took a few weeks before it was complete but once finished he was keen for us to see it. Mitchell opened the door at Gun Lane, eager for us follow him to the garden, which Bob did, whilst I stayed to say hello to the cat. I heard a cry of disbelief from outside and my name called.

'Megs, quick, come out here!'

Thinking something bad had happened I rushed to where they were standing, both looking at the pond. There, floating right in the middle was a large white feather, giving the stamp of approval.

There have been many times we have been taken aback by similar happenstances, but none more surprising than during a visit to Cape Town, South Africa. We had been on a trip to the top of Table Mountain but decided to watch the sunset nearer the coast. As we made our way up by car to Lions Head, which looks west over Camps Bay, we discovered that hundreds of others had decided to do the same and the viewing area was becoming very crowded by the time we arrived. Bob dropped me off for me to find a good sunset viewing space whilst he parked the car. People were gathered two-deep across the long stretch of wooden fence which protected the steep drop below, but I managed to spot a space and quickly made my way there before anyone else took it. I looked out across the glorious spectacle of mountain, beach and water, the colour of the sky beginning to change as the sun lowered itself towards the horizon. Bob found me and squeezed himself into the space next to me leaning his elbows on the wooden fence. After a few seconds he suddenly let out a cry of astonishment and I turned wondering what on earth had happened.

'Look! Look between my arms!'

I looked down and there, exactly in the centre of the space bordered by his forearms and carved into the top of the fence were the words 'Willow'.

There must have been several hundred people doing exactly the same as we were, leaning on the fence waiting for sunset to arrive, but I doubt whether 'Willow' was written anywhere else along the perimeter.

I am sure that when I recount these incidents to others their reaction is likely to be – you don't really believe that do you? My only answer would be to say that although I have no certain knowledge about the possibilities of an after-life, all I do know is that I need comfort, and if white feathers and carved happenstance letters bring such comfort to us, then what is the harm?

There were two main catalysts which sparked the creation of Special Days. The first was Anna's reaction to Bob's *This Is Your Life* programme. For ten days afterwards her symptoms vanished and quite miraculously she appeared well and happy. The preparation before the programme, the taking part and the excitement of recalling the day all contributed to her temporary relief from the pain and tiredness that were her constant companions. It demonstrated so vividly how mental distraction can sometimes take precedence over the physical.

And the second catalyst penetrated my mind like no other statement has ever done before or since. The family have always quoted Nan Wilson's heartfelt belief that 'It will all turn out for the best' no matter what life has thrown at you or what tragic event has taken place. It was towards the end of Anna's struggle for life whilst lying in a bed at the Brompton that I queried the logic of Bob's mum's heartfelt belief.

'What good could possibly come out of all of this, Anna?'

'You'll do something Mum, something related to all of this, I know you will'.

Willow Foundation – The First 20 Years

GOVERNANCE

Chair of Trustees:

1999 - 2008   Megs Wilson
2008 - 2010   Tina Tietjen
2010 –   Richard King

Trustees through the years:

Bob Wilson OBE	Brian Hilton
Megs Wilson	Greg Hall
Terry Mitchinson	Oliver Peterken
Kate Baldwin	Dr Philip Lodge
Sarah Price	Maurice Gammell
Pippa Forster	Rachel Jones
Chris Measures	Nick Aldridge
Louise Hickson	Farine Clarke
Sue Mitchell	Andrew Unwin
Heather Coladangelo	Stewart Bennett
Ken Haddon	Andrew Harvey
Dean Barratt	David Waddington CBE
Richard King	Elena Ciallie
Tina Tietjen	John Wilson
Nicki Swan	Glyn Taylor
Gina Tress	Daniel Hunter

CEO's: 1999 – 2003 Megs Wilson - voluntarily
2003 - 2010 David Williams OBE
2010 – 2012 Gill Edelman
2012 – 2013 Jeff Kaye
2013 – 2016 David White
2016 – 2017 Interim
2017   Jonathan Aves

We are so grateful to all our Ambassadors for the support and time they give to Willow:

David Seaman MBE

Natasha Kaplinsky OBE

Mary Nightingale

Linda Lusardi

Sam Kane

Simon McCoy

Jim Rosenthal

Gary Mabbutt MBE

Pat Jennings OBE KSG

Martin Chivers

Ian Poulter

Ian Wright MBE

Ossie Ardiles

Lee Dixon

Lee Mears

Gary Lewin

Hardeep Singh Kohli

Theo Walcott

Frankie Seaman (formally Poultney)

Alfie Boe OBE

Katie Swan

Leah Williamson

Special Day Recipients Illness Type by Percentage

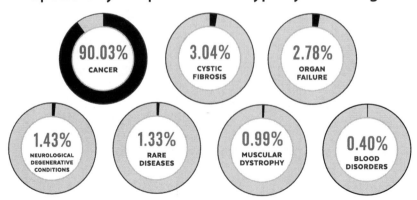

90.03% CANCER

3.04% CYSTIC FIBROSIS

2.78% ORGAN FAILURE

1.43% NEUROLOGICAL DEGENERATIVE CONDITIONS

1.33% RARE DISEASES

0.99% MUSCULAR DYSTROPHY

0.40% BLOOD DISORDERS

Every year in the UK more than 15,000 young adults aged 16-40 are newly diagnosed with a life-threatening illness. That equates to more than 40 young adults every single day who could be eligible for a Special Day. Every Special Day is completely bespoke, no two days should ever be the same and should be unique and unforgettable.

Special Day Types

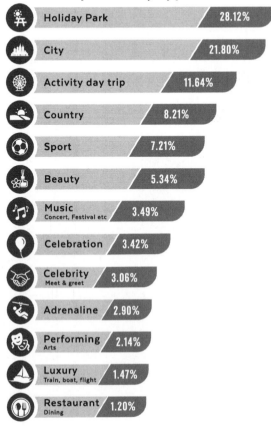

Type	Percentage
Holiday Park	28.12%
City	21.80%
Activity day trip	11.64%
Country	8.21%
Sport	7.21%
Beauty	5.34%
Music (Concert, Festival etc)	3.49%
Celebration	3.42%
Celebrity (Meet & greet)	3.06%
Adrenaline	2.90%
Performing Arts	2.14%
Luxury (Train, boat, flight)	1.47%
Restaurant (Dining)	1.20%

Working Across the UK

REGIONS

- North West
- South East
- Yorks & Humber
- East
- South West
- West Midlands
- East Midlands
- Scotland
- London
- Wales
- Northern Ireland
- North East

16,500+
TREASURED EXPERIENCES
FULFILLED SINCE 1999

66,000+
SMILES CREATED FOR
SERIOUSLY ILL 16-40
YEAR OLDS AND THEIR
FRIENDS AND FAMILY

4
PEOPLE ON AVERAGE
ATTENDED EVERY
SPECIAL DAY

130+
APPLICATIONS
RECEIVED EACH MONTH

Twenty Years of Monies Raised
and Special Days Provided

YEAR	DONATIONS & LEGACIES	EVENT SALES	RETAIL SHOP SALES	OTHER TRADING ACTIVITIES	INVESTMENT INCOME	INCOME	SPECIAL DAY NUMBERS
1999	-	-	-	-	-	-	-
2000	194,000	-	-	-	3,000	196,000	17
2001	326,000	175,000	-	-	16,000	517,000	57
2002	340,000	423,000	-	-	29,000	792,000	73
2003	580,000	164,000	-	-	36,000	779,000	205
2004	1,601,000	421,000	-	-	90,000	2,112,000	287
2005	989,000	440,000	-	-	74,000	1,503,000	407
2006	1,081,000	255,000	-	-	85,000	1,421,000	890
2007	1,954,000	1,431,000	-	-	88,000	3,472,000	1,054
2008	1,937,000	896,000	-	-	109,000	2,942,000	1,315
2009	1,741,000	613,000	-	-	82,000	2,436,000	1,325
2010	1,477,000	928,000	-	-	77,000	2,481,000	1,381
2011	1,748,000	1,114,000	-	-	66,000	2,929,000	1,395
2012	1,452,000	648,000	-	-	70,000	2,170,000	777
2013	1,699,000	567,000	-	-	50,000	2,316,000	843
2014	1,792,000	907,000	-	41,000	55,000	2,795,000	980
2015	2,171,000	953,000	139,000	52,000	52,000	3,366,000	1,029
2016	2,793,000	1,140,000	250,000	52,000	52,000	4,287,000	1,278
2017	3,106,000	1,073,000	293,000	31,000	52,000	4,556,000	1,300
2018	2,274,000	1,016,000	340,000	31,000	55,000	3,716,000	1,199
2019 (to date)	-	-	-	-	-	-	808

VOLUNTEERS

Our delivery of over 1000 Special Days each year is only possible thanks to a team of dedicated employees and loyal, hard working volunteers.

Volunteers are the lifeblood of any charity and central to all the activities at Willow. They contribute their time and skills to a range of areas including the Trustee Board and Committees, Development Board, celebrity supporters and ambassadors, in the retail shops, at events and in the Head Office.

In 2018 the number of hours given by the amazing volunteers in one year was 17,680

the equivalent value of £248,000

which equals 198 Special Days.

Thank you on behalf of Willow but particularly on behalf of all those whose ability to smile is challenged daily and who will benefit from your generosity of time.

Bob and Megs
September 2019

Acknowledgements

This book began as a diary but over time, was expanded to chart the creation of Willow, the charity we founded in 1999 inspired by our daughter as she lived her life with cancer.

However, I needed much help in turning this rough diary into readable book form and I would like to acknowledge and give huge thanks to my dear brother Peter Miles, for the patience, time and effort he has put into typesetting the text and the layout of the photographs. I'm sure he felt he was contributing to his niece's memory but his encouragement and wisdom have gone a long way to helping my own confidence in the process of publishing this book.

I would also like to show my appreciation to Dick Eadon for giving so much of his time in proof reading my first draft of the text, and meticulously correcting my own inadequate stylistics and grammar.

I am truly grateful also to Gabby Morley for her excellent work on the cover and statistics designs.

I also send all my love to our two sons; John the journalist who, in the early days, always urged me to keep writing and our son Robert, for the use of his stunning photographs, exemplified by the cover of this book. Then there is my ever loving husband Bob, who has always been totally supportive and encouraging in all that I have ever done – from the day we met and fell in love, aged 11 and 12 respectively.

Finally to Anna, our beautiful and courageous daughter; I miss you although you remain with me every day.